The Copy Generic

The Copy Generic

HOW THE NONSPECIFIC
MAKES OUR SOCIAL WORLDS

Scott MacLochlainn

The University of Chicago Press   CHICAGO AND LONDON

The University of Chicago Press, Chicago 60637
The University of Chicago Press, Ltd., London
© 2022 by The University of Chicago

Published 2022
Printed in the United States of America

31 30 29 28 27 26 25 24 23 22   1 2 3 4 5

ISBN-13: 978-0-226-82275-4 (cloth)
ISBN-13: 978-0-226-82277-8 (paper)
ISBN-13: 978-0-226-82276-1 (e-book)
DOI: https://doi.org/10.7208/chicago/9780226822761.001.0001

Library of Congress Cataloging-in-Publication Data

Names: MacLochlainn, Scott, author.
Title: The copy generic : how the nonspecific makes our social worlds /
Scott MacLochlainn.
Description: Chicago ; London : The University of Chicago Press, 2022. |
Includes bibliographical references and index.
Identifiers: LCCN 2022018126 | ISBN 9780226822754 (cloth) | ISBN
9780226822778 (paperback) | ISBN 9780226822761 (ebook)
Subjects: LCSH: Generic, The (Philosophy) | Generic, The (Philosophy)—
Social aspects | Generic, The (Philosophy)—Social aspects—Philippines |
Christianity—Philippines. | BISAC: SOCIAL SCIENCE / Anthropology /
Cultural & Social | SOCIAL SCIENCE / Sociology of Religion
Classification: LCC B105.G46 M33 2022 | DDC 128/.6—dc23/eng/20220610
LC record available at https://lccn.loc.gov/2022018126

♾ This paper meets the requirements of ANSI/NISO Z39.48-1992
(Permanence of Paper).

Contents

⌐

PART I

The Copy Generic

Copies Generic, Templates, and [Insert Text Here]

the important
thing
is
the obvious
thing
that
nobody
is
saying

—*Charles Bukowski, "Always" (1990)*

It is an odd concept, "the generic." Commonly used, but rarely thought about: at times its meaning is obscure, at others, simply multiple. There are those famous examples, such as elevator music, off-brand consumer products, internet memes, and cultural stereotypes, as well as its more formal designations, within copyright and patent law, for example. For the most part, however, the term is used loosely and often, without any great specificity, mirroring its very own meaning. It is a remarkably common concept, with some version of it found in most languages and in most places, sometimes nudging closer to the meaning of "general" than in others. But what exactly is "the generic"? And what might its importance be for how we understand contemporary social worlds?

Much of the time, the generic suggests the copied and worn out—the unauthentic. In this light, it is seen as the husk of meaning, left over and unwanted. Often serving as a designation for what things are not—original, new, or unique—the generic exists as a pejorative, devaluing term. It is the culturally exhausted—those objects, meanings, and spaces that have been overused but are still lingering in the world. We unsurprisingly tend to look elsewhere when trying to understand a particular social context, especially if that context is seen to be important and generative of new meaning. While anthropology often looks to the understudied and the underappreciated, even at times the deviant, the generic is none of these; it is neither the underappreciated nor the overappreciated. Rather, it has already been appreciated, but now has been cast aside, lingering in the semiotic cracks of culture, between "non-" and "post-" meaning. Assuming some sort of process, it is a byproduct, the leftover. The generic is the waste from the culture machine.

But this is only one lens through which to view the generic. In another sense, the generic is simply the nonspecific. Scraped of particularity, it can come close to meaning "universal," or at least a certain type of universal. It is the starting point, the template and background, upon and against which we build and create—again invoking a process of some sort. Presupposing an all-encompassing quality, it emphasizes type over token. It is a category of encompassment, inclusive of multiple specificities, but always itself remaining stubbornly nonspecific. While we often look upon the essentialized and reductive as problematic, they are nevertheless key to how meaning circulates, and are predicated on the semiotic practices of stripping away specificity. While the singular and unique are so often held to have more intrinsic value, the flip side is of equal, maybe even of more importance. The ability to summarize, substitute, and generalize— these are the engines of the social. To strip away surface detail and begin to order and classify the world in meaningful ways is also the generic. Thus, it is not just the culturally discarded, but in many ways the beating heart of how we make sense of things.

In our everyday ordering of things, we have the generic, indeed, scales of the generic. Lexically, for example, in English there is *fruit*, which is more generic than *an apple*, which in turn is more generic than *a Braeburn* or *a Golden Delicious* apple. Or consider the common phrase "blah blah blah," proclaiming boredom and meaninglessness, simultaneously highlighting the separation of generic form over content by way of substitution. We often seem to need generic terms and categories to move through the world. They are also, it seems, the workhorses of everything from cognition and psychology to infrastructures and technology. At times the generic seems to erase difference, and at other times it becomes a starting point from which to make further differentiation of the world. In this neutral sense, it is about similarity and difference, types and universals—the shared and common grounds of meaning. At other times, it is still about sorting, but of sorting value—determining what is to be valued and what is not.

Within these two roaming definitional spaces of the generic—that of depreciatory evaluation and that of abstracted classification—there emerges a concept of the generic as something fundamentally necessary to the circulation of meaning, something crucial to sociality. When we see the generic enacted in the world as a concept, it most often moves between both definitions, simultaneously neutral and pejorative. It is sort of everywhere, the generic, and so it goes unnoticed. It is as if the concept of the generic is itself generic. There is of course the risk of fetishizing it— seeing everything thusly, overloading the concept with all that is similar. If it is understood as having some aspect of mimesis and similarity, what then is not generic? It is undoubtedly a slippery slope, and one that I wish to avoid. Instead, I shall describe the inherent importance of the generic as a driving factor of the social. Here it moves past just similarity and mimesis, merging them, repeating them, warping them, until it might emerge as its own concept—a concept crucial to an anthropological project of understanding the nature of how things repeat, circulate, and are ultimately classified in the world.

Taking a word from the language and place in which I mostly work, the Philippines, *banal* in Filipino/Tagalog is a linguistic false friend in English, and denotes not the common,[1] but rather the holy. In this book, then, I want to make a pitch for the generic as something holy rather than banal—a strange and potent space. I want to explore the concept of the generic, and consider what sorts of spaces it occupies both in anthropology and in the milieus in which we study. I do so by examining how the generic is at play in the interwoven contemporary modes of technological and media formation, design, and ideologies of classification. Ultimately, I stake a claim for the importance of the generic as a space of analysis within the social. Indeed, as I will show, the generic is not something that we should begin to study in earnest, but rather something that we already do study. We would be well rewarded for bringing it into focus. Perhaps not intentionally, it has lingered here and there in the anthropological shadows, whenever people have spoken of "patterns" in culture, "traits," and indeed the general, ubiquitous, and universal. As I describe, the generic is ethnographically alive. It is there every time we roll our eyes upon hearing a clichéd song, in the similarities in architectural design, or the ease with which a person who has lived all their life in Manila can so easily read a map of the New York City subway system. It is in the engagement anthropology has had with metaphor and tropes (Fernandez 1991), and analogy (Jones 2017), as well as with broader, often implicit projects of comparison, extrapolation, and generalization. It serves not only in the highlighting of difference, but in the multiple forms of replication, mimesis, and similarity.

Not only is a better accounting of things generic essential to any understanding of a social world, but also it underscores the need to push back against a problematic trend in anthropology (and a classic problem in media) of emphasizing the sensational. That is, to attend to the generic is equally a political and ethical project of realigning anthropology with a clear and fundamental humanism—moving away from a focus on exceptionalism, and instead assigning ethnographic and conceptual value to everybody and equally, challenging increasingly accepted, though often implicit hierarchies of what and where constitutes the culturally important. If we think through more fully the importance of generic social forms, we might then ask anew: what constitutes the compelling anthropological subject or object of study? And what compels anthropology itself as a project (Pandian 2019; McLean 2017; Ortner 2016). To that end, and to somewhat contest a marketplace of newness and arguably a troubling logic of relevancy and irrelevancy—indeed, the importance of trends in anthropology—I use the concept of the generic as a way to theoretically deepen those spaces we too often gloss as the quotidian, mundane, and everyday, terms that do so much heavy lifting for us descriptively but that demand a fuller conceptual engagement.[2]

This book, however, is not simply about the ordinary, or the normative, but rather is an argument for the need of a conceptual space—the generic—that fundamentally resituates how we think about copies as related to templates and blueprints of the social. While the generic moves in and out of focus, and overlaps with several other conceptual spaces, critically it tethers a number of ethnographic and theoretical spaces that are too often seen to be distinct. If we move beyond ideological contestations over originality, and the indictment of social contexts as disenchanted, no longer sacred in their authenticity, what happens if we simply assume that cultural milieus, spaces, and contexts in fact often lose their originality and authenticity, becoming a commingling of replication and the quotidian, no longer sacred in their unfamiliarity? What then? We know that the culture machine does not stop. Having to step out of the confines of conceptual oppositions of new and old, mimesis and replication instead assume new roles in a semiotics of meaning-making. Originals and copies cease to be oppositional, or even distinct. For it is arguably how we derive from, circulate, and play with origins and sources—how they constitute shorthands—that constitutes our social worlds, not the origins and sources themselves.

Much of this book is ethnographically located in the Philippines. At first glance, the Philippines might easily be associated with the generic. With its colonial histories vast and multiple, the country, and in particular its capital, Manila, has both willingly and unwillingly always looked outward, consuming and being shaped by external forms of language, economic trade routes, architecture, food, and art. Famous in the eyes of many as a mishmash culture of Taglish, smartphones, call centers, karaoke and dancing prisoners, Americanized culture, shopping malls, dubbed South Korean television shows, and self-styled Mexican tele-novelas, the Philippines often stands as an icon of the everywhere and nowhere. Ostensibly lacking in the cultural specificity of its Southeast Asian counterparts, such as Indonesia or Laos, and without the economic and cultural force of South Korea, Japan, or China, its cultural exports are commonly predicated on digesting the cultural practices and tropes of elsewhere. Even in the small towns, appearing strangely South American, with Spanish architecture, plazas, and street names, and at the same time thoroughly Southeast Asian, with rice fields and water buffalo, there are seemingly endless moments of disjuncture within the cultural stereotypes of Filipiniana.

Or at least that is how the story goes. Within this narrative, the Philippines stands in the middle, a conglomerate of colonial pastiche and outside influence. Of course, I would strongly argue against such a narrative, if for nothing else, for how it is predicated on an outsiders' view, if not an outright imperial gaze. Such a narrative is also deeply determined by a hierarchy (and definition) of "cultural" value that relies on difference and exceptionality as inherently more worthwhile. At the same time, I would suggest there is the need to move beyond the tropes of the swirling cultural amalgamation of globalization and global cities. Something more important, I argue, is at play—in how sameness and difference is semiotically transacted and circulated. It is precisely the ideology of "generic culture" with which the Philippines has often been labeled that hides other forms of genericness that are not as queasily evaluative, but rather are critical to understanding the vectors of universalism that are central to social practices not only in the Philippines, but everywhere. Within the smaller world of anthropological genealogies, the Philippines is also important for thinking through the generic. As I describe in chapter 1, in the 1950s the Philippines was a key ethnographic (although classically and problematically othered) space in which a burgeoning cognitive anthropology emerged—a subdiscipline that would increasingly depend on ideologies of universalism that were seen to embody the category of "generic." It was also the ethnographic space, two decades later, in which that same cognitive anthropology came under severe critique (for example, through Michelle Rosaldo's work on language and metaphor [Rosaldo 1986, 1982, 1973]), a critique that I argue is particularly useful in thinking through contemporary issues around the politics of naming. And it is within a contemporary politics of naming, and of identity, that we can arguably begin to consider the ethics at play within the generic. For there are inevitably structures and inequalities relating to who gets to constitute and rely on the generic. As I show, to be able to choose when and how to reside in specificity and nonspecificity, to define the very parameters of such, and to be able to determine others along such axes is a striking mode of power.

Part II of this book is likewise, and more fully ethnographically, situated in the Philippines, famously "Asia's only Christian country."[3] The history of Christianity highlights these global, colonial histories of the Philippines, missionary projects of attempted homogenization, as well as the inherent universalist ideologies that run through Christian doctrine. Moreover, as the long dominance of Catholicism in the country slowly gives way to a more pluralist Christian context, the increasingly multiple forms of Christian affiliation that exist (ranging from Pentecostal, Methodist, and Iglesia ni Cristo to Mormon and Jehovah's Witness) redefine the very rubric of Christian ubiquity and universality. As the shared backdrops of Catholic predominance are contested, the generic becomes ever more useful in how people engage one another across lines of religious and ethical difference. For these reasons contemporary Christianity in the Philippines offers an immensely fruitful context—one that moves among linguistic, media, ethical, political, and ideological spaces—in which to think through the generic as something critical for how we navigate the fluid worlds of universality, sameness, and difference.

Formality and Informality

There are any number of spheres in which the generic is not only important, but used explicitly as a definitional term, often with partial overlaps of meaning. For example, *generic swaps* in finance, often referred to as the most basic form of derivative swap, are also known as vanilla, or straight, swaps. In this meaning of the term, generic clearly has less to do with universals, and more to do with basic and nonspecific forms of practice. In psychology, the term *generic knowledge* refers to that form of knowledge distinct from personal experience. Here, elements of the abstract and nonspecific combine. In programming, the term *generic type font* describes those fonts that are expected to be shared by a computer and a webpage. This, obviously, has connotations of the universal and basic, but not of the inclusive.

Given the multiple contexts in which the generic formally appears, there are two that would necessarily appear as first ports of call for an anthropology of the generic. First, the most widely known use of the generic over the last two decades has occurred within patents and branding, in particular, the enormous growth and popularity of generic drugs (Hayden 2013, 2007). The explosion of the global generic drug market, accounting for 88 percent of US prescription drug purchases (Conti and Berndt 2020), has brought a new legal encounter with the generic as a concept. As discussed in chapter 2, fake and generic knockoffs of consumer products are part of the branding landscape and are constantly pushing at the lines of patent and copyright infringement. Unsurprisingly, pharmaceuticals are highly regulated. As a result, the legal concept of the generic is more fully realized for prescription drugs than other commodities. For example, when patent protections on a branded drug expire, widespread production of generic versions is common. However, in several countries, the generic copy is specifically refused the right to sell under any type of branded name and must use a lowercase form of the nonbranded drug name to mark it as generic (Greene 2014; Hilliard et al. 2012). Such regulatory separation of the generic from the "real" brand coexists with the fact that generic drugs are thus increasingly associated with the "real" ingredients, and are at times viewed as the actual drug, purified and stripped of its brand. In this way, the generic emerges as something other than the knockoff or fake, and is constituted as a type of space in and unto itself—at once both the imitation and the original. Throughout this book, I describe how the generic negates the classic oppositional framing of original versus imitation. While much critiqued in social thought (Auerbach 1953; Benjamin 1968), and more recently in anthropology (Taussig 1993; Urban 2001; Nakassis 2012), the problematics of original and copy remain stubbornly in place in the social worlds most of us inhabit.

The second port of call is arguably linguistics, in which generic(s) is not only a technical term, but a subfield and a sustained focus of scholarship. Linguistic approaches to the generic have emphasized not only the difficulty in pinning down its precise nature, but the wide range of hugely important and deeply social concepts that are implicated when we think, even peripherally, about the generic. Linguists have highlighted how the marking of specificity and nonspecificity in language is key to understanding the complexities of how we think and speak about types, kinds, and categories of things. The generic has perhaps most often been associated with ethnosemantics, language development, and the concepts of subordinate and superordinate prototype categories, as well as "kinds" of things (Pelletier 2010). This is not to say, however, that it has a precise meaning in linguistics. Outside of semantic and lexical scales, clearly delimiting the generic in the much broader and informal spaces of language is quite difficult. For example, what determines a "kind" of thing? A space of entanglements and ambiguity, the generic is nevertheless one of immense productivity in understanding how language works (Carlson and Pelletier 1995; Croft and Cruse 2004; Gelman 2009; Leslie 2007; Mannheim and Gelman 2013; Mari et al. 2013).

For many linguists, the importance of the category of the generic lies in its ability to provide shorthands for kinds of things that are otherwise lacking in sufficient detail. In the absence of more information, generics are enacted as a way to characterize, afford general properties, and delineate kinds of things. Enacted not so much as background but as backup, the generic is the minimal basis of agreement and understanding. This, of course, runs counter to the generic as something overly specified to the point of being useless and culturally discarded, and exists as something of a shared semiotic ground. Charles Zuckerman, for example, has noted that a fuller engagement with generics allows us to better understand not only how people linguistically categorize things, but the nature of abstraction in the social (Zuckerman 2020).[4] I pay particular attention to language practices throughout this book for this very reason. Language is a compelling space in which to understand how the generic is constituted in the world. Not only is the study of language central to understanding how people configure the consortium of generality, shorthands, and background worlds, the generic itself is essential to language, ever-present in the pull and play of talk and text.

That is not to say however, that outside of semantic and lexical scales, clearly delimiting the generic in the much broader and informal spaces of language is necessarily easy. For example, in an American context, is the phrase "whassup" generic, because it has cycled through so much appropriation and parody that what once had a niche and temporary cache (perhaps) now no longer does?[5] How is it different from "hi" or "hello"? Are they the more generic salutations, given their remarkable ubiquity, or do they lack the discarded and diminished affect of "whassup" that is often accorded the generic? Or, in the Philippines, what about the phrase "It's more fun in the Philippines!" originated by the BBDO Guerrero advertising agency for the Department of Tourism as the slogan for a government-led global tourism campaign, but subsequently the wry and universally chuckled response to everything that goes wrong, from national financial scandals to when someone spills coffee on their shirt? Does that form of appropriation and ubiquity see it fall under the rubric of generic, or is that simply satire through mimesis? What of a slogan such as "Make America Great Again"? For many people in the United

States, such a political tag moved beyond trite and into meaninglessness, and became a classic example of the generic, in both its denotative components and its connotative motivations. It seemed almost designed to be generic. Does meaninglessness enable language and objects to become placeholders? And yet, in part because of that supposed meaninglessness, the phrase became famously pointed and instantly recognizable, not as a free-floating idiom, but as a marker of a distinct political affiliation—arguably the inverse of the generic.

One important question that runs throughout this book is whether the generic needs to be widely read as such. Are elements of explicitness necessary, or inherent, in the generic, and what types of attention does it draw to itself? Like internet memes, is the explicitness and citation of its own replication necessary? Or are there forms of concealment involved? For sure, much of what we understand as generic is called just that. One of the most famous and regularly used examples of genericness are placeholder names, such as "John Doe" and "Jane Doe." As placeholder names, John and Jane Doe are fully generic in the United States, known as such, and only function because of the widespread acknowledgment that they are generic. They are dependent on the transparency of their genericness. Similarly, for example, with their Philippine equivalents, Juan dela Cruz and Maria dela Cruz. These terms are used within legal, medical, and bureaucratic spheres as placeholders. Serving as proxies for the universal and nonspecific Filipino, gendered but nothing else, they are inclusive of everyone, but pointing to no one in particular. Moreover, they align easily with their US counterparts. This is no accident. Juan dela Cruz has a specific history, emerging from a US colonial context, in which the author, and sometime editor of the *Manila Times*, Robert McCulloch-Dick coined the term Juan dela Cruz as an everyman Filipino. Culling the names from what he perceived to be the most popular first and last name at the time, Juan dela Cruz was represented in cartoons as wearing traditional Filipino clothes, including a salakot, a type of wide-brimmed hat. Depictions were sometimes comical, sometimes sympathetic, but always portrayed the naïve native, and more often than not ran closer to the representational economy of Jim Crow. Unlike Jim Crow, however, Juan dela Cruz (and later Maria), was rehabilitated, or reappropriated, not necessarily within a charged political context, and has come to inhabit the same generic space as John Doe, arguably without any racializing intonations. Thus, both the explicitness and particular histories of the generic are at play. Moreover, the history of Juan dela Cruz points to how the rolling stone of genericness does indeed gather semiotic moss, shifting in meaning and open to appropriation and reinterpretation and erasure, all the while maintaining its usefulness as a generic artifact.

But what of those things and spaces that are not widely viewed as generic, but still might be? In chapter 1, I describe how, for some cognitive social scientists, the generic exists as a "covert category" (Whorf 1945) enacted by us in our perception and memory, but not consciously so. I argue, however, that we need not reach that far to find the generic. The generic exists in blueprints and templates, and in shorthands all around us (Mattingly 208; Wilf 2016). For present purposes, in this book, I want to look beyond the explicitly generic, and past the classificatory tensions of what falls into and out of it in the strictest terms, and rather make a case for the expansiveness of the concept and its usefulness in thinking about how things are meaningful and meaningless, and the movement back and forth between the two.

In arguing for a prominent role of genericness across social contexts, I do not mean to curtail the social. For example, accepting even the most basic remit of an ethnographic landscape is to accept the expansive ecologies that engage and are engaged by the social. Infrastructural environments are one such space. For example, consider the MIFARE series of microchips, manufactured and designed by the Dutch corporation, NXP Semiconductors. Over the last fifteen years, MIFARE chips have been key to the global expansion of smart cards. Notably used in urban transport payment and ticketing systems, MIFARE chips are also used in everything from library cards to social welfare and medical IDs, as well as passports and driver's licenses. The technology, while simple enough, is in no way legally generic. MIFARE chips are most definitely patented. And yet, there is something determinedly generic about the use and universality of the chips—that is, their situatedness in the world. They are everywhere, used in nearly every country—and with an estimated ten billion cards produced in just the last decade, there are more MIFARE chip cards than people in the world.

It is not just their universality. MIFARE chips have become so embedded within our lives that the technology is wholly indistinct and unnoticed. That is the generic. Indeed, unlike smartphones, which have particular forms of constant self-referentiality of the technology inherent in their use, including branding and popular discourses on the role of phones in culture, MIFARE technology, though ubiquitous, is rarely mentioned.[6] As a technology, it is not explicitly thought and talked about as generic and universal. Arguably, it is not thought about or talked about much at all, and yet it has significant consequences in the world. MIFARE chips are central to large-scale pushes toward a cashless society, integrated public transport systems, and of course biometric surveillance, and private and state data collection. That a technology such as MIFARE chips might not be legally generic, but socially so, points to the slippage not only within legal frameworks, but more broadly.

This slippage, or intangibility, of what constitutes the generic— specifically in the merging of infrastructural spaces with the social—is a theme taken up by AbdouMaliq Simone (2016), in his engagement with how logics of "generic blackness" are co-inscribed on urban infrastructures and black bodies. Generic blackness, for Simone, is something different from blackness, and in describing it, he captures the difficulty in pinning it down. He is interested in eliciting forms of blackness that are at once everywhere and nowhere, located within particular geographies, and yet move beyond them:

> I want to explore this generic aspect of blackness—exploring, and by no means solving, a conundrum that entails extending a seemingly intangible aspect of blackness across peoples and cities that are not black while remaining within all of the convoluted histories and meanings that seem "most black." How do you detach something so rooted in piles of evidence and affect? How do you make something potentially belong to those who may want no part of it, who have no concreted basis to claim it, and which could detract from the concrete nuts and bolts of dealing with those "real" black bodies struggling every day? How to make the resource embodied by blackness into something that is not necessarily dependent upon that embodiment? These questions define what the generic means here.

What Simone captures here is the simultaneous sense of presence and absence, of embodiment and abstraction, that is often the hallmark of the generic: how, as a concept, it points to types of meaning that are ubiquitous and yet intangible. He points to how genericness moves between, for example, the discursive aspects of race through text and talk, and its material forms, such as urban infrastructures. And yet, although the generic crisscrosses several different conceptual spaces, this does not negate its potency as the bedrock of the social, nor indeed its importance as a broader anthropological concern.

Rules of the Generic

So how might the copy and nonspecific be configured within a useful concept of the generic? How might the generic be understood as an end-point of meaning as well as a beginning? As a classificatory project as well as an evaluative one? Anthropology and its dual engagement with ethnographic detail and abstraction is a remarkably useful space in which to think through the generic. Moreover, this dual engagement, as well as a long history of extraction of general rules, and specificity-free extrapolation, mirrors a particular project that seems to be inherent in the generic. But before turning to how the generic has retained something of a furtive presence throughout the history of modern anthropology, and has generated many of its persistent fault lines, I wish to briefly sketch some of its more normative and popular spaces that might provide something of a map, or at least might gesture to a conceptual expansiveness.

I describe three examples, seemingly arbitrary and a little slight, drawn from music. I do so, in part because taken together, music and sound form an increasingly fruitful avenue in anthropology through which to understand the types of indexicality and convention that I suggest are at play with the generic (Eisenlohr 2018; Harkness 2014; Wilf 2014). Moreover, music is a particularly rewarding arena in which to think about the generic. No doubt this is related to the fluid auditory worlds in which we move, and the wholesale cultural practices of music listening that are common the world over—in that we listen to music in focused and chosen ways as well as in spaces without consciously doing so. The same is less true of many visual media, such as television and film, although product placement is a good example of how this is changing. Moreover, when compared to many other forms of art, music sets itself apart in its preponderance for genre-marking and boundary formation. The genres listed on the music-streaming service Spotify, for example, dramatically outnumber those for television and film on Netflix (Erikson et al. 2019; Seaver 2022). The space between the shared characteristics that define "genre" and the over-shared characteristics that define the generic is inevitably an overlapping one. Is the rhythm of a hip-hop song or the pedal steel guitar of a country song a generic feature, enabling one to recognize the type of song within seconds? Or is it a matter of custom, tradition, or convention? How do we understand the classificatory practices of particular social worlds? In many ways this is the crux of this book—not to circle the roundabouts of the term "generic," but rather to explore its remit as a concept.

Generic 1: The Universal Building Block

In 1969, the funk-soul group, the Winstons, released the single "Color Him Father" in the United States on the Metromedia record label. The song itself was very successful, selling more than a million copies and winning a Grammy award, but faded quickly from US collective musical memory. However, it was the flip side of that single, "Amen, Brother," a generally uninspired and instrumental filler, that has become famous, and of elemental importance in the history of modern music. Having gone nearly entirely unnoticed for more than a decade, it was revived in the 1980s amid the emergence of sampling technology and hip-hop. A very brief 6-second, 4-bar drum break, seemingly a throwaway moment, occurring between 1:26 and 1:33 minutes into the song, subsequently became known as the "Amen Break." A listener might easily miss it, and certainly one would not describe it as a particularly important musical moment. However, it is now widely regarded as by far the most globally sampled piece of music in history, and would likely be recognizable to most people with even a passing interest in contemporary pop and hip-hop music, or indeed anyone who has listened to radio in the last three decades. The Amen Break continuously circulates and recirculates through music and ears the world over, and has been sampled by the likes of NWA in the 1980s, David Bowie in the 1990s, the theme tune to the cartoon *Futurama* in the 2000s, and more recently by artists such as Diplo and Skrillex. Nevertheless, few people would be aware of it, and yet they would know it when they hear it. The break itself is now thoroughly generic, learned by beginner drummers, ubiquitous across musical genres. What type of generic is it, though? It is less the culturally wasted, and more an accepted building block of modern music—a template. One might argue that there is at least some form of citationality at play, one that is inherent in sampling itself, with the use of call-backs and gestures of musical anchoring central to how artists position themselves within musical genres, but there is also an element of universal building blocks at work. Like, for example, the ubiquitous role of chorus and verse progressions within the three-minute pop song, the Amen Break has become a generic formation upon which originality rests.

There are numerous reasons behind the explosive ubiquity of the Amen Break. Its uptake and circulation rested in part on the material infrastructures of sampling, such as the release of the E-mu SP-1200 sampler in 1987, which went some way in democratizing cultures of sampling in music. The drum break itself is also not particularly difficult to replicate outside of direct sampling of the original record, and it is thoroughly amenable to slowing, quickening, and reinterpretation, allowing it to retain a musical usefulness. Significantly, it is not particularly notable, limiting its distinction and thus the risk of overdetermination, and continuing its appropriation and use. Moreover, it did not circulate until it was involved in a project of collation, on the first official *Ultimate Breaks and*

Beats (SBR 501, edited by "Breakbeat Lou" Flores, and released on LP in 1987). While there is something of a rule book as to how things become generic according to definitions of patent and copyright law (although that is still ambiguous and relies heavily on an interpretation of an agreed societal common sense as to usage), there is no rule book for how things become generic in a broader sense. But if there were one, the Amen Break would surely tick many boxes: the material infrastructures, such as sampling machines; its amenability to large-scale replication and circulation; and projects of collation, all of which are often part of what constitutes the generic.

Generic 2: The Ubiquitous

It is difficult to overstate the reach of Hillsong Music Australia. Wander into nearly any Evangelical or Pentecostal church in the world, and you will hear one of its songs being sung. It might be in the original English, or perhaps a translation into a local language. In my fieldwork among Christians in the Philippines, just as many, if not more, people are involved in translating, reading lyrics, and listening to Hillsong music as in reading the Bible. Beginning as an offshoot of Hillsong Church, a megachurch in Sydney, Hillsong Music has emerged as an engine of global Christian music since the early 2000s, only recently perhaps faltering in its dominance of the market. A record company in a classic sense, it maintains a highly regulated roster of quasi-bands.[7] Heavily influenced by early 2000s pop music, Hillsong's music is remarkably similar across the sixty-plus albums it has released. Locating Hillsong's music within a genre is problematic, as its influence is so prominent that it has in large part itself constituted the genre of contemporary "Christian music." Dominated by anthemic ballads, in a standardized American pop accent, with lyrics explicitly emphasizing faith, songs such as "Only You" (2013) and "By Your Side" (1999) mimic song titles (for example "Only You" by Yazoo, and "By Your Side" by Sade), lyrics, and sentiment from pop music genres. Hillsong music seeks to present faith and love in Jesus and salvation within the conventions of a love song. And there is obvious leakage between pop and Christian genres. Songs such as "The Climb" (2009), by Miley Cyrus, not only resemble Christian pop, but are aimed at that very audience.

There is the question of directionality in how Christian music mimics and indexes other genres. The likes of pop stars such as Miley Cyrus aside (she subsequently sought to move away from courting such an audience), in a classic assignment of the generic as a value statement, Christian pop is assumed to be fully generic, aping the worst parts of pop. Christian music is often unoriginal, clumsy, and overwrought in sentiment, so that few people would look to any Christian music scene as a space of musical originality and experimentation. This was not always the case, of course, and the history of music is obviously shot through with Christian innovation. Even within twentieth-century pop music, one can easily point to gospel, blues, and country (emerging fully or in part from Christian worship music) as influencing pop music trends. But this is for the most part no longer true. Christian music is presently and widely viewed as generic. It is wholly derived *from*, and not originating *of*. But there is clearly more to the story of mimesis and genericness here. For one thing, no longer does the Christian music scene mimic so many different genres. In the early 2000s, there was a Christian version of nearly every mainstream musical genre, from nu-metal to emo and hip-hop. Christian pop existed as a shadow music scene, Christianizing whatever musical trends were currently popular. And yet, over the last decade, there has been a winnowing of what constitutes the genre of Christian pop. Less is derived from multiple musical genres, and there has been an evident consolidation—in part because of Hillsong, and at the least wholly aligned with its sound— that has seen Christian pop declare ownership of the genre it once was viewed as copying.

More important, rather than simply viewing Christian pop as derivative, if one looks to the ethnographic context in which it is listened to and circulates, there are far more complex practices, scales of indexicality, and mimesis at play. In the Philippines, for example, mainstream Filipino pop has in many ways mimicked US mainstream pop, much as Christian music has, thus blurring the positionality of Christian pop itself to other genres. Likewise, cultures of music listening for Christian pop are different in the Philippines than in the United States. The meaning of a Christian identity itself is, unsurprisingly, different in Mindoro than in Mississippi.

Generic 3: The Discarded

One of the more infamous examples of a generic form that circulates in many parts of the world, emerging from the United States, is muzak—or a capitalized and registered Muzak, which is very much part of the story. A well-known descriptor of soulless, derivative music, muzak is famously synonymous with background music of a certain low-valued type, such as elevator or supermarket music. There is a doubled type of generic at work here with regard to muzak. Muzak, a music brand and corporation, produced generic music, while the lowercase term "muzak" has become a generic term for generic music. But while it is used as a generic term, it was a registered trademark, and was a leading proponent of background music in the United States for most of the twentieth century.

Stripped of anything that might make it distinctive, muzak and elevator music has always been designed to be backgrounded. Muzak, as Joseph Lanza has noted, "shifts music from figure to ground" (Lanza 2004, 3). At best ambient, at worst inane, muzak characterizes a widely held value determination, and indeed conceptualization, of the generic. And yet, as I discuss in chapter 2 with regard to on-screen branding design in California, such an emphasis on the generic as the culturally devalued often misses the semiotic work and precise labor that is sometimes devoted to achieving the unmarked and backgrounded life of these artifacts. The capitalized Muzak—much like prop designers in Hollywood—was self-consciously engaged in producing such generic forms. This is where Muzak and muzak diverge. Although its reputation indicated otherwise, Muzak was never simply involved in producing cheap and inane music to fill the silence in shopping malls. Rather it attempted to redesign how people listened to music.

Muzak emerged from an attempt to challenge radio by piping music directly through electrical wires rather than over the airwaves, but by the 1940s it had begun to actively use, and finance, psychological and behavioral studies of how people unconsciously listened to music. Manufacturing music to directly manipulate people's behavior (see, for example, a published report titled *Effects of Muzak on Industrial Efficiency* [Case & Co. 1964]), such as increasing labor efficiency among factory workers, or music that would slow the pace of customers walking in supermarket aisles (through its "Stimulus Progression" music), Muzak unsurprisingly faced a backlash and accusations of "brainwashing" (Barnes 1988). As a result, from the 1960s on, Muzak moved toward releasing work by original artists (though most remained anonymous), and segued into producing mimetic and "easy listening" forms of music genres, notably jazz, thus fully aligning itself with the generic, and the type of generic that is associated with the unoriginal, overappropriated, and clichéd—the culturally discarded. Of course, since muzak gestures to the manifestly inane forms of music eroded of originality and creativity, the inheritors of muzak are also all forms of background music, notably ambient music, ranging from Brian Eno's work in the 1970s to Max Richter's *Sleep* recordings in 2015, to meditative music played in yoga classes, to more recent ASMR (Autonomous Sensory Meridian Response) YouTube videos.

Thus, what exactly do we mean when we use the term "muzak" (in its general sense) or "elevator music"? It is the generic, not as the ubiquitous, but rather as the culturally wasted. It is about the slip from originality to unoriginality. What is the relationship between easy-listening music, the popular use of songs (such as Leonard Cohen's "Hallelujah," mostly by way of Jeff Buckley's version) in TV shows and movies, and intentionally produced background music, ranging from actual elevator music to innovative ambient music? Is "Macarena," the 1995 one-hit wonder, generic, or just ubiquitous? If the "Macarena" dance at weddings is generic, are "Despacito" or "Shape of You," two of the most watched music (or any other type of) videos in the last decade, generic as well? Or is it not the universality of the music, but rather the intent of its circulation that deems it generic? Perhaps "Despacito" is not generic, but the musical and visual forms it is predicated on are? Does one dig deeper and locate the generic within shifts from major to minor chords in sad songs? Is the use of E-minor in melancholic pop songs the same as the Amen Break? All in all, it would seem that to parse the exact borders of the generic is a losing battle. And yet it is a determining factor in the social. It is not just the discarded, but the process or alchemy through which the discarded becomes strangely normative and continues to circulate in ways that become templates.

Within the three musical examples presented here, we might start to see the types of spaces the generic inhabits more broadly—identifying the differences and similarities between (1) Muzak, the discarded and overproduced, and at the same time the semiotically skilled and purposefully designed; (2) Hillsong, the Australian Christian music corporation whose music has become so successful among Christians globally that is ubiquitous in Christian worship and is teetering on ownership of the genre, constantly engaged in classificatory practices of what constitutes that genre; and (3) the Amen Break, a drum sequence that has become so sampled that it has become a foundational and universal, if latent, template.

Anthropological Histories of the Generic

Somewhat surprisingly, aside from work on branding, patents, and copyright (Coombe 1998; Manning 2010; Mazzarella 2003), anthropologists have been less than keen to engage directly with the concept of "the generic," especially in its guise as the nonspecific but nevertheless encapsulating quality of all. I say directly, for as I argue throughout this book, anthropologists and social theorists have long been searching for "the general" and "the fundamental" within the social. Of course, we find the generic as far back as Plato's theory of forms (later, order theory), in which all instances of things in the world are only known in terms of the generic idea or form of the thing. Similarly, we might look to the potentiality and purity of category and concept in Kant (2008 [1781]). That is, the individual horses we see in the world are ultimately knowable because they correspond to a generic, ideal type—the essence of the thing. Within the intellectual genealogy of a modern anthropology, something close to the concept of the generic, if not the term itself, can be traced back to at least the nineteenth century as a going concern. Think here of Max Weber's own concept of "ideal types," gesturing to the abstracted and common, reduced and purified of specificity (as well as, for Weber, a classically utopian form) (Weber 1978 [1921]). Or of Edward Burnett Tylor, who cut out an early space for modern anthropology and gave currency to the term "culture" as a theoretical concept: he likewise ignited a century-long concern within the discipline for "minimal definitions," which continued up to and including the work of Clifford Geertz (for example, his definitions of both "culture" and "religion" [Geertz 1973]). Indeed, such definitional concerns enabled these terms to become load-bearing forms of social classification and taxonomy. For Evans-Pritchard, as for the vast majority of his contemporaries and predecessors, the purpose of studying "the primitive" was not just to see the complex (of civilization) writ simple, but to see how, for example (and repeating a famous nineteenth-century phrase), primitive religion was "a species of the genus religion," enabling an insight into the "nature of religion in general" (Evans-Pritchard 1965).

The same might be said of many early twentieth-century anthropologists. Early machinations of the classificatory fetish might now be most famously associated with Durkheim and Mauss's *Primitive Classification* (1903). It is worth remembering, however, that the English translation arrived much later, by way of Rodney Needham (1963), amid the enclosed universe of structuralism—another time in which remarkable amounts of intellectual labor were invested in uncovering the elemental nature of classification. Similarly, contemporary manifestations of classificatory concerns might be best highlighted within the quick boom of the ontological turn in the mid- to late 2000s (for example, Holbraad 2012; Viveiros de Castro 2004). Whether we consider the nature of red powder in Cuban divination, the ability to distinguish the borderlines of ontologies, or the definitional differences between humans and animals (Kohn 2013), throughout the ontological move, we see the universal, general, assumed, unmarked, and de facto—and of course, equivalency—all hovering near the surface.

My goal here is not to critique. Rather, it is to highlight the generic as an ongoing concern. Something like it is ubiquitous in the history of ethnographic theory. For example, in Durkheim's "elementary forms" of religion (1915), in Lévi-Strauss's "mythemes" (1958), or in Paul Radin's framing of the trickster myth as a universalized archetype (1972 [1956]), we find ideologies of the generalizable, which in turn is dependent on a (sometimes implicit, sometimes explicit) view of how meaning is reducible to its form—without necessarily its content. And how it is, of course, replicatable. Replication is inherent to any concept of the generic. Anthropologists associated with the Culture and Personality school of thought were often, to greater or lesser degrees, working on projects of abstraction—decoupling the empirical specificity from general rules and patterns of human psychology. Ruth Benedict, of course, was famous in this regard, and her *Patterns of Culture* (1934) and *The Chrysanthemum and the Sword* (1942) sought to elicit the fundamental psychologies of particular groups, as well as universally circulated types. Some anthropologists, such as Alfred Kroeber, used the term "generic" often, as well as "general," and actually described Tylor's definition of culture as useful because of its generic qualities (Kroeber and Kluckhon 1952), while others, such as Franz Boas and Edward Sapir, preferred instead to write only of "general patterns," and "general laws."[8] Such language and theoretical approaches all fit comfortably into a view of a classical ethnography/ethnology divide: the ethnographic project as a record of the lived specificities of culture, the ethnological concerned with comparison and contrast, to attain an understanding of how culture works, but also of what it is when reduced to its most generic form. If there was a difference between Kroeber's generic and the general, it is how the general is fully abstracted, while the generic is inevitably materialized in practice. It assumes an adjectival frame. Thus, one finds generic terms, concepts, and objects. That is, there are generic Mayan ceramic pots, but Mayan culture itself is not generic (Kroeber 1948). In this reading, the generic is abstracted, but always still to be found in the world.

At some moments the generic has risen to the fore, however briefly—for example, by anthropologists using linguistic data to make larger claims regarding the role of the generic within particular social contexts. One such was Dorothy Lee in the 1940s (publishing as D. Demetracopoulou Lee), on the role of the generic for Wintu people in Northern California. Now forgotten, her 1944 article in *American Anthropologist* staked a claim for the generic, inverting our assumptions of the concept, suggesting that the generic is sometimes much more highly valued than the particular. Drawing a definitional line between generic and universal, Lee argued that it is the generic that is hugely orienting for people, enabling them to navigate the world in ways that a focus on particularity cannot—a point I return to throughout this book. In fact, just such an argument motivates this book: that often the socially devalued forms, reproduced and copied into oblivion, are overlooked, but nevertheless are crucial to the contemporary lived experience. Working primarily within a linguistic context, Lee suggested that the inferences drawn from generic categories within the linguistic and categorizing practices of Wintu people, while recognizably generic, are contextually implicated in unique ways. Both overlapping and resisting social categories such as animate and inanimate, Lee described how a reliance on the generic resulted in different formations of, for example, self and object. The opening paragraph is worth quoting in full:

> To the Wintu', generic concepts are primary and the particular is derivative. I use the term *generic* rather than *universal* advisedly. To the Wintu', the given is not a succession of particulars, to be conceptualized and classified under universals. Rather, it is immediate apprehension of qualitatively differentiated being. For the Wintu' speaker, the phrase *there-is-fog,* with a separate word for the subject and the predicate, is only a grammatical alternative for his other expression, *it-fogs.* He prefers an expression such as *it-roes* to *roe exists, it-darks* to *it-is dark;* he will say *she-soups* instead of *she-makes soup. Round* is derived from *to-be-round, thunder* from *to-thunder,* nest from *to-build-a-nest.* Actor and result are one with the act. Substance is one with existence; it cannot be said to be particular, as it is conceived of in European thought. Substances, as for example roe, fog, wood, deer, are originally differentiated but since they are not delimited, the particular is a secondary concept.

While Lee's subsequent discussion of linguistic data is difficult to summarize, indeed difficult even to parse, the takeaway is not only that can we see the generic at work in the world, but also that it exists simultaneously as a classificatory practice and as a way of assigning and discerning value—and not always as repository of the nonvalued. In highlighting a context in which the generic is not necessarily defined in a different manner, but located within a different semiotics of value, Lee pointed the way for an understanding of the generic as something malleable, and far more collectively and socially constituted than we might think.

Lee's brief but important work aside, throughout the anthropological canon, we still get to see how something similar to a concept of the generic has been at play. In truth, however, it was unfortunately less a concerted project of engaging the generic in the world, and more the creation and classification of things as generic. It was always the outside in, never as an emergent and in situ concept in the world.

If, as I describe in chapter 1, the generic emerged most fully in anthropology within the problematic frame of "folk taxonomies" and cognitive classificatory practices, there are other, more recent thematics that are important to fleshing out the concept of the generic. One of the more interesting anthropological uses of the term, as I describe in chapter 2, can be found in Robert Moore's (2003) discussion of brand genericide, and Krisztina Fehérváry's (2012) and Paul Manning and Ann Uplisashvili's (2007) examinations of genericness as related to socialist and post-Soviet economies. For Moore, the generic is the decoupling of object and specificity, in this case between product (material and otherwise) and originating brand producer. Similarly, Fehérváry notes that the generic label on consumer goods, as commonly understood, "simply identifies a product, conveying nothing more than its use value ... it offers no contextualization of the item beyond its existence on the store shelf" (Fehérváry 2013, 117). And yet, for both Moore and Fehérváry, the inclusion of the generic within semiotic contexts does not stop there. The generic will always convey, in its material instantiation, much more than nonspecificity (Fehérváry 2009). In a similar vein, Marilyn Strathern (2014), in her discussion of relationality, focuses on the role of generic kinship concepts and terms. Viewing generics as abstracted types employed for purposes of both inclusiveness and opacity that may give recognition without specificity, she notes there is nothing inherently vague about generics: "generics are rather more than metaphorical extensions of ideas calling out for concrete expression" (14). While not all authors use the term or concept directly, the abstracted forms of practice that Strathern calls attention to are likewise important to scholars such as Anna Tsing, who seeks to understand global processes outside predominant thematics of universalism and classifications (Tsing 2011). Moving from plant taxonomies to Indonesian discourses on universal rights, for example, Tsing engages the remit of universal templates through an ethnographic critique of the "logics of classification" (Tsing 2005, 14; see also Li 2019; McIntosh 2009). It is in such anthropological spaces, sometimes invoking classical (and heavily critiqued) anthropological topics such as kinship and taxonomies, that we find a very different but nonetheless crucial concern with how specificity and nonspecificity, as well as naming and classifying, are at play in the social.

One of the most important spaces within anthropology to think about the generic has been the study of genre. The term "generic" is actually common within the scholarship on genre (for example, "generic intertextuality"). In this sense, the generic is simply that which makes up a genre—that is, a genre must have apparent and well-known contours in order to be constituted as such. The generic is those contours. The generic is constituted within the forms and practices of enregisterment (Agha 2005; Gershon and Prentice 2021). If a romantic comedy must have a meet-cute, or a passionate kiss as the denouement, or if a pop song must have a verse, chorus, and bridge—these are the generic aspects of a genre. The generic constitutes the identifiable features of a genre. In a foundational paper, Charles Briggs and Richard Bauman (1992) provide an argument for the importance of attending to genre as a mechanism of the social, as well as an etymology of genre in anthropology. Similar to what I am outlining here with regard to the generic, they identify genre where it was not explicitly used as a term, but where its definitional spaces were clearly encountered. In highlighting the inherent classificatory aspect of genre, they show how it was enacted as a "sorting principle," especially within the early Boasian school and the concern with collecting texts. Myths, legends, and folktales, for example, were some of the genres used, with the dividing lines between each often drawn by the anthropologist, rather than emergent from those people with whom they worked. As Bauman and Briggs note, "the genre brings into special relief the way in which generic categories and textual forms are correlated by the ethnographer and the consultant" (1992: 133).

Additionally, genres inside and outside of anthropology "provide powerful means of shaping discourse into ordered, unified, and bounded texts. As soon as we hear a generic framing device, such as 'once upon a time,' we unleash a set of expectations regarding narrative form and content. Animals may talk and people may possess supernatural powers" (Briggs and Bauman 1992, 147). One can quickly see how this focus on genre aligns with spaces in which semiotically inclined anthropologists have worked, such as citationality (Nakassis 2013), intertextuality (Hanks 2010), fractal recursivity (Irvine and Gal 2000), scales of indexicality and iconicity (Silverstein 2003a; Carr and Lempert 2016; Inoue 2004), and entextualization (Haviland 1996). Similarly, the "ground" in Charles Peirce's semiotics (Keane 2018), and John Searle's use of "background" in the assumptions people make in interaction settings (Searle 2002), or Erving Goffman's description of presuppositions and pragmatics, as well as frames (1983, 1974), all highlight the taken-for-granted aspects, the necessary conventions, and shared understandings essential to communication.

Moreover, as one begins to think about genre in terms not only of how lines of difference between genres are constituted, or what falls within one or the other, but also of how they structure and shape practice, the importance of genre, beyond its ex situ classificatory role, is evident. As Orlikowski and Yates (1994) note, in their discussion of communicative genres in workplace organizations, "a genre established within a particular community serves as an institutionalized template for social action—an organizing structure—that shapes the ongoing communicative actions of community members through their use of it" (543). Staying within the workplace of the office (even if it exists in a more imaginary or aspirational form) Ilana Gershon has ethnographically engaged genre (and the generic) in ways that seek to merge and expand genre as we know it in textual terms into spaces of language interaction, media, and the ordering templates of sociality. Situating genre as template and type, she writes that "genres not only shape how information is organized in the moment of interaction, but they also shape how the knowledge discussed in one interaction will be able to travel into other interactions" (Gershon 2017, 68).

If genres produce templates, what semiotically becomes of those templates as they increasingly circulate, out and beyond their original intent, is of equal importance, and a question this book pursues. Rather than differentiating the generic from genre in this book, I am more interested in aligning them. They are not exactly the same, but they certainly breathe the same conceptual air. Like genre, the concept of mimesis, along with simulacrum and verisimilitude, is of huge import in thinking about the generic. Some anthropologists in the 1990s, such as Greg Urban, Michael Taussig, and Benjamin Lee, working within varying intellectual traditions, highlighted the relationship between reproduction, mimesis, and circulation—especially of certain images, sounds, narratives, templates, and memes, an issue I describe in chapter 3 in relation to nineteenth-century world's fairs.[9] This literature, while wide-ranging, has often centered on the theoretical and ethnographic explication of publics and mass mediation (Cody 2013; Mazzarella 2017; Warner 2005; Shryock 2004; Hull 2012; B. Lee and LiPuma 2002), and intersects more broadly with scholarship on mass media (Boyer 2013, 200; Mazzarella 2013; Strassler 2020). And before them is perhaps the most famous work on mimesis, that of Eric Auerbach (2003 [1953]). For all that has been written and said of his work *Mimesis*, drawing subterranean parallels and discontinuities across sometimes opaque literary genres, he highlights some fundamental, if often forgotten, aspects of experience and representation—notably for our purposes here, the play between backgrounds and foregrounds, how they are constituted, and for what end. Moreover, as I discuss throughout this book, mimesis, in its full, multifaceted nature, often draws attention to distinctions between form and type, reasserting the force of templates and formal structure.

Replication is inherent to the generic. Jean Baudrillard (1994 [1981]) and Gilles Deleuze (2004 [1968]) emphasized in different ways the entropy and mirroring of meaningfulness—of semiotic signs themselves— merging and emerging. Similarly in the work of Jacques Derrida, we see the breakdown in the durability of authorship, text, and originals (famously in Derrida 1977 [1972]). It comes as no surprise to anyone that categories of originality and unoriginality are absorbed into worlds of discerning value. Walter Benjamin (1968) famously articulated, not only how the replicated is tethered to the original, and the machinery (literal and ideological) that enables such tethering, but the irresistible large-scale ascription of value to both. It is not that I wish to remove the generic from its position within the spectrum of value and nonvalue, but I do want to better understand it, both as an evaluative tool and as a way of seeing (ordering) the world. There are undoubtedly elements of the derivative, fake, and inauthentic at play in the generic, of mimesis of forms as well as content, but surely the generic is at its most potent when, unsettling Benjamin's famous temporal trajectory of original and reproduction, it exists simultaneously as both the original and the copy. Instead, the question is how practices of mimesis and replication begin to constitute copies, not as fakes or unoriginals, but as backdrops and templates. Templates both emerge out of, and are the engine of, replication. One might think here of website templates, common type fonts such as Times New Roman, or the circumference of bicycle wheels: they are all the outcome of particular cultures of (re)production, as well as their source. This is a matter I discuss in more detail in part II of the book, in relation to Christian forms of practice, in which the generic begins to depart from discourses on inauthenticity and originality, and instead generic Christian forms are circulated as the shared, nonspecific essential aspects of Christian belief.

It is within these contours, thus far described, that I explore the resonances and importance of the concept of the generic over the course of this book. In making a case for its necessity for understanding the social worlds we inhabit, I move among several ethnographic and conceptual spaces. The reader will undoubtedly find that I often return to language throughout the book. At times I focus on the legal definitions of particular terms, at other times I turn to a more finely grained linguistic anthropological framing, as in chapter 5. In doing so, I try to make a case for the usefulness of language, and of media and semiosis more generally, in understanding the complexities of the generic as a concept. Indeed, one aim of this book is to bring the analytic spaces of media and language more closely together, and push back against seeing most ethnographic contexts as anything but wholly saturated by language and media.

The book is organized into two parts. Part I seeks to conceptually delineate the generic, describing its nature and boundaries in social theory. Much of this first part of the book is concerned with the generic in its more explicit forms, self-consciously constituted as a concept in the world. Although distinct in subject matter, chapters 1 through 3 are perhaps best thought of in a simple semiotic triad of type, token, and circulation. Ultimately, as I describe, the generic essentially exists in the connective tissue and play, not only between types and tokens in the world, but in how that relationship type and token itself is constructed, deconstructed, and ultimately circulated (Silverstein 2005). A famous distinction generally credited to Charles Sanders Peirce in 1906, "type and token" is a useful semiotic tool, though it does, if one is not careful, risk an easy binary that overdetermines everything. Unsurprisingly, Peirce was seeking to do anything but imagine a reductive binary. For example, he saw type and token as part of an informal triad with *tone* (Peirce 2009 [1906]). As I discuss in chapter 2, and as noted by other scholars, the contemporary brand is hugely dependent on types and tokens, and the play between them (the Nike brand as type, and its actual sneakers as instances, or tokens, of that type). Or take Peirce's own famous example of the word "the" as the type, and all the instances of "the" (for example, on this page) as tokens of that type. Though the two are dependent on each other—a type needs tokens to be a type, and tokens need types to be tokens—Peirce himself was much more interested in the ambiguities, tensions, and plays between them.[10]

In chapter 1, I describe how the generic has come to occupy a unique position in how we understand the nature of category and classification in social thought, often existing as a "covert category." This is notable, for example, in relation to a contemporary politics of language, in which the unmarked categories in language are increasingly foregrounded and contested. I engage a particular genealogy of the generic. I describe how the generic, emerging as a normative concept within systems of classification in the natural sciences in the eighteenth century, always had something of an ambiguous existence as a classifier, especially when compared to its typological cousins, genus and genera. While forms of classification were always popular in a burgeoning sociocultural anthropology, their broad evolutionary nature saw them always looser in their schematics, with terms such as "primitive" and "savage" never attaining the scientific precision that a Linnaean binomial nomenclature promised. I relate how the generic, under the guise of "folk taxonomies," in many ways both rose and fell in the Philippines, albeit in a sometimes problematic rendering of the Philippines as a static fieldsite by American anthropologists. I describe how Harold Conklin, working on the island of Mindoro, prompted a wide-ranging interest in ethnobotany and folk taxonomies. Such a focus on how people classified plants (and colors, and so on) immediately called to attention a larger question of how universal are the ways through which we see and order the world and our experiences. I then turn to the work of Michelle Rosaldo, who also worked in the Philippines, and describe how, through a focus on language practices, she thoroughly critiqued such spaces of generic universality. I discuss how a semiotics of the marked and unmarked, while enjoying something of a limited currency within linguistic and semiotic anthropology in the 1980s, emerges now as a component in how we understand contemporary media and politics of the social, notably in relation to race and gender, and a politics of naming.

In chapter 2, I turn to the work of prop designers in Hollywood. This industry offers a particular insight into the world of the generic. My interest here is in understanding their work in providing on-screen, non-branded representations of consumer products. In taking up the work of Independent Studio Services, a large prop house located in Los Angeles, I look at how fake and generic alternatives to "real" brands essentially replicate brandedness without any brand, reconfiguring the very definitions of token and type. I describe how the design teams at ISS navigate the problem of copyright infringement on screen, and how they are explicitly engaged in the semiotically specific work of creating generic forms. In building a believable on-screen universe, these prop designers must immerse themselves in the complexities of collective aesthetics and social norms, without marking anything as overly specific, and in the process they cut out a unique semiotic space in which the generic is a crucial component. In this dynamic between trademarking and unmarking, we begin to see not only a fracturing of the spaces between real and fake, original and copy, but also the critical role of nonspecificity.

Chapter 3 explores the generic in perhaps its most famous guise—the mimetic—describing how within replication, new forms of nonownership and nonauthorship emerge. Here we see the generic emerging within practices of circulation. I describe how such ideologies of replication are deeply entwined in how we think about authorship and ownership—for example, in the Obama "Hope" poster controversy in 2008, in which the very concept of ownership fractured, as the artist, Shepard Fairey, used an unauthorized photo of Barack Obama as a basis for his poster—and how this is in stark contrast to current discourses on the emergence of a market for digital nonfungible tokens (NFTs). I argue that forms of the generic are crucial to both, and begin to dissolve the boundaries of ownership. I then turn to how ideologies of collective ownership and of genericness suffuse larger social projects—with mimesis enacted as a form of commensurability. In particular, I take up the projects of colonial design, mimesis, and genre in nineteenth- and early twentieth-century world's fairs, and in particular the case of Ireland, which sought to overcome stereotypes of an impoverished and famine-beset country through inclusion in the international circuit of world's fairs, with the promise of a particular modernity that those exhibitions embodied. In doing so, however, it unexpectedly achieved the cosmopolitan modern by performing its inverse, a bucolic and commodified Irish heritage, in what became a complete, functioning, and traveling Irish "village" named Ballymaclinton. The fact that such new "types" of heritage were constituted in a space of exemplar cosmopolitanism (world's fairs), in ways similar to the Obama "Hope" poster controversy, reveals a fundamental estrangement between form and content, creating a space in which the generic "nonauthor" and "nonowner" emerges. I frame this chapter through the semiotic lens of form/content, and of type/token, exploring how contestations over representational authority and ownership, as well as processes of abstraction of people and publics, highlight the productivity and circulation of generic forms.[11]

While part I describes the generic in its different twists and turns as a concept, part II changes tack. Here, I offer an experiment in what a sustained ethnographic engagement with the generic might look like. That is, what are the benefits of taking the generic seriously as a conceptual tool and as a fundamental ethnographic concern? How might we ethnographically grapple with how the generic is embedded within the contours of sociality? How do people live with and through generic forms? In order to explore these questions, and in offering this ethnographic experiment, I turn to what is perhaps one of the most famous spaces in which universals, copies, type and tokens, and ubiquity are at play: Christianity. In many ways, Christianity can be located within the generic, while at the same time having a unique and forceful history in the Philippines. Over the course of three chapters, I move between sites of Christian formation in the Philippines, specifically on the island of Mindoro, where I conducted two years of ethnographic fieldwork. I do so in order to engage with how such a famously and historically global practice has become a space for the generic while maintaining a fundamental claim to an overarching universality and similarity. How does Christianity, subjected to large-scale exportation, importation, and appropriation, as well as mimicry and redefinition, nevertheless circulate as a shared universal? Such universality is inherent in the theological claims of Christianity, but also in its lived and negotiated forms. To that end, in part II, I describe how a research project that set out to explore the emergence of religious difference in Mindoro became the study of how such difference was continuously predicated upon a particular shared semiotic of a "generic Christianity."

Part II begins not so much with what is categorized as Christian, as with what is classified as non-Christian. And *who* is categorized as such. In chapter 4, I sketch the story of an annual performance in Mindoro, in which Indigenous Mangyan actors replay a collective moment of salvation by Catholic missionary sisters—missionaries who are themselves sitting in the audience watching the Mangyan actors dressed as Catholic sisters reenact that exact missionary moment. Such mimesis is central to how Mangyan people are constituted in terms of Christianity. I then relate the history of how Christianity became legally defined in terms of its negation through a 1919 Philippine Supreme Court case, in which the US colonial administration decided that the forcible relocation and imprisonment of Mangyan communities on the island of Mindoro was legal. In doing so, the courts established the appellation "non-Christian" as the generic legal term for referring to all Indigenous groups and thus establishing Christians as the foremost unmarked group. I then return to present-day Mindoro, and explore how Jehovah's Witnesses use sign language in proselytizing among deaf and hard-of-hearing people. I describe how they inhabit a specific language ideology, viewing sign language as more natural than vocal languages and reliant on generic forms of gesture. Chapter 4 concludes with a description of how this view of language and gesture as generic is deeply implicated in their view of what a "generic Christianity" entails—a Christianity stripped of denominational and doctrinal difference. In both cases, the generic is employed as a means to differentiate and define what is not.

In chapter 5, I examine the practice of Bible translation and the underlying sets of Christian ideologies regarding the commensurability of linguistic forms. Ethnographically situated around a Bible translation workshop in Mindoro in 2013, during which the Bible was translated into three Mangyan languages, the chapter argues that the degree to which the actual linguistic forms in the scriptures are divinely inspired often exists as an irresolvable semiotic problem for Bible translators. To this end, I discuss the means through which the Holy Spirit is taken as an essential mediator between the fallible work of Christian translators and the Bible as a language-instantiated form of God's presence. I show how the employment of "generic" language by Christian translators is not only dependent on a particular view of what generic is and how language works, but also enables them to achieve their goals in translation, and mirror and circulate the divine universality of scriptural meaning in earthly form. So, while I make a case in part II for the circulation of, and dependence upon, a type of "generic Christianity" in the Philippines, it does not align with any generic class of religious forms, or minimal definitions. It is not particularly classificatory in nature. Rather, generic Christianity includes those worship practices, beliefs, habits, and norms that are shared by everyone, whatever their denomination. It is the ubiquitous. It is also reduced to the essence of the thing, stripped of specificity. It is this project of purification, of distilling type from token, that enables ubiquity to be cited and circulated through shorthands.

In chapter 6, I stay within a setting of Christian conversion, and indeed Christian pluralism, on the island of Mindoro. Rather than look at how a "generic Christianity" is circulated, or relied upon, I instead focus on a moment in which it changes. I examine the emergence of a Christian pluralism in a small rural community. I describe how the community, nearly entirely Catholic, has experienced the arrival and establishment of a born-again Evangelical church. I explore the conversion strategies of this new church (Jesus Is Lord Church), and one pastor in particular, working to establish a religious alternative to the dominant Catholic faith. I consider the critique of Catholicism that is on display, notably in the setting of church services. In particular, I address a practice of discursive omission, whereby an explicit critique of Catholicism is wholly avoided, thus steering clear of a conversionary rupture, and instead a set of practices that rely on a more implicit stance of valuation of Catholicism take place. I discuss the formation of religious backdrops, in this case, the universal and ambient presence of Catholicism, against which Christian evangelists must enact techniques of conversion. These unspoken, backdrop forms of Christianity are, I argue, at the core of what constitutes contemporary spaces of genericness. Moreover, such a context helps reveal how the generic not only enables acts of silence and omission, but is often a fundamental characteristic in sociality and, in particular, forms of social rupture and upheaval.

I embark on this journey, in chapter 1, by describing how the generic came to inhabit a unique space of tension in how we understand the nature of category and classification in social practice. How has the concept of the generic come to exist as something ever-present, yet overlooked—a ubiquitous "covert category," to borrow a phrase from the linguistic anthropologist Benjamin Lee Whorf? In outlining a genealogy of the category of color and classification, I show how the generic might help us understand better a contemporary mode of media and language, in particular, the politics of naming and unnaming.

CHAPTER 1

Roses Are Red

THE SEDUCTION OF ORDER AND
THE COVERTNESS OF CATEGORY

I do not remember whether I ever told you that some years ago when comparing the culture of northwest California and southwest Oregon, I found fully as much that I was able to use in your fragmentary Takelma notes as in all the rest of the literature put together because statements in the latter were generic.

—*Alfred Kroeber, writing to Edward Sapir, July 8, 1922*

If there is a presumed context in which to immediately locate theories of the generic within anthropology, it is arguably that of long-held concerns over classification and taxonomy. There has never really been a time in which anthropology has not been concerned with classification, even as these terms have changed their valence and target over the course of a century. Historically, whether it was the classification *of* cultures, or the nature of classification *in* them, lines of a classificatory fetish can be drawn throughout the anthropological canon. To some extent, every ethnographic project is ultimately concerned with describing the generic features of a society, group, subculture, social context, or style, no matter the scale or theoretical orientation of the analysis. That is, in any project that seeks to encapsulate or extrapolate from, one often finds anthropology, intentionally or unintentionally, rendering microcosms of the social. As described in the introduction, there existed an abiding concern in the nineteenth and early twentieth centuries for root explanations, generalized patterns, and minimal definitions. Likewise, definitional debates over concepts such as culture and religion were primarily informed by greater projects of establishing universal categories that would allow all forms of specificity to fill them up, and in the process be ordered. Such concerns were intimately interwoven with the concept of the generic. As discussions of classification and typology are understood essentially as projects of studying similarity and difference, underlying assumptions of genericness are often nearby, even if furtively so. In this chapter, I track a small corner of anthropology's genealogy to do with language and naming, and its relationship to classification across social milieus more generally. I describe how the utterly lived aspect of language, stubbornly refusing it any stagnancy, should fully inform how we understand the nature of social categories and practices of classification. Moreover, I gesture to the importance of accounting for the covert categories in social worlds, especially those seen to be universal, generic, and all-encapsulating.

Many anthropologists in the nineteenth and twentieth centuries, ranging from Frazer, Tyler, and Rivers to Boas, Sapir, and Benedict, were directly interested in the overt classification and taxonomy of peoples and their kinship systems, beliefs, myths, and languages. Such explicit classification reached its high-water mark in the 1950s, a brief period when "folk taxonomies" emerged as a prominent subject of theorizing and discussion (Frake 1961; Berlin et al. 1973; Hunn 1976). This literature was not a critique of classification, but rather a full engagement with the nature of *how* people classify things, pulling in linguistic, ethnographic, and, as time moved on, increasingly cognitive approaches.[1] Much of the time, the generic was an explicit and formal part of folk taxonomies. Necessary for any classification, or order theory, was the identification and collection of inclusive, universal, and unspecified categories that could be said to be typical and recurring. If in the introduction we saw a latent view of the generic emerge from within classificatory projects and a burgeoning anthropology, here I want to briefly sketch how biological concepts of the generic, from outside anthropology, slowly began to inform ethnography and how cognitive theories of the generic began to take hold. I then describe how linguistic anthropology, and more generally an anthropology concerned with language and *naming*, came to highlight the inadequacies of cognitive approaches, pushed back against universalist claims, and has offered a grounded critique of the taxonomic and generic as they emerged within folk taxonomy and cognition. A focus on language provides an immensely productive space in which to understand the covert categories of the social and points the way to a much broader and dynamic view of the generic. For instance, we might ask whether the classificatory underpinnings of color terminology and taxonomies in the 1950s have something to say about the present covertness of whiteness as a racial category in United States. Inasmuch as we understand the need to account for the forms of power that inhere in having the authority to name and define, accounting for the intentionality behind silence and omission is likewise critical. To that end, I describe how a contemporary politics of naming has made use of the categories of *marked* and *unmarked*, and how the overt/covert aspect of markedness sees the emergence of something uncannily similar to the generic. If formal categories are socially power-ful forces, the covert ones—occupying the spaces of the unnamed and unmarked—are often even more so. We can then ask not only how covert categories rely on generic unmarked and unspoken backdrops, but how we can understand more broadly the ways that categories and naming are reliant on generic types. Indeed we can ask how generic types are made.

While etymologically linked to and contiguous with *general* and *genus*, and more directly emergent from the French term *générique*, the mean-ing of generic was always, it seems, surprisingly slippery. Arising out of biological nomenclature, the term itself, if not the concept, assumed some prominence within the Enlightenment growth of taxonomic stud-ies in the aftermath of Carl Linnaeus's *Systema Naturae* (2003 [1735]). Although Linnaeus himself would not use the term *generica* until his subsequent botanical taxonomy, *Critica Botanica* (1737), he regularly used the terms *genus* and *genera*. The use and meaning of *generic*, as a descriptive adjective, however, was always somewhat more ambiguous. We find different definitional emphases throughout its early use, which continue to this day in contemporary debates regarding the meaning and purpose of, for example, generic taxa (Randall 1987; Van Pool and Van Pool 2009; Louwrens 2004). While the concept itself permeated the bio-logical sciences and taxonomies, there has been very little historical dis-cussion of the emergence of the term. The nature of taxonomic systems, of course, was an engine of debate across eighteenth- and nineteenth-century science, in which people such as Darwin and Lamarck were seri-ously invested, but the role of the generic was never properly clarified. It was deployed, albeit in different ways, without strict definition.

In a rare piece explicitly engaging the concept, Harley Harris Bartlett (1940) described the emergence of the generic in scientific taxonomies. Naturalizing the concept and making a claim for its universality across time and cultures, he also highlighted the inextricable role that language and naming have within any understanding of the generic. Aligning folk botany within scientific taxonomies and nomenclature, he noted:

> The grouping of distinguishable but similar kinds into genera seems always to have been a linguistic necessity if there was to be a reasonable flexibility and precision in the nomenclature of plants and animals . . . in speaking of the generic concept in folk botany as needing little change to become essentially the generic concept of modern science, I

must of course guard myself by inviting that the inclusiveness or size of genera, now as in the past, is less a matter of science than of linguistic preference and convenience. (Bartlett 1940, 350)

This is a point I will return to later, but it is worth noting how Bartlett conceptualized the relationship between universal ideas of the generic and language. Here, while language is often prioritized as essential to how the generic exists (what terms and names people use), it is a surprisingly static version of language. Whether the concept of the generic was viewed as intrinsic in people (in language or cognition) or intrinsic in the world (morphological similarity and contrast), or as an externally imposed scientific form of classification, the generic and language were often presented together, as in Bartlett's history of the concept. There is another way, although less common amid the history of scientific classification, and one that, whether universal or not, is rather a meeting place or ground upon which similarity and difference begins to get sorted. This form of the generic is discernible in the work of geologist Abraham Gottlob Werner, a notable figure during his day, but for the most part now forgotten.

Werner was an early enthusiast of the term, employing it in a categorical manner in his 1774 work, *A Treatise on the External Characters of Fossils*, translated into English in 1805. Werner is useful for recognizing perhaps an originary purpose of the concept itself, as a categorical default that was itself empty of contents. Using the term *generic* (*generischen* in the original German), Werner outlined a classification system of fossils based on their external features. His use of the term is interesting. In describing their "generic characters" based on categories such as color, cohesion, unctuosity (greasiness), coldness, taste, and weight, he made it a notable ordering term. In figure 1, one can see how the term is used—not as a taxonomic rank within a classificatory hierarchy into which something is ordered, as *genus* might be, or as Linnaeus used the term, but more as a universal category of relatedness. In this sense, the generic category is not that something might be solid, but that it can defined in relation to solidness. It is not a cognitive category, in the human mind, nor is it in material forms, but something between people and the world. In doing so, Werner was one of the few early taxonomists to directly address the meaning and nature of the generic:

But Genera of External Characters, or generic characters, are those which direct us to what is to be determined in a fossil, such are Colour, Cohesion of the particles, Weight, Taste, &c. Thus in saying Copper-

Pyrites has a colour, I have not determined any thing, but merely pointed out what is to be determined. Again Generic Characters are *common and particular; common* are those which point out what is to be determined in every fossil, and *particular,* what is to be determined in *one branch of fossils only;* of the former, those adduced above may serve as an example; of the latter, we may notice *solidity, sound,* &c. which are solely applicable to *one branch of fossils,* viz. the *solid.* Species of External Characters, or *specific characters,* are those which determine what may be said of a fossil with respect to a generic character; as e.g., saying that Copper-Pyrites, with respect to its colour, is *yellow;* or, with respect to its hardness, is *half-hard.* It is from these *specific characters* that we form the External conception of a fossil, and that we frame its External description; whereas the *generic characters* serve merely to class the specific under Genera in the System, and to indicate those for which we are to seek. (Werner 1805, 69–70)

In Werner's reading of the term here, the generic character "direct[s] us to" something, but is not necessarily a category inherent in matter. It is more about attuning the human senses and cognitive orderliness to salient features of material objects. It is a term through which we might best think about matter, in this case fossils, allowing a baseline from which the details of difference might be catalogued—an orienting push toward focusing and categorizing difference from a framework of shared qualities. For Werner, specificity is predicated on the unmarked shared, something that points to a much more useful way of thinking about the generic and aligns with contemporary thinking on naming and unnaming. In this sense, it is general. It is common. But the play between human senses and forms of ordering, and the physical details and "objective" ordering in nature of matter, is nevertheless always evident in Werner's writing.

By the mid-nineteenth century, moving away from Werner's ambiguous and sliding interpretation of the term, the generic resisted a unitary meaning, but began to solidify in several ways. For the most part, its use continued to remain within the worlds of biological taxonomy and classification. Charles Darwin, for example, relied on the term, but in a very straightforward manner. In his work, it refers to the shared and universal, standing in binary opposition to the specific. As he wrote in *Origin of the Species:*

If some species in a large genus of plants had blue flowers and some had red, the colour would be only a specific character, and no one

TABULAR ARRANGEMENT

OF THE

GENERIC EXTERNAL CHARACTERS OF FOSSILS.

Common generic external characters.

I. The Colour.

II. The Cohesion of the particles, in relation to which
Fosils are distinguished

into

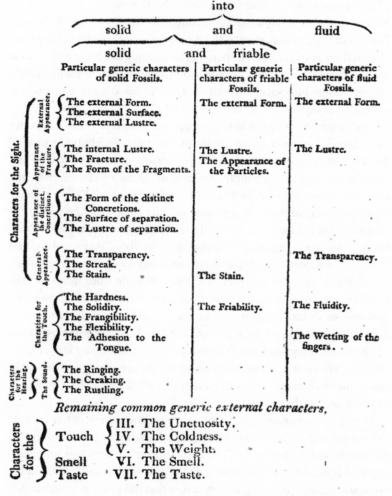

	solid and		fluid
	solid and friable		
	Particular generic characters of solid Fossils.	Particular generic characters of friable Fossils.	Particular generic characters of fluid Fossils.
External Appearance.	The external Form. The external Surface. The external Lustre.	The external Form.	The external Form.
Appearance of the Fracture.	The internal Lustre. The Fracture. The Form of the Fragments.	The Lustre. The Appearance of the Particles.	The Lustre.
Appearance of the distinct Concretions.	The Form of the distinct Concretions. The Surface of separation. The Lustre of separation.		
General Appearance.	The Transparency. The Streak. The Stain.	The Stain.	The Transparency.
Characters for the Touch.	The Hardness. The Solidity. The Frangibility. The Flexibility. The Adhesion to the Tongue.	The Friability.	The Fluidity. The Wetting of the fingers.
Characters for the Hearing. The Sound.	The Ringing. The Creaking. The Rustling.		

Characters for the Sight brackets the first four groups. *Characters for the Touch* and *Characters for the Hearing* label the lower groups.

Remaining common generic external characters.

Characters for the {
Touch { III. The Unctuosity.
IV. The Coldness.
V. The Weight.
Smell VI. The Smell.
Taste VII. The Taste.

FIGURE 1. Generic characters, from Abraham Gottlob Werner's *A Treatise on the External Characters of Fossils*, 1774. University of Michigan Library.

would be surprised at one of the blue species varying into red, or conversely; but if all species had blue flowers, the color would become a generic character, and its variation would be a more unusual circumstance. (Darwin 2009 [1859]: 122)

Determinedly contrasted with the specific, the generic here, in Darwin's reading, is also not inclusive—it is the baseline shared. Its meaning has no purpose in distinguishing between objects. This is not the generic of genus and genera, occupying a hierarchical position of order, which he uses in the same paragraph. I highlight the examples of Werner and Darwin to suggest that even in the nineteenth century, the concept had little in the way of a coherent, stand-alone meaning as a category in and of itself—that is, "the generic." While essentially synonymous with genus/genera within biological taxonomic systems, as Werner and Darwin showed, it always had other connotations.[2]

The naturalness of generic taxa, or genera, or of taxonomic categories more broadly, raises a set of questions that immediately point to matters of language, cognition, and the universality of human sociality and meaning-making. For example, are generic forms of classification the result of limitations of cognition and human memory? Do we need to start conceiving of things in a generic manner to manage the vast forms of specificity? For example, we need to have the generic category of "car" because humans cannot sort through the details of shape, colors, and brands of different cars. Are generic groupings a cognitive, human act, or are things grouped like that in the world, aside from human intention? For example, there are biological lines of division between many species—or to locate the matter in grander philosophical terms, there is order in nature aside from our linguistic and cognitive interventions. Or in the often repeated words of Robert Lowie, mostly by way of Lévi-Strauss, "We must first inquire whether we are comparing cultural realities or merely figments of our logical modes of classification" (quoted in Lévi-Strauss 1963b: 10).

While, as previously noted, one can trace the generic, or at least its lurking presence as a concept, throughout the history of anthropology, it was mostly as a mishmash of botanical classification, cognitive and philosophical concerns over the universality of perception, and ethnographic engagements with meaning and structure that the generic, as an explicit term, was taken up in anthropology, notably under the rubric of "folk taxonomies."

Homilies for Taxonomies

Sociocultural anthropological research on folk taxonomies arguably began in earnest in the Philippines, with the work of Harold Conklin in the 1950s. It was here that a classic biological framing of classification most fully merged with an ethnographic, sociocultural engagement. Conklin conducted his research among Hanunoo people, one of eight Indigenous ethnolinguistic groups in Mindoro, collectively known as Mangyan.[3] Pursuing an ethnographic understanding of botanical classifications among Hanunoo people, with a noted talent for the precise work of collecting data and identifying thousands of taxa and plant categories and terms, Conklin has been lauded for opening up the field of ethnobiology. Although Conklin published several monographs and papers on Hanunoo agriculture and botanical categories (Conklin 1969, 1957), this phase of his career is perhaps now most famously associated with a very short paper on color categories (Conklin 1955b), in which he examined the nature of color classification in the Hanunoo language. This paper elaborated as much on the nature of Hanunoo classification as it did on how one might go about studying it. Opening up an ethnographic space in which cognitive, linguistic, and cultural perspectives merged, an explicit focus on classification seemed to promise a systematic and standardized (and diagrammatic) anthropological method. However, while this ostensible "sciencing up" of anthropology through folk taxonomies would gather speed in the 1960s, early engagements, such as Conklin's, hewed surprisingly close to a more contemporary and broadly relativist understanding. For example, in his discussion of color, Conklin notes that

> under laboratory conditions, color *discrimination* is probably the same for all human populations, irrespective of language; but the manner in which languages classify the millions of "colors" which every normal individual can discriminate *differ*. Many stimuli are classified as equivalent, as extensive, cognitive—or perceptual—screening takes place. Requirements of specification may differ considerably from one culturally-defined situation to another. (Conklin 1955b: 340)

Moreover, he suggests that "color, in a western technical sense, is not a universal concept and in many languages such as Hanunóo there is no unitary terminological equivalent" (Conklin 1955b: 339). "Color terms," he notes, "are part of the vocabulary of particular languages and only the intercultural analysis of such lexical sets and their correlate can provide the key to their understanding and range of applicability. The study of isolated and assumed translations in other languages can lead only to confusion" (340). Nevertheless, Conklin believed that there existed "basic" categories, emergent from structural contrasts, and at two levels. Interestingly, Conklin suggested that color classifications among Hanunoo people "have certain correlates beyond what is usually considered the range of chromatic differentiation" (343), including, famously, dryness (rara?) and wetness (latuy). One can see a similarity here to how Werner was understanding basic categories through which comparisons and contrasts can be made. Conklin located the basis of his research and classification within a tradition of a quite straightforward linguistic relativism, and he continuously emphasized throughout his work the potential dangers in seeing superficial equivalencies between linguistic systems as a measure of universality in how people see the world.

While the ideological resonance of color has been reinserted into the discipline through recent debates on ontology (what does the redness of powder really mean? [Henare et al. 2007; Keane 2009]), many scholars forget that anthropology has long had an odd obsession with color, with many articles and books on color and perception, color and linguistic categories, color and cognition, and so forth (Hardin and Maffi 1997; MacLaury 1997; Randall 1987; Witkowski and Brown 1977; Berlin and Kay 1969). In a way, this is hardly surprising, if one is concerned with questions of culture and universality. Color is a conspicuous and neatly bounded topic to look to, shared even by children in their play: how do I know that you see the same color that we both call "blue"? From Goethe's interest in the early nineteenth century, to the contemporary anthropology engagement of Michael Taussig's discussion of the deeply colonial and ideological battles over color and its meaning (2010), to the color of socialism (Manning 2007), we see how the object of color has woven into and between classic and overdetermined spaces of objective and subjective claims. Johannes Itten, for example, famed for his association with the Bauhaus school, sought to commingle the affective tenor of color and tones with a more diagrammatic and classificatory guise (figure 2). Lest one think, however, that folk taxonomies favored the more cognitive and sensorial topics, one should note that in the 1960s, even the likes of cooking methods received such treatment (Perchonock and Werner 1969). Any object could fit within a broader taxonomy. It was the emergence of taxonomic research, with its cognitive tilt, that essentially took Conklin's theory of "basic" categories and moved toward a full engagement with those categories that are viewed as unmarked, unreferenced, and unspoken. The intent here was that establishing basic generic categories allowed for difference to be better understood. And yet, to fully engage the classificatory, especially when claims to scientific objectivity were already seeping in, posed a danger of imposing rather than revealing the ways people order their worlds.[4]

Cognitive Meanders

Ignited in many ways by Conklin's work, the literature congregating around folk taxonomies in the 1960s and early 1970s was hugely diverse, including linguistic work (for example, on ethnosemantics), ethnobiology and ethnobotany, the emerging subdiscipline of cognitive anthropology (associated with anthropologists such as Roy D'Andrade but stretching back to A. I. Hallowell, and W. H. R. Rivers), and, perhaps most famously, the role of folk classification in structuralism (most innovatively in Lévi-Strauss's *The Savage Mind*). Collectively, this literature on folk taxonomy made several large claims about how humans cognitively and socially interrelate, constitute, and categorize their worlds. Soon, however, the emerging role of cognitive and structural anthropology expanded into larger claims about the cognitive regulation of cultural experience. Conklin's hesitancy to frame specificity within overarching universal systems of cognition was matched by the likes of Dell Hymes, who warned of abstracted universal classificatory systems. Hymes noted that "the study of folk taxonomies, and of ethnographic semantics generally, needs specification of communicative contexts if it is to achieve the implicit goal of discovering the structure of vocabularies as wholes" (Hymes 1964). He suggested that the linguistic impetus for a broad structuralist approach in anthropology had given rise to interest in "folk taxonomies" in the first place (Hymes 1983).

There is no doubt that mainstream anthropological interest in folk taxonomies has thoroughly waned. The term itself is problematic. "Folk" in such a context notably tilts toward a racializing and exoticizing hierarchy, while "taxonomy" suggests a locatable scientism that is static, holistic, and ultimately reducible to a chart of words and arrows. The multifaceted approaches to folk taxonomy by cognitively inclined anthropologists and psychologists, however, remain bluntly problematic for contemporary sociocultural anthropology. In many ways, this is because it rests in part in the language of engagement. There is little in the way of a discursive reflexivity and politics of representation that sociocultural anthropologists are generally, and at least partially, adept at. Sometimes, it is the particularity of the subject matter itself. While it might be an admirable job to catalog the thousands of terms a fishing community might use for maritime

FIGURE 2. Johannes Itten's diagrammatic "Color Star in Seven Light Levels and Twelve Tones," here in black and white tones, from *Utopia: Documents of Reality*, 1921. Courtesy of the Smithsonian Libraries and Archives.

purposes, the reader might often want more ethnographic description of the play and politics of such terms. That is, the lived context of such linguistic categories is viewed by most as paramount, and the rendering of an acontextual schematic is challenged as a myopic form of abstractive knowledge. At its most uncompromising, the critique of this literature and these approaches rests on a fundamentally different way of understanding how humans and meaning work. Such critiques emerge directly out of 1960s and 1970s culture critique and the rise of interpretive modes of ethnographic theory, and question the basic tenets of psychological and cognitive approaches to how human sociality works. One notable arena in which this critique occurred was within approaches to language, with strong versions of linguistic relativism and poststructuralism used to undermine the rigid views of cognitivists. Taxonomies, particularly of the folk variety, have slipped out of view for most anthropologists since the 1980s—with good reason. But, of course, even the preeminent proponent of interpretive approaches, Clifford Geertz, ultimately remained committed to charting a generic story (Balinese cockfights, for instance) that was being told, perpetuating the notion of a generic something in anthropological accounts.

And yet, as cognitive anthropologists such as Roy D'Andrade have argued, there is also good reason for an anthropological focus on taxonomy, rather than on the features of biology. Understanding how people themselves understand "x as a *kind* of y" is a hugely important way through which people organize the world. And we move through the world in part by organizing it (Bowker and Star 2000). When we view anthropological concerns with infrastructure or medical concepts, for example, as a space of human and nonhuman interaction, material and immaterial world-making, and the subjectivities of sensory ordering, the taxonomic classification of things and people appears closer to contemporary interests than not. Thus, whether understood as a cognitive means of enabling humans to manage large amounts of information, as the innate tendency toward experiencing the world through a gestalt-like system, or as social meaning-making projects, both big and small, through which we make and discern things meaningful and important, the taxonomic doings of people would seem to be of some relevance.

As noted, interest in folk taxonomies, while mostly migrating away from sociocultural anthropology, is alive and well in certain quarters, such as ethnobotany, and in some ways crosses paths with the cognitive and linguistic approaches to the generic (Forth 2016; Pakia 2006). Even in reading modern work on folk taxonomies, most sociocultural anthropologists would likely not make it much past the opening paragraphs without taking issue with some of the major assumptions upon which such taxonomies are conceptualized. Nevertheless, given the prominent role the concept and category of the generic plays in this literature, it is an important mode of thinking. Indeed, I argue that the version of the generic running throughout this cognitive science literature points to the sheer slipperiness of the term (even if unrecognized by many using it), its intrinsic ubiquity, and its presence as something important in the world.

Scott Atran has written about the use of the generic within folk biology and taxonomies. Perhaps known to sociocultural anthropologists more for his work on terrorism and violence (Atran 2010), which runs against many anthropological discourses on violence and agency, he has long been interested in the cognitive backdrops to the classificatory goings-on of humans. His interest, for example, in understanding the convergences and divergences between folk biology and scientific biology sounds alarms for many, including an assumption that the classificatory practices of all people are essentially similar. With opening sentences such as "In every human society, people think about plants and animals in the same special ways" (Atran 1998), Atran runs counter to a vast ethnographic literature that suggests otherwise (Tsing 2011; Viveiros de Castro 1998, 2004; Kohn 2013). Nevertheless, as with Werner, there is something of the generic more as a concept, rather than only as a passing term, at play in such work. In attempting to describe how a universal cognitive process of biological classification exists, and to argue for the centrality of the classificatory level of "generic species" within such a universal process, Atran explains why he uses the term "generic" in the first place. First, he notes that in practice, people do not differentiate between the level of genus and species, and that such a distinction came from a limiting European context. Rather, people are classifying "monospecific genera," so the use of "generic species" is a preferred term. Interestingly, for Atran, they are the more useful group—cognitively, linguistically, and culturally—they are the "salient mnemonic group" (1998: 550). And significantly, he argues that the term "generic species" is salient as "people" (unmarked/generic) see each member of a generic species as sharing a "unique underlying nature, or essence" (550). All of which is to say that these types of cognitive science engagements in "folk" or "ethno" classificatory practices give rise to a constant, and highly problematic, slippage between cognitive categories, both scientifically objective (claims of morphological equivalency), and linguistic. However, they also highlight some of the partial definitions and stakes of the generic, arguing for the generic as an essential component to how we see and move through the world (figure 3).

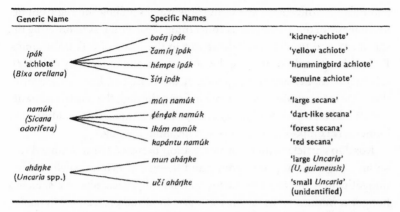

Generic Name	Specific Names	
ipák 'achiote' (Bixa orellana)	baéŋ ipák	'kidney-achiote'
	čamíŋ ipák	'yellow achiote'
	hémpe ipák	'hummingbird achiote'
	šíŋ ipák	'genuine achiote'
namúk (Sicana odorifera)	mún namúk	'large secana'
	¢énʈak namúk	'dart-like secana'
	ikám namúk	'forest secana'
	kapántu namúk	'red secana'
aháŋke (Uncaria spp.)	mun aháŋke	'large Uncaria' (U. guianeusis)
	učí aháŋke	'small Uncaria' (unidentified)

FIGURE 3. Brent Berlin's use of the generic in describing the "binomial specific nomenclature in Aguaruna folk botany," 1976. Courtesy of *American Ethnologist*.

As described in the introduction, running somewhat concurrently with the concept of generic in cognitive anthropology, or the cognitive social sciences, has been the use of the concept in linguistics. While perhaps never fully aligning with sociocultural concerns over the deeply embedded particularities of lived contexts, collectively, cognitive and linguistics explorations of the generic have pushed for an important focus on how to understand similarity and difference. Moreover, several terms and concepts actually point to a space in which to understand the generic outside of rigid taxonomic hierarchies. Concepts such as "unique beginners," (Berlin 1992), (the basic, most inclusive category), and "covert categories," (categories that arguably exist but are not referenced through any single term [Lucy 1992, Lee 1996]),[5] all gesture to the complex and fascinating ways through which we might start accounting for the centrality of the generic in our social worlds. But I want to stay in the 1970s for a moment, at the high-water mark of cognitive anthropology, and describe how sociocultural anthropologists for the most part turned away from the ostensible objectivity and universality of folk taxonomies.

Michelle Z. Rosaldo and the Critique of Taxonomy

If the boom in an anthropological literature on "folk taxonomies" found its footing in the Philippines, it maybe lost it there also, at least in American sociocultural anthropology, with the work of Michelle Zimbalist Rosaldo. While perhaps best known for her writings on gender and language, as well as on headhunting among Ilongot people in the Philippines (Rosaldo 1984, 1982, 1980a, 1980b), in a 1972 article titled "Metaphors and Folk Classification," she went some way in pulling the rug from beneath many of the assumptions concerning the usefulness in ordering the specificity and the nature of difference in the study of folk taxonomies. Rather than simply contesting the universality and objectivity of botanical categories, her article suggests that the shared and social categories that appear to be essential for maneuvering through the world and easily discerned (such as "color") may emerge from unique, cross-cutting, and immensely complex constellations of meaning-making.

Rosaldo's article centers on the relation between the interlinked taxonomic practices of plant naming and the use of magical spells among Ilongot people in Northern Luzon in the Philippines. She first sketches Ilongot communities as for the most part fluid and unstratified in family, political, and religious structure, and as a society in which most adults are well versed in, and regularly use, popular spells, or *nawnaw*. These *nawnaw* are not the specialized spells of shamans, but are available to all and commonplace in their usage. Rosaldo describes the widespread use of *nawnaw*, and how a practitioner, without any proclamation or notice, will set about gathering the correct herbs for the spell, indicating the linkage of plant taxonomy and spells. Some spells are for curing certain aliments, such as diarrhea, while others serve to either invoke or repel spirits. Then, alone or with a patient, the practitioner "beats, rubs, steams, or smokes his magical materials" (Rosaldo 1972: 85). The practitioner shouts or whispers a somewhat improvised spell for about ten minutes. And in many ways, that is that—a quite unremarkable and ritualistically stripped-down use of magic. But if one focuses less on the authority or efficacy, for example, of these spells, and instead on the language forms used, *nawnaw* become more interesting. Two parts of Rosaldo's research collide here: her interest in spells and magic, and her work on botanical knowledge. With regard to the *nawnaw*, the two were obviously connected, and she became interested in understanding both the structure of the spells and why certain plants were chosen for certain spells.

Unfortunately, not only did Rosaldo find a lack of any regularity in magical usage, including the linguistic aspects of the spells, but also the matching plant/herb recipes for the spells similarly lacked any noticeable pattern. The same names were even attributed to different plants and herbs by different people. Thus, the situation appeared as something of a free-for-all when it came to the taxonomy of plants and to their use in magic spells. Moreover, Ilongot people did not appear to be concerned with irregularities and slippage in either spells or in plant naming: "when two men called one plant by different names and I asked for an explanation, they answered that each had learned the words from his own father—of course they didn't agree!" (86). Rosaldo added that "it is hardly surprising that in a loosely structured community people in different homes or different hamlets diverge in their botanical knowledge. But the amount of variation was striking. Plants used only in spells, like orchids, might be identified by one or as many as 13 different labels" (86).

It appeared that the categorizing of orchids *as* orchids had little to do with any biologically shared characteristics, but rather emanated from one the two types of spirits invoked in *nawnaw*. One of these, the *Lampuŋ*, existed in geographically high places. While all plants used for a *nawnaw* calling on the *Lampuŋ* were recognizably members of the family *Orchidaceae*, or orchids, they were referred to by parts of the human body, such as "thighs," "fingernails," and "braids," and throughout the *nawnaw*, the names of parts of the body played an important role. Here is an excerpt of Rosaldo's translation of a *nawnaw* to the *Lampuŋ* (85):

> He calls out the spirit; then, rhythmically, sometimes shouting and sometimes whispering the words which come so fast they take his breath, he begins to chant:

> Hey, all you spirits come listen now!
> Here are your thighs, spirit;
> May your thighs be twisted, spirit, if you do not make this child well.
> Open his heart, spirit, make him light spirit.

The "thighs" here are a metaphorical employment of body parts for the orchids used, and, by extension, for those body parts of the spirits. As Rosaldo notes, it was through this use in *nawnaw* that these orchids formed a taxonomic class for the Ilongot, emanating from a unique intersection of body metaphors and their shared use in relation to the *Lampuŋ*, representing "a recognized natural category, even though the category itself is not named" (88). Echoing Ludwig Wittgenstein's description of *Familienähnlichkeit*, or familial resemblance (2010 [1953]), through metaphor, in this case the body, Rosaldo argues, people "discover relevant resemblances between categories which are not ordinarily related to one another" (92). The forms of reference and signification—here emanating from a context of body-part naming and the high spatial location of certain plants and certain spirits—align for the most part with the taxonomic family *Orchidaceae*. The taxonomic family, however, is arrived at by way of divergence, disagreement, and difference of interpretation—not through necessary forms of agreement of objective and biological similarity. For Rosaldo, "plant names may 'refer' insofar as their range corresponds to 'real' or holistic categories in nature; sets of semantically related lexemes may be used to label morphologically related kinds of plants. But semantic discriminations within these categories may have little to do with the constant cognitive partitioning of objective experience" (96).

The motivation here, and indeed the explanation of lexical variation, is not by way of any cognitive determination of biological species of plants, but is rather located within the metaphorical uses of language and magic and materiality. Rosaldo argues not against objective categories and biological schemas, but rather against the linguistic relationship to and reference of them. Similarly, it is not that morphological similarity and difference are not at play in determining botanical taxonomies, but rather that this is sort of beside the point. One can take this down quite a normative Whorfian path in terms of linguistic relativism and emphasize the interpretive modes of world-making that exist within linguistic structures.

This is the common cry of linguistic anthropology since Whorf (who seems to have coined the term "covert categories")—a rejection of the role of language as a simple reflection of reality.[6] Instead, language is viewed as a constitutive mode of thinking and reality—making it, processing it, and interpreting it—where little is free of language, and language in its own way, though having its own internal structures, logics, and systems, is likewise fundamentally tethered to the world. Conklin, in his own way, articulated a version of such linguistic relativism, highlighting the fallacy of trying to view particular cultural categories as universal, and using linguistic evidence to do so. As described above, he pointed out that with respect to a Western concept of color, among Hanunoo Mangyan groups in Mindoro in the 1950s, what was previously labeled as "confusion" among the Hanunoo was actually a linguistic sorting of colors based on general categories of lightness, darkness, wetness, and dryness (1955b: 343). But while Conklin was interested in showing how different language communities constituted categories differently through linguistic systems, Rosaldo is concerned not just with different languages doing different things, but with a series of uniquely intersecting spaces from which a taxonomic category might emerge. Language is very much involved, through the use of lexical items and the use of metaphor, or broadly what, for Rosaldo, would be termed a particular ethnosemantics, but there are also the material conditions of the spatial remit of orchids, of the Lampuŋ spirits, and the practice of nawnaw.

She goes further than Conklin, arguing that it is not just a case of how linguistic categories map onto objective categories of things in the world, but that these are simply not discrete systems of categorization, or categories. Arguing against an ethnographic semantics that had been predicated on the "notion of reference," that "assumed that names, whatever their use in naturally occurring contexts, are primarily labels for well-defined objective categories" (1972: 83), Rosaldo presented a much broader and socially lived context in which to understand any ethnosemantic project. In her articulation of Ilongot practices of *nawnaw*, we see how ostensibly objective categories are not that objective at all, or how they are inevitably experienced through culturally specific modes. Rather, both the names and the categories of things emerge from immensely cross-cutting and complex modes. What she describes are not only Ilongot categories, and sets of practices—of body parts, plants, and spirits—that are wholly interrelated, but ones that are fluid and idiosyncratic even among and between Ilongot households themselves.

If the work of Rosaldo and a number of her contemporaries (Gumperz 1971; Fernandez 1974; Ochs [Keenan] 1979, 1976; Hymes 1974) signaled a move away from the ordered diagrammatic ideologies of taxonomy, and clearly showed the need to locate language amid its lived contexts, the generic seemingly got lost in the mix, assigned to a view of seeing the world that most anthropologists have no interest in propagating, one that is inherently nonethnographic, decontextualized, and shunts people and their words and their meaning into quasi-scientific categories. But, in a case of baby and bathwater, what gets lost is how people engage with concepts of the generic, not as a scientific taxonomic category, but as a core means of making sense of things. The literature on folk taxonomies went some way in eliciting and filling out the concept of the generic, if perhaps failing to capture any lived sense of the concept, its uses and complexities, and its stubborn slipperiness, casting it instead as an objective term, always applied from the outside in.

We can also see the tussle between taxonomic attempts to provide overarching schemata of similarity and difference, and the questioning of the secluded forms of data such schemata are based on, namely language. Ultimately, it is never a simple case of objects and naming. And this is the point. No matter what one thinks of either folk taxonomies or the prime theoretical location afforded to metaphor and poetics by linguistic anthropologists in the 1970s,[7] the use of the generic inevitably highlights the nature of, and the immense complexity of meaning involved in, naming and unnaming.

Generic Unmarked and the Politics of the (Un)Named

In chapter 4, I describe the consequences of naming and unnaming in the Philippines, especially with regard to early twentieth-century US colonial legal definitions of Indigenous groups in the Philippines as "non-Christian." But we do not need to look so far back in time to find how naming and unnaming are seen to be critical to social meaning. Current discourses on race and gender reveal how naming (and the refusal to name) can involve much more than referential meaning, instead relying on forms of indirect and implicit assumptions.[8] In such practices of naming, we can begin to see the importance and force of linguistic shorthands and proxies.

Although the generic has never played a particularly prominent role within linguistic anthropology, outside, as noted, some forays into ethnosemantics (although this is changing [Zuckerman 2021]), several important concepts within linguistic anthropology—register and stance, and, of course, semiotic understandings of indexicality, convention, and thirdness—clearly speak, at least in part, to how the multifaceted generic is constituted. When framed in terms of naming and unnaming, one strand of the literature in linguistics, and linguistic anthropology, seems to speak most wholly to thinking about the generic, and that is the literature on markedness (or more important here, unmarkedness). It speaks to the generic, not so much within contexts of similarity and dissimilarity, but in terms of the general, basic, and universal—all those things that, for whatever reason, are understood as having no, or needing no, specificity. Not only are the marked and unmarked immediately situated within the nature of naming and unnaming, but also they enable us to think about a generic space as it is socially constructed through projects of contrast and alterity. For many linguists, markedness is of only limited use, having become so polysemous and general as a concept that it inhibits the level of specificity needed (there is just too much going on to linguistically to be able to simply mark forms of text and talk as marked and unmarked [Haspelmath 2006]). Yet it has seen a resurgence in how we understand contemporary discourses on unstated cultural backdrops.

Emerging out of the work of Roman Jakobson and Nikolai Trubetzkoy, and linguistic studies of phonology, markedness was made more prominent among anthropologists in the 1980s by scholars such as Linda Waugh (1982, 1980). Elaborating on the work of Jakobson, Waugh sought to provide a clarity and cohesiveness to the concept of markedness within language and semiotics (figure 4).

At its most basic, markedness concerns the asymmetry between pairs of linguistic features, where one feature is more specialized than the other. This can occur at the level of voiced and unvoiced phonological features, or it can move right through to semantics, where, for example, in the relationship between nouns and their plurals, the plural is for the

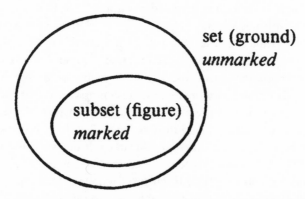

set (ground)
unmarked

subset (figure)
marked

FIGURE 4. A now classic diagrammatic representation of the marked/ unmarked, from Linda Waugh, "Marked and Unmarked: A Choice between Unequals in Semiotic Structure," *Semiotica* 38, nos. 3–4 (1982).

most part unmarked. That is, the plural is seen as more specialized. While markedness theory originated within the closed and very specific thinking on linguistic systems, as Waugh notes, Trubetzkoy and Jakobson from the very beginning saw the expansive role of the thinking about the marked and unmarked beyond linguistic features. As Jakobson wrote to Trubetzkoy in 1930:

> It seems to me that it has a significance not only for linguistics but also for ethnology and the history of culture, and that such historic-cultural correlations as life~death, liberty~non-liberty, sin~virtue, holidays~working days, etc., are always confined to relations a~non-a, and that it is important to find out for any epoch, group, nation etc., what the marked element is. (Jakobson, quoted in Waugh 1982: 300)

He wasn't wrong. There is an obvious and immense appeal to viewing not only linguistic but also social categories through an (un)marked lens (an example in itself here, as the "un-" prefix in English is marked against the adjective "marked"). The politics around "standard" ways of speaking indeed highlight the interwoven nature of social categories and language.[9] Jakobson himself not only noted the intricacies of markedness within linguistics, but also outlined some aspects of a broader interpretive mode, in his discussion of the "zero-sign" (Jakobson 1984 [1939]) and "minus-interpretation," or the "non-signalization of x" and the "signalization of non-x." Waugh elaborated on this, using an example of present and past tense in English, where the present tense is often unmarked (and zero-interpretation), and the past is marked. As Waugh notes of the present tense in statements such as "two and two is four," "the time axis remains vague, and the present tense is used not so much because it expresses a given time period but because it is the only tense that can be used with a minimal reference to time" (Waugh 1982, 303). Minus-interpretation is concerned not with vagueness or nonspecificity, but rather with the basic term. Similarly, the present tense in English is assumed to be the basic, default tense. It is unmarked, not because of an absence of specificity, or markedness, but rather because it includes all of them. It is basic, and given that every language has such unmarked distinctions, also universal. It is about how things become naturalized and no longer noticed— referenced to, and circulated through, assumption. Interestingly, such oppositional contrast and alterity can be seen to run through a literature in structuralism, from Saussure, to Lévi-Strauss, to Louis Dumont, who argued for a very similar understanding of markedness theory in his postface to *Homo Hierarchicus* (1980 [1966]), and can be seen as well in Gregory Bateson's description of schismogenesis, in which meaningful dissimilarity between social groups is predicated on a more fundamental similarity (Bateson 1958 [1936]).

One can clearly see here how close the unmarked comes to definitions of the generic, situated within a world of specificity and nonspecificity, universal and basic meaning, and of tacitness. It is not simply about categorizing, although it includes that. Rather, it is about what the consequences of such categories are. What effects and affects do such categories, emergent from thinking universals and practices of naming, have on how people navigate social and material worlds? In the use of markedness as a concept outside of linguistics and in the politics of naming in the last decade, one tends to find foregrounded a discussion of un/markedness centering on the politics and ideologies of race and identity, for example within a US context (Rosa 2019; Zerubavel 2018; Urciuoli 2009; Dávila 2008).

Indeed, a politics of naming highlights the potency of the indexical relationships between the names, signifiers, and reference points we use to articulate social forms. At the same time, we likewise see the instability of that of those relationships and social forms. The "politics," then, within these contexts is often to argue that there exist naturalized, unmarked backdrops against which certain groups are set (Shankar 2019), with some form of implicit othering involved. Such covertness of category is notably enacted within the play of ideological intent. The forcefulness of the implicit, unspoken, and absent has been well articulated in critical thought (Spivak 1988; Derrida 1976 [1967]). To that end, we find that the act of naming is often tethered to that of unnaming. While we might often align the unspoken with forms of erasure, by highlighting the nature of markedness, we also see its force.

For example, take the proposal of replacing "Filipino" with "Filipinx."[10] We see numerous forms of highlighting and replicating of covert categories here. In one sense, as with the term "Latinx," the replacement of "Filipino/a" is an attempt to resituate the politics of markedness. It is an explicit attempt to achieve gender neutrality in linguistic form. It is also a challenge to the predominance of the masculine *o* of "Filipino" to exist as the unmarked category of "Philippine-ness," encompassing both male and female forms. Such projects of introducing nonbinary nomenclature see scales of complexity abound, however. In one sense, having more currency in the United States, the promotion and use of "Filipinx" raises questions regarding the relationship between the Philippines and its diaspora. Indeed, given the Spanish and American colonial histories of the Philippines, is "Filipinx" or "Pilipinx" a reinscription of those histories or a positive reappropriation and redefinition of them? Does the relationship between "Filipinx" and "Latinx" need to be accounted for? Is it one of copying and appropriation, or one of commonality? Should the term stand alongside "Filipino/a" as a nongendered option, or should it fully replace gender differentiation? That is, who is "Filipinx" for? Moreover, while the Filipino language has the gender-marked forms of the masculine "Filipino" and the feminine "Filipina," the language itself is famous for being grammatically gender neutral, with its pronouns and possessives having no marker for gender. At the same time, one can also make the case that while pronouns in Filipino might be gender neutral, the language is hardly free from gender asymmetries, and like many other languages it is saturated with masculine norms. And should we even look to the Filipino (Tagalog) language as a space in which to achieve forms of equality at all? Its history in becoming the national language (Tupas 2015; Hau and Tinio 2003), in which the language of urban Manila and the Tagalog-speaking groups was favored over all other languages, arguably further constitutes a hierarchy of language and ethnic identities in the country.

Thus, part of the project at hand is to mark, or remark, such backdrops (Jackson Jr. 2005; McIntosh 2014). Tacking back to the earlier discussion on taxonomies of color, we may look to contemporary "white" forms of sociality as a notable example. As Jane Hill has noted, in a US context, "whiteness" is enacted as "an invisible and unmarked 'norm'" (Hill 1998: 684). In discussing controversies over how the use of mock-Spanish is described by many as just "the way people talk," here "'people' can only be that group that is unmarked and thereby 'white'" (687; see also

McElhinny 2001).[11] But while one would say that white forms of sociality in the US are unmarked, one wouldn't quite say they are generic. The representational practices or, perhaps better, instantiational practices of that sociality, however, are certainly often generic. That is, the musical Amen Break, discussed in the introduction, is not itself generic, but its circulation is. The importance for purposes here, however, in understanding the generic is that we find how powerful the construct of the unmarked is (S. Scott 2017). We are well acquainted with the social force of the unspoken and indeed half-spoken (aposiopesis, for example) but I am suggesting a space more mundane. It might be political, and infamous, but it might not. It might not be a space of contestation at all. It is, however, about how unstated backdrops are active agents, and are often socially constituted through forms of analytic practices.

As Mary Bucholtz (2019) and Susan Gal (2019), in the same journal issue, have described, the resituating of whiteness from a presupposed background to a discursive foreground highlights a wide array of linguistic tools that draw on circulating norms of whiteness. Gal, with Kathryn Woolard, has previously described the forcefulness of how ideologies of universality suffuse a standardized American accent as a "voice from nowhere," but in actuality push against any universality in practice (Gal and Woolard 2001). The projected "normal" accent or accent-free way of talking, claiming objective authority in its availability to everyone, is in reality the production of language hierarchies. Linguistic anthropologists have long studied how language ideologies are fundamentally concerned with constituting differentiation and sameness (Kroskrity 2000; Gal and Irvine 2019). It is in such spaces that the generic is a useful concept in seeing how ways of ordering the world become unstated and assumed.

I have tried here to trace, in a small way, how the generic emerged as a concept in anthropology (and more broadly in the social and natural sciences) as an empirical means of sorting similarity and dissimilarity. But these engagements missed an important if obvious point—that people themselves, acting within social milieus, are equally dependent on something amounting to the generic in order to sort similarity and difference in their lives. While employed as an outside-in, objective form of classification, it has always carried with it an ambiguity in definition, or at least a multiplicity in meaning. Moreover, language has always been attached to the generic, either as an empirical means to locate it, or as its repository. The problem, for present purposes, with the concept of generic within cognitive and taxonomic approaches is that it is ultimately concerned with, first, the best ways to categorize similarity and difference, and, second, with whether such ranking and categorizing of things is universal.

But even if the first were achieved, and the second were true—that is, even if we grant a social or cognitive universality to the generic—it remains a remarkably static view of how meaning works. We do not get the sense of the generic doing anything, or of the consequences of things in the world being thus classified. Things simply are or are not generic. But my argument throughout this book is that things being classified as generic is the result of a huge amount of semiotic work, sometimes intentional, sometimes not. That is, in some ways, nothing *is* inherently generic, it is always made to be so, just as scientists have to work to construct generic folk taxonomies. If we understand the ideologies, practices, and politics of how linguistic forms become marked and unmarked, how people shift in register and stance with regard to particular contexts and people, why would we think for a moment that a living conceptual space that is the generic would be static? Moreover, the generic is thoroughly constituted amid the social. It is a process of collective under- and overdeterminacy.

In chapter 2, where I describe the work of movie and television prop designers in Los Angeles, I highlight a setting in which people are actively engaged in producing the generic. They are, obviously, not concerned with universal cognitive or linguistic categories, but they are fully invested in navigating similarity and dissimilarity, universals of meaning. And they are critically aware of the legibility, and potency, of the unmarked. As I describe, the threat of copyright infringement in on-screen uses of branding forces an explicit engagement with branding and markedness, within which mimesis and the generic emerge. It is in these types of spaces, I argue, that the generic begins to appear as a project—a large-scale and collective one—that is less to do with the simple ascription of things as generic, and more with the making of them as such.

CHAPTER 2

Generic Goes to Hollywood

TRADEMARKING, UNMARKING,
AND THE BRAND DISPLACED

Nothing ever had been, was or would be in the universe outside it but was already present as virtual, or actual, or virtual rising into actual, or actual falling into virtual, in the universe inside it.

—*Samuel Beckett,* Murphy *(1938)*

In Manila advertising firms that work closely with American brands, it is generally accepted that the danger of brand genericization is greater in the Philippines than in the United States. One of the great fears of brands is that they will become so associated with a product that their trademark will lose value and distinction, sometimes to the extent of losing their legal rights to the trademark. This is said to occur more often in the Philippines. The reasoning goes that because of the widespread usage of English in the Philippines alongside the non-American context of brand consumption, there is a greater tendency for Filipinos to use a brand name as a generic descriptor and adjective for a product. That is, circulating your sneaker brand—say, Nike—in the Philippines carries the risk of Filipinos using "Nike" as the generic term for any and all brands of sneakers, and thus creating an existential threat to a brand trademark.[1]

Whether or not this is actually the case, it highlights how in many ways the brand exists as antithetical to the generic, with the need to be fully marked in the world, its value rooted in its ability to differentiate itself. It also shows that both branding and the generic are active spaces, with definitional lines in constant flux. The practice of genericization, or "genericide" (death of the brand), has been eloquently described by Robert Moore (2003). In his discussion of an unnamed marketing firm, Moore defines genericide as when "a brand name has lost its source-identifying power and has become just another word in the language, a term identifying not a single producer's products but the product class to which they belong (hence, 'generic')" (336). This is not simply an informal label, but a legal one, with fundamental consequences as to the validity of a trademark. That is, if the courts decide that a trademark has become generic, they can and do vacate it. As a death knell of a brand, examples of genericide abound: think of Aspirin (in the United States, though not in Europe), Linoleum (trademarked in 1864, declared generic in 1878), or Flip-Phone (originally trademarked by Motorola). Here we see not only the classic play between (and policing of) type and token, but how circulation is essential to their coherence. A court's decision on whether a trademark has become generic is solely dependent on how it views the cultural circulation of that trademark (when people ask for a Kleenex, are they referring to that particular brand, or to tissues in a generic sense?). Thus, we can immediately see the generic as something that emerges out of the social—especially through people's engagement with language and media. We all see its value and potency, even in highly regulated, commodified, and financialized spaces, such as corporate branding.

Engaging the concept of the generic allows us to better understand wide-ranging but seemingly disconnected sets of social practices. As with branding, for example, how do we understand the universality of crucifix regalia across Christian denominations in the Philippines, as relating to the striking similarity of social housing architectural plans across Europe, or the predominance of the Times New Roman type font? Or how the subtle eyeroll in response to a cliché is connected to copyright law, or how we understand contemporary forms of identity-making? But to do so, we need to move past viewing the generic as something static, the result of other social forms and processes. And one space in which we see the generic as immensely active and contested is in the practices of contemporary branding—where the mark, and identity of difference, token and type, brand and product—are necessarily foregrounded.

Probably the best known and most widespread type of generic in the world is indeed connected to branding: generic prescription drugs. The coexistence of branded and unbranded drugs, as well as proprietary and nonproprietary drugs,[2] underlines how the very nature of trademarks, patents, and copyrights—so forcefully concerned with specificity, distinction, and limitation of circulation—seems to inherently constitute their inverse, the generic. But the directionality here—that the generic is the leftover, or waste product, of branding and trademarks—recalls the broader narrative of the generic as the culturally overused. In this chapter, I push back against that narrative, or at least look at it from the other side. I describe a context in which the generic is the desired outcome, one that people consciously labor toward. I aim to show how at times making the generic can be remarkably specific semiotic work. While maintaining its unmarked nature, the generic here is revealed to be hugely effective in enabling types of world-making. Thus, while this chapter is situated in the world of branding, it describes something of the broader nature of the generic and its centrality to the world of shorthands and proxies. Echoing the discussion of markedness and unmarkedness in chapter 1, branding is often immersed in the marking and unmarking of commodities. Nowhere is this more evident than in contexts in which there are ongoing threats of copyright and trademark infringement. It is just such a space that I will describe in this chapter: a movie and television prop company in Los Angeles, Independent Studio Services (ISS), and its engagement with providing fictive, generic on-screen alternatives to branded products (or, stated otherwise, providing specific semiotic tokens to generic types).

These generic on-screen alternatives include fictional brands ("Heisler Beer") as well as generic replacements (just "Beer"), which might together be best described as nonbrands.[3] These nonbrands are used as on-screen proxies for actual, trademarked brands. These nonbrands, portrayed through the work of ISS, reveal the porous boundaries of trademarked images and brands. They also allow us to better think through the consequences of the "generic" more broadly as a circulating form, particularly in terms of how tokens relate to types. My goal here is not to provide an ethnographic portrait of the prop industry in Hollywood, so much as it is to highlight the semiotic spaces in which the nonbrand circulates. I will explore here the generic as the forms of substitution, resemblance, and nonspecificity that surround us, particularly within media spheres. My discussion of the generic nonbrand is set against the well-known up-turn in brand-sponsored product placement in television and film ("that's a Coca-Cola your favorite movie star is drinking . . .") (Meyer et al. 2016). But as on-screen product placement has grown in importance as a mechanism of advertising and movie financing, a more strategic practice has emerged of withholding trademark rights for on-screen use by the brands themselves. Thus, media spaces have become not only an increasingly important space, but a highly contested one in which the brand circulates. Because of such brand management, product placement has seen the rise of its inverse, or perhaps strange cousins—nonbrand, fictive, and generic alternatives.[4]

The fictional universes of television and movies offer a unique means of understanding what semiotic spaces and processes the generic (and the brand) can and cannot occupy. In particular, the generic brand highlights, in Constantine Nakassis's terms, the space between brand identity and the overarching role of the social ontology of brandedness (Nakassis 2012). I suggest here that this separation of brands and their particular mechanics from the broader concept of "brandedness" is useful in thinking through how the semiotic relationship between type and token is breached, or at the very least redefined. Rather than viewing this separation as an exercise in abstraction, however, the Hollywood prop-brands actually inhabit such a distinction in practice. These nonbrands are essentially engaged in the unique project of constituting ideologies of the brand without the brand itself. Indeed, although commonly understood as mimicking, copying, stealing, and otherwise appropriating brand identities and commodity value, the creation of fictive and generic brands points to a semiotic space that is more concerned with erasing the projects of distinction that are intrinsic to particular brands than with imitating them. Thus, instead of framing the generic as existing as semiotically underdetermined, vague, or nonspecific, these nonbrands show how the concept of the generic is often anything but vague—in fact, on-screen generic products are remarkably precise, and indeed distinct, in how they semiotically locate themselves in relation to brands. While on the surface this play between branding and its generic offshoots is contained within the space of movie and TV set design, I suggest that the legal spaces of copyright law and ownership are implicated, and that the role of "the generic"—in social practice generally as well as in the disciplinary spaces of anthropology—is necessarily foregrounded. Moreover, such a foregrounding of the generic is important, given that it occupies, as described in the previous chapter, a unique commingled space of evaluation and classification within broader frames of sociality.

In the wake of a critical upsurge in political and activist attention paid to brand and corporate practices in the 1990s (epitomized by the Kathie Lee Gifford and Nike sweatshop scandals, Coca-Cola union-busting in Mexico and the *Sinaltrainal v. Coca-Cola Co.* case, and the popularity of Naomi Klein's 2000 book, *No Logo*), anthropology (like much political and media discourse) initially engaged with branding through the wide lens of globalization, as well as in particular subfields, such as legal anthropology (Miller 1998; Lury 2004).[5] Subsequently, over the past two decades, the brand has in many ways become something of a thematic cynosure in anthropology. This makes sense, given that the brand intersects with several critical concerns of the discipline, ranging from the nature of the commodity, exchange and consumption, law and corporations, to the circulatory and ideological remits of materiality. It is also unsurprising that several anthropologists have taken a semiotic approach to the study of brands and branding, as discourses within corporations on branding are, as Paul Manning has noted, eerily similar to anthropological discourses on semiosis more generally (Manning 2010). That is, talk of signs and interpretation, and of the inferences and connotational value of particular images, words, and gestures, is as common in corporate advertising boardrooms as in graduate anthropology classes.

More recently, anthropological attention to the brand has often looked to the so-called "edges" of brand consumption and production, such as spaces in which the concept of the brand is stretched—materially, socially, and legally. For example, the production of counterfeit brands (Nakassis 2012; Pang 2008), the "death/genericide" of brands (R. Moore 2003), and the branding of that which is not usually viewed as being brandable, such as "cuteness" (Allison 2004), have all received attention. In such spaces, we see the brand wrested from the control of official brand managers. Admittedly such edges problematically presuppose a center, the composition of which has likewise come under scrutiny (Wengrow 2008; Crăciun 2012; Luvaas 2013). This focus on the edges of the brand emphasizes that to the extent the branded commodity is indexical of its brand, it is simultaneously indexical of the structures of its own formation (even if that formation is one that seeks to erase forms of labor). Moreover, such indexicality—as is the way with indexicality—is open to appropriation and reinterpretation. In this semiotic coalescing of brand and product that is core to the success of a brand, the relationship between commodity and production is minimized, while that between commodity and brand is emphasized, perhaps much more than in traditional forms of production and commodity.[6] It is within this opening and closing of interpretive space between the brand and the commodity that the fictive and generic can be located.

The fictive and generic products produced by ISS can be aligned with such "edges" of brand commodities. The space that these brand (or actively nonbrand) formations constitute between the ideologies of brandedness and the commodity is a remarkably useful one in understanding the circulation and ideological contingencies of branding and genericness more broadly. While they emerged as a response to the branded world, such nonbrands are now clearly engaged, semiotically and economically, with real brands (and real economies). In some ways, they bear similarities to the counterfeit, the fake, and the knockoff—such as fundamentally engaging in projects of verisimilitude and replication— but they also differ from those in that there is no attempt to replace or supplant the real. Moreover, the prop-brand originates from an overarching attempt to avoid crossing legal boundaries and infringing upon trademarks, whereas the counterfeit intentionally crosses those bounds.

As I describe in this chapter, ISS and its production teams move past the replication of brands and are engaging in a new semiotic space of brandedness, in which brandedness is actually produced without the brand itself. That is, ISS creates generic and fictive forms, not only as a means of avoiding trademark infringement, but because it wishes to avoid the overdistinction of branded identities in the shows and movies it services. The company wishes to constitute a version of the world in which the concept of branding exists, but in which the semiotic play of distinction, in which brands must compete, does not. If branding obscures the relation between the commodity and its production, it reveals the relation between the brand and the nature of brand production (a branded commodity foregrounds the practice of branding in the world). But is it possible to foreground this practice of branding in the world—to highlight that things are branded—without the use of brands? That is the project of ISS's engagement with brands. As several authors have argued, while we might read the can of Coca-Cola in our hand as a token of the Coca-Cola type, there is another type/token relation at work, where the Coca-Cola brand is the token, and brandedness itself is the type (the citationality of the brand as per Nakassis 2012; see also Fehérváry 2013). Through this lens, the fictive and generic stand as attempts to produce type without token (or only token and ontology)—essentially, brandedness without the brand.

In what follows, I take up several cases of props that in some manner stand in relation to the world of branding. In particular, I look at fictive beers produced by ISS. These are by far the most widely circulated of the company's fictive brands and have taken on something of a branded life of their own, being themselves subject to counterfeiting. As I discuss, this is an odd inversion of the real-to-fake brand, whereby the knockoff is the real and the original is the fake. Here, the original is a fictive brand that does not exist in any real commodified manner or circulate in any normal understanding of a market, and the fictive is real merchandise that is "knocking off" the fictive brand. However, my aim here is not just to highlight a simple quirk in the grand scheme of contemporary branding practices, in which the fictive and generic brand is appropriated in real and commodified forms; rather, I hope to show how prop-branding reveals the semiotic intricacies of the fictive and generic to be much more complicated, and ultimately implicated in the normative practices of brand management.

The Prop House

Independent Studio Services (ISS) is one of the larger Hollywood prop houses, located in a nondescript red-brick building in Sunland, at the foot of the San Gabriel Mountains, at both the geographic and economic edge of Los Angeles. Unlike some prop houses that specialize in particular sorts of props, for example, 1950s Americana (diner booths, soda fountains, jukeboxes, etc.), ISS has a stock of hundreds of thousands of props, and a factory capable of building almost any prop requested. ISS will make and rent out anything from mummy caskets and treasure chests of golden doubloons to SWAT team assault rifles. It has built a particular reputation for fictional brands, and is adept at producing both the labels and the packaging for normally branded commodities—milk cartons, soda, bread, candy, and alcoholic drinks. If one flicks through American TV channels or streaming services on any given evening, one is bound to find ISS products lurking somewhere on the screen.

The prop industry in Los Angeles is decentralized, and for the most part is independent of the entertainment studios. This was not always the case. In the first half of the twentieth century, as Hollywood became a major industry, props (derived from "properties," as in theater or stage properties) were owned and housed by the major studios themselves. Most often located on the large studio lots, each prop department would cater only to that studio's movies. This was part of the centralized format of the studio system, which likewise had full control of production and actors' contracts and movie distribution. As these were integrated conglomerates, maintaining control of every aspect of movie production and circulation was a guiding principle, and for the major studios (notably the "Big Five" of MGM, Warner, RKO, Paramount, and Fox), having an internal prop department made sense, given the prevailing use of sound stages and backlots for filming (think here of an actor dressed as a hotdog, on a cigarette break with another actor dressed in top hat and black tie). However, after a string of legal cases, and ultimately a 1948 Supreme Court ruling in *United States v. Paramount Pictures, Inc.*, the major studios in Hollywood were limited in their ownership and monopolies of movie theaters. Such changes initiated the large-scale "vertical disintegration" of the Hollywood studios (Bloch 2005). While such decentralization (or disintegration) of the studio system is now most often associated with the end of studios "owning" actors through stringent contracts and with the rise of United Artists and independent production companies, the prop industry was also affected by these changes in movie production.

Having thus originated as part of the studios themselves, the prop houses began to exist as their own adjacent industry in Los Angeles, and since the 1960s, most have been owned independently of the Hollywood studios and television networks. There are now hundreds of prop houses in Los Angeles, ranging in size and specialty. In addition to building their own sets and reusing basic props, such as characters' clothes, any network or major cable television show, or major studio movie, will on average use approximately ten prop houses during a production (Bloch 2005). Due in part to this economic and organizational independence from the studios, the same fictive branded props are used across networks and studios. To this end, because of the wide (and widening) scope of fictive brands, a verisimilitude of fictive branding has grown up, independent of and larger than any movie, television show, or studio. One can see an ISS "Heisler" branded beer on a Fox sitcom on a Thursday evening, in a political drama on NBC on a Friday evening, and in a Warner Brothers rom-com movie in the cinema on a Saturday night. In semiotic terms, the fictive and generic brands are no longer simply indexical of particular real brands (Heisler to Heineken, for example) but constitute and circulate within an iconic-indexically interrelated universe of fictive brands. That is, the prop-brands are not only gesturing to a specific brand but replicating the semiotic ideologies of branding writ large (Keane 2003).

Brand Displacement

The existence of prop-nonbrands is deeply connected to trademark law in the United States. Without delving into the legal intricacies, it is important to note that while trademark law is long established and expansive— although notoriously inadequate to meet the changes in media and technology—there is an inherent ambiguity and difficulty in determining what constitutes "fair" and "incidental" use of trademark (and sometimes copyrighted) brands on screen (Seiter and Seiter 2012). Thus, although it is possible to display trademarked brands in limited ways on screen without permission, it is notoriously difficult to "get it right," especially if the brand company is litigious and particularly controlling of its brand. Added to this difficulty is the nature of filming, where the risk of having to reshoot because of incorrectly judging the fairness of a trademark use is so costly as to be prohibitive. Rather than tease out the complexities and risk infringement of trademark use, studios, production teams, and the prop designers often find an easy solution in the fictive and generic forms of branding.

In general, the prop houses shunt the legal work surrounding their use of brands and the risk of infringement onto the studios. Nevertheless, because of this intersection between real and counterfeit brands, ISS and the prop designers and prop managers employed by the movie and television productions are all thoroughly adept at engaging with the world of brands. Most people are now well aware of the increasingly important business of "product placement," whereby a branded product appears on screen and is embedded within the context of the universe portrayed on screen. Such is the success of product placement as an advertising technique that by many accounts it has often doubled in value year on year (Al-Kadi 2013). Product placement thus makes sense and is becoming probably the most viable and important means of advertising available to brands. While television and print advertising are seeing decreasing revenues, and internet advertising fails to live up to its expectations, the placement of brand identities within the fictive universes of television and film is a booming industry. To have a well-loved character or actor engage with a branded product is thought by many to be much more effective than actual advertisements (La Ferle and Edwards 2006).

There is nothing new, of course, to the relationship between TV or movies and the economics of consumer goods. And such a relationship is not limited to product placement or traditional forms of advertising. Product placement has not in itself produced the ground upon which it exists. That was in place since at least the 1930s. For example, one famous (although possibly apocryphal) story is that of Clark Gable and men's undershirts. According to legend, when Clark Gable removed his shirt in front of Claudette Colbert in It Happened One Night (1934) and revealed a bare chest rather than an undershirt, sales for undershirts across the United States plummeted by three-quarters. Although the story is likely untrue (undershirts did fall dramatically out of fashion at this time, but the trend almost certainly began before 1934), it does highlight the intricate and accepted relationship between on-screen action (consumption) and the indexical relationships (in terms of both influencing and being influenced by) of fictive and real universes of consumption. Contemporary product placement is predicated upon this established ground. It comes as no surprise, then, that brand managers would wish to have their brands associated with particular characters and contexts in television and film. The most prominent examples of product placement involve fictitious characters using real brands, such as Daniel Craig's James Bond using a Sony VAIO laptop to send an email in Casino Royale (2007), or Chris Pratt's character in Jurassic World (2015) drinking a bottle of Coca-Cola (figure 5). Indeed, in the case of Sony and James Bond, as is common, the advertising went beyond product placement and into cross-promotional tie-ins when, for example, Sony released a version of that

FIGURE 5. Coca-Cola product placement in the film
Jurassic World, 2015. Universal Pictures.

laptop with James Bond insignia and the number "007." Another James Bond movie, *Tomorrow Never Dies*, is noted for its excessive use of product placement, with estimates between a quarter and its entire budget coming from placement revenue (Kardes et al. 2014).

Product placement can be motivated by either party. While Coca-Cola, for example, might pay to have its product in a movie, television and movie productions may request permission from and possibly also pay a brand company to have its product on screen. The latter is less common, and usually occurs only if the brand is viewed as central to the narrative or scene. For example, in AMC's television show *Mad Men* (2014), Coca-Cola was deemed a necessary plot device in the series finale, and an alternative or fictive brand would not have worked, given the centrality of the brand to the story. Another example is the common use of real brands (Hershey, Pez, and Junior Mints) in the *Seinfeld* TV series (1989–98). Such product placement instigated by the screen productions themselves often gives a desired sense of reality (that is, greater verisimilitude) to a movie or television show. But such a move can be costly (although sometimes permission is granted without payment, as was often the case with *Seinfeld*), and the brands themselves often simply refuse, notably if they have little to no control over the brand's on-screen portrayal and are unwilling to leave the presentation of their brand to the whim of screen production teams. For example, Apple apparently refuses to have TV or movie villains use iPhones. Such a problematic for prop managers, designers, and directors has led to the inverse of "product placement," perhaps unsurprisingly known as "product displacement."

There are several ways one can displace a product in order to avoid trademark infringement. The most basic way is known as "greeking." This is simply covering a branded item enough on screen so as to not infringe upon a trademark. Simple in theory, but often difficult in practice. There is an art and expertise to greeking, covering just enough and revealing just enough of the branded item so that the viewer can detect it (albeit unconsciously at times, or "noticing without noticing," as one person I spoke to described it), and there is a constant pushback from brand companies themselves, as they try to retain a "firm grip" on their brand circulation (Luvaas 2013). Greeking can take several forms, some more subtle than others, and can be done in postproduction if necessary. For example, a casual viewer of television may well have noticed a sports jersey logo or sponsor's name pixelated on screen, particularly on reality television shows where there is less control over the on-screen appearance of branded items. This is perhaps the crudest version of greeking, and exists outside of the fictive universe, being superimposed in editing. A person wearing a New York Giants or Manchester United jersey on camera in a reality television show will have to be greeked in postproduction if the rights cannot be obtained, and the options of subtly greeking are limited as a result. Pixelation also occurs in television shows (much more often than in movies) due to different international trademark agreements and law. Thus, any viewer of American reality television shows in Europe will find many more pixelated items than if they were viewing the same shows (or music videos) in the United States. Of course, this form of greeking is generally far from the preferred outcome, as it draws attention to the matter of product, and violates many assumptions of the suspension of disbelief and the verisimilitude of reality laid claim to by television productions. The expense of more nuanced postproduction greeking effects covering up a trademarked logo is often prohibitive. Much cheaper and often more effective, for example, is the can of Coca-Cola with a sandwich placed in front, obscuring much of the Coca-Cola trademark on the can, or a price sticker placed atop most of the "HERSHEY" label on a Hershey-branded chocolate bar. Not only is suspension of disbelief retained, but the viewer is judged to be adept enough in the ways of branding to decipher the redness of a can of Coke, or the Hershey-ness of a chocolate wrapper.

Important for our purposes here is that branding on screen, whether product placement or displacement, relies on a certain presupposed expertise[7] of the viewer in navigating the world of branding and being acclimated to the slippage between real brands and fictive universes, not only the particularities of specific brands. Such expertise, and indeed such exercises in branding, however, are not limited to the fictive universes of product (dis)placement, as witnessed, for example, by the controversy over Michael Phelps wearing Beats headphones at the 2016 Rio Olympics, resulting in Phelps having to "greek" the logo of the headphones with American flags.

The second means through which to achieve product displacement and avoid trademark infringement is to design a generic (or nonbranded) form of the branded product for on-screen purposes. This is often done for products that might be branded, but whose brand identity is not high. Milk is a good example (figure 6). While an average consumer is likely to have a preferred brand of milk, and is likely to have a reasonable knowledge of the specificities of the product (full fat or 2 percent, almond, oat, or coconut, price per quart or half-gallon), they may not know the brand name, or at least not to the same extent as their knowledge of and loyalty to soda or car brands. While even a person who neither drives nor drinks soda would likely be able to name three brands of each product, the average milk drinker would likely be hard put to do the same with milk brands. Here, the descriptive or referential component of the product is emphasized over the value of brandedness and brand identity. Milk companies, of course, know this and tend to present descriptive aspects of their product in much larger type than the logo or brand name.[8] As a result, prop companies tend to produce generic forms of such products. Where the product carries a foregrounded generic form, so too will the prop version. "Bad" props (those that the viewer readily identifies as a prop) are often found when a generic form is replacing a highly branded product, which calls to mind the role of generic branding in socialist markets (Manning and Uplisashvili 2007). Thus, when the generic form is enacted as a proxy for highly branded commodity (a can of "cola" where one would expect "Pepsi" or "Coca-Cola"), the prop has failed to do its job in constituting a simulacrum of the original. Suspension of disbelief is broken.

The third type of product displacement is the "fictive brand." As already noted, the fictive brand, along with the generic, is perhaps the most interesting practice, at least for our purposes here, in revealing a particular set of indexical properties that are deeply implicated in "real" branding. ISS produces a wide array of fictive brands, but all are intricately tethered to real brands. This is perhaps the traditional way of viewing fictive brands, and can be aligned with greeking, for the two appear to be engaged in a similar project: come as close as possible, without infringing on the trademark. But as I suggest below, this is not all that is at work in the prop-brand. On the one hand, the fictive brand (for example, Heisler

FIGURE 6. ISS generic/fictive milk cartons. Photo by the author.

Beer) appears to be a straightforward mimic of a real brand: that is, it is "fake" in a straightforward sense, being directly tethered to a real brand (namely, in this example, Heineken). On the other hand, these fictive brands are not so much "fake" or "virtual" as they are attempts to achieve an instantiation of brand type without any token. They are not copies of brands, but rather improvisations on them and, importantly, instantiations of categories of objects without any object—as is the generic. That the fictive brand is taking advantage of a generic space is significant and is what allows the prop-brand to succeed. Both are denying what might be termed "semiotically leapfrogging," or otherwise avoiding, brands.

Fictive alcohol brands occupy a notable position within the prop-brand world. There are several reasons for this. On-screen consumption of alcohol is of course near ubiquitous, especially in certain genres of television, such as the sitcom. Based on talk rather than action, such genres regularly present consumption of alcohol as a means of indexical framing and context for friendship and sociality, as well as a plot device for enabling character advancement. Compared to food, for example, alcohol consumption is much preferable: it facilitates control of continuity between shots and retakes, and it does not hamper talking as eating food does. And alcohol consumption is simply a much wider and legible indexicality of sociality than food can be. Easy indexicals of alcohol consumption include a character's declining state, for example, after losing a job (show them getting drunk at home on the couch), a plot device for a mistaken romantic entanglement (show them drinking in a club and waking up hungover in bed with said entanglement), youthful abandonment (show them binge-drinking), or postaction solidarity (show characters raising a glass or a beer to one another).

ISS does produce fictive brands of spirits, but the vast majority of its fictive alcohol brands are beer. This makes sense given the general consumption of spirits in nondescript glasses, which calls for nothing in the way of brand replication. And aligning with the drink of choice for Americans—at least on-screen Americans—beer is by far the dominant alcoholic beverage on US screens. But given that the on-screen representation of beer consumption regularly includes drunkenness, drunken fighting, throwing up, regretted dalliances, it is unsurprising that alcohol brands are often unwilling to allow their brands to be represented in such an ostensibly negative light.[9] And when trademark owners are either being paid for, or themselves paying for, the placement of their product, they are notably controlling in the on-screen management of their products. Thus, if a brand wants to have Brad Pitt drinking its beer in the manner it wishes, a TV commercial is often the preferred choice (for example, the Heineken 2005 "Beer Run" TV commercial, directed by David Fincher and starring Brad Pitt).

Of course, there has been widespread critique of product placement for numerous reasons, including the growing influence of brand companies in seizing control of plot and narrative from writers and producers. One of the interesting outcomes of such critiques is that TV shows and movies often include product placement while at the same time critiquing its practice. Examples range from *Arrested Development* (2003–6) and *30 Rock* (2006–13), in which no subtlety or naturalness of placement is attempted, to the extent that in one episode of the latter, Tina Fey's character says "Verizon" and then breaks the fourth wall and asks the camera, "Can we have our money now?" to movies and music videos that overincorporate product placement. In doing so, they call attention to corporate, branded, and commoditized norms (for example, the music video for Lady Gaga's song "Telephone" in 2010).

In order to show how the prop-brand is engaged with trademarks, current branding practices, and the concept of the generic, I offer three examples of ISS prop design, in which the semiotic slippage that such prop-brands incur is notable.

EXAMPLE 1

In March 2016, during pilot season (in which a multitude of first episodes of shows are produced with the goal of being picked up for a full season), everyone at ISS was very busy. While I was speaking to an assistant designer in her office, the phone rang, and she needed to take the call. A television show was on location in Atlanta, and the assistant director had called her to ask for a custom-made prop. The script called for a character to be sprayed in the face with an antibacterial spray. They informed ISS that they needed the bottle to be larger than a real spray and were planning to use a small bottle of Evian water. They needed ISS to design an antibacterial spray label to fit the bottle. But what label was most suitable? They agreed that the brands Neosporin and Bactine, for example, were neither culturally dominant nor indeed sufficiently descriptive or linguistically referential enough in their brand names to be open to imitation, or partially obscured (for example, by a $1.99 price sticker) so as to be greeked. That is, a label with a fictive brand name such as "Newsporin" or "AntiBactea" would be illegible to the viewer as having an indexical and iconic tethering to a real brand. For this reason, ISS and the TV show's production team decided on a generic and explicitly descriptive title, "Triple Antibiotic Spray" with a similar design and color scheme to Neosporin (figure 7). In this way, the generic form was chosen as having more connotative value, which could not be achieved by using a fictive brand that aligned itself with and hewed close to a real brand. Thus, in this scenario, the generic nonbranded form is viewed not as less meaningful, but as more so, than either the real or fictive brand. It is this use of the generic form that shows not only how the fictive brand is determinedly different from the counterfeit (the counterfeit cannot successfully instantiate the generic), but also how the generic itself is not limited

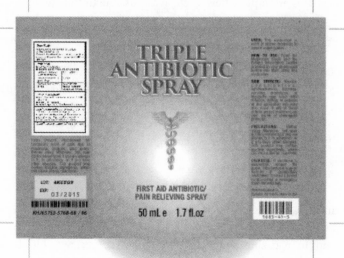

FIGURE 7. Label design mock-up for an antibiotic spray.
Courtesy of Independent Studio Services.

to running a semiotic spectrum of specific to nonspecific in order to attain indexical and iconic value.

EXAMPLE 2

ISS had been working with the production teams on the new series of *Twin Peaks* on the Showtime network. I was asking designers about the degree of engagement production teams generally had with ISS. Did the production teams co-design the props, or was ISS given a wide latitude in their design? As in example 1, many times it was a joint effort, but at other times, I was told, ISS staff were left to their own devices. The director David Lynch was mentioned as an example, unsurprisingly, of a director who took pains to involve himself in the process. For *Twin Peaks*, he had wanted exact replicas of FBI badges and ID cards. He had been unhappy with the ones used in the original series. Because of Lynch's insistence, ISS contacted the FBI, and requested an example on which to base the prop design. The FBI responded that it could not assert whether FBI agents even had badges or not. After a lengthy conversation, apparently the person at the FBI informed ISS that it should (wink-wink) copy the badges used by *The X-Files* production, as those were by far the best replicas. This attempt to hew as close as possible to the iconicity of the "real" was similar to that of an often repeated story that circulates at ISS and beyond, regarding the printing of fake money. During the filming of a Las Vegas explosion sequence in *Rush Hour 2* in 2000, a truck stacked with fake money printed by ISS was blown up. A small riot apparently ensued in which the money was grabbed by bystanders and subsequently began to appear in stores across multiple states. In consequence, a federal enforcement agency ordered ISS to cease producing any form of fake money. The money was not fake enough.

EXAMPLE 3

The third example is ISS's fictive beer brand, Heisler. As discussed previously, while ISS produces a multitude of fictive brands, ranging from tortilla chips to magazine covers, often for one-off scenes, reusable alcoholic drink brands occupy a prominent position at ISS, and Heisler is arguably the company's most successful (figure 8). Heisler Beer, with its iconic red label, has appeared in numerous television shows, such as *Brooklyn Nine-Nine* (2013–21) and *CSI: Miami* (2002–12), as well as movies such as *Training Day* (2001) and *The Social Network* (2010). So successful has Heisler become, in fact, that in recent years increasing attention is paid to it within shows, such as a character explicitly asking for a Heisler in the television show *New Girl* in 2015. Not only this, but Heisler, like many "real" beer brands, has itself been replicated, imitated, and circulated outside of its managers' own intentions, often with a recognizably ironic/cult sensibility. Heisler Beer is now a well-known "fake" brand, with its name and design adorning t-shirts and clocks for sale on Amazon. Moreover, Heisler Beer is trademarked.[10] The popularity of Heisler has supposedly caused several movie and TV productions to choose ISS brands other than Heisler. The reasoning, as given by people at ISS, was that Heisler may now draw attention away from the scene. It has been marked. It is not generic enough.

Realities of the Fictive Brand

These three brief examples point to some of the tensions and ambiguities in which the prop-brand, and its varying shades of mimicry, fakeness, and genericness, engage with the semiotic mediation of "realness" and trademarked brands. As example 1 shows, the goal of the prop-brand is not simply to avoid trademark infringement (or similar legal infringe-

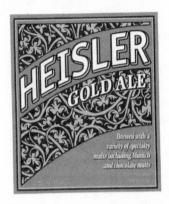

FIGURE 8. Heisler Beer, a fictive beer brand created by
ISS. Courtesy of Independent Studio Services.

ments on US federal identifications). Many movies and TV shows prefer
not to use a real brand, as brands are embedded in semiotic practices of
distinction, and distinction risks disrupting the suspension of disbelief in
a given scene. Instead, these production teams wish to produce brandedness without instantiating an actual brand. The generic and fictive brand
enables such indexical leapfrogging. In Peircean terms, this might be
viewed as an attempt to instantiate the legisign of brandedness without
really having to account for that instantiation, or perhaps to produce type
without token, or at the very least to mimic the token to achieve a real
legisign. Or similarly, while the brand famously excels in achieving all
three Peircean categories of firstness, secondness, and thirdness (from
initial sensation, or qualia, to the highly mediated social fact), the prop-
brand is concerned with firstness and thirdness, but in many ways not
with secondness (in this case the actuality and instance of a brand).

That is, the prop-brand tries to draw a straight line between the feeling
and sensation of a brand and the world of brandedness (in which there
is general agreement that commodities can be branded, and that brands
mean certain things), without the brand itself. The role of materiality is
also at play, given that within the brand–commodity relationship, the
brand token is often assumed to take a material form (the can of Coca-
Cola). Indeed, the materiality of the prop-brand is notable, as it exists
and circulates in both material and immaterial forms. Similarly, in the
double, or mediated, market through which it is sold and consumed (first
by the screen production or studios, and subsequently by the viewer), the

bottle of Heisler has a material form (there is a bottle and label) but also does not (there is no beer in Heisler Beer), and its ultimate consumer, the viewer, only consumes it as a visual form. However, this is an over-simplification, not only of what constitutes the material form, but also of how it weaves in and out of causation and result, form and content. Much of the work in the anthropology of design, such as that of Keith Murphy, highlights this aspect of material form. For example, in thinking through how concepts such as collaboration and imagination are grounded in material forms, he highlights the very fluidity within the interactional modes of talk, gesture, and visuality that the organizational materiality of workspaces is predicated upon (Murphy 2005, 2015).

Example 2, concerned with approximating as closely as possible a real FBI badge or real dollar bills, appears to highlight the more expected role of the generic and fictive with regard to branding. That the prop-brand is constituted as a generic form of a brand is noteworthy in that it points to a unique semiotic space that is constituted by a combination of fictiveness, specificity, and nonspecificity, as well as brand alignment with material form. The antibacterial label produced by ISS is both more generic and more specific than any real brand. Generic in its replication of branded form without a brand name, the label of the antibacterial spray is oddly more specific in its linguistic description of the product (and also in its size—more iconically available). It is worth considering this form of the generic in light of more accepted norms of how the term "generic" is used in relation to branding, namely, through the marketing of pharmaceuticals. While some anthropologists have taken up the relationship between brand identities and their generic counterparts, we often see the generic as more explicitly replicating the brand itself. For example, in Cori Hayden's work on generic medicines, the generic is used to imitate (as nearly as possible) the trademarked product without risking infringement and postpatent (Hayden 2007, 2013). In the work of Fehérváry (2013) and Manning (2012; Manning and Uplisashvili 2007) on generic branding in socialist and post-socialist contexts, we see much more slippage in the indexical scales at play, with socialism, capitalistic luxury, and nationalism all marked within the congruence of the im/materiality of the brand and the contexts in which it circulates. But, as each of these authors notes in different ways, the generic is always in some fashion replicating the nature of branding, even if doing so by the negation of the indexicality/iconicity of a particular brand. Through this lens, the generic stands as an attempt to produce type without token—essentially, brandedness without the brand (figure 9). Thus, I want to highlight here how prop-brands (for example, ISS's Heisler Beer) are doing much more than "replication without encroachment," that is,

FIGURE 9. Animated generic/prop-brand, from *Dan Vs.* (animated TV series, 2011–13), 2011. Starz Media.

simply providing a fictive version of a real brand (for example, Heineken). Instead, they are indexically leapfrogging (rather than piggybacking) an object, independent of cycles of semiosis associated with the brand, albeit ultimately implicated in it. To whatever degree brands are inherently self-distinguishing, as Rosemary Coombe notes, they simultaneously produce the structures of their own existence (Coombe 1996: 202). Likewise, for Nakassis, the brand cites its own brand identity as well as an ontology, or overarching schema, of brandedness. It is at this general and all-inclusive scale of branding, outside its particular instantiations, I suggest, that the prop-brand and potency of the generic exists.

While other authors have thoroughly excavated the complexities of branding practices and commodity value (Mazzarella 2019, 2003; R. Moore 2003; Manning 2012), there are two particular and uncontroversial aspects of branding that are useful to highlight here in understanding the prop-brand, and by extension the concept of the "generic." First, there is some sort of intentional, and nonunidirectional type/token relationship at work, whereby the can of Coca-Cola in your hand is semiotically tethered to the brand of Coca-Cola, and vice versa. That is, just as the can in your hand is an instance of the meaning of the Coca-Cola brand, it is likewise constitutive of that very meaning, and thus its circulation in the world affects the social meaning of other cans of Coca-Cola. As Daniel Miller has noted of Coca-Cola specifically, it has emerged as a meta-brand, and meta-commodity, gesturing more explicitly to the basic process of branding than would normally be the case. As he writes, "the term Coca-Cola comes to stand, not just for a particular soft drink, but also for the problematic nature of commodities in general. It is a meta-commodity" (Miller 1998: 170).[11] Second, the "meaning" of a brand is always multiple in its indexical orders (Silverstein 2003a). Indeed, the ability of prop-brands to scale such indexical orders is part of the replication of the semiotic ideologies of branding overall.

Core to branding is the ability of the brand to work simultaneously at different scales, ranging from formal signs of authentication of source (this is a "real" Apple iPhone) to particular claims of product value (the new iPhone is the best phone on the market), to much wider claims of inhabiting and fulfilling moments of modernity, the zeitgeist, and the definition and desires of self (your iPhone enables you to achieve both a better fidelity of online video and a better fidelity of self). Again, there is nothing controversial about such statements, but the ability of brands to simultaneously inhabit scales of indexicality, as well as relying on some form of type/token relationship between commodity and brand, is core to understanding the leapfrogging that the prop-brand attempts. The question is whether an ostensibly fictive brand can mimic not only the real brand, but also the indexical orders that brands are implicated in, or in Rosemary Coombe's terms, "the logic of the trademark's communicative mode" (1998: 216). There is little reason to think otherwise, given that the brand itself is engaged in projects of mimicry. It raises an important point about the generic as a label—that it denotes that which is not authentic. But as we see, even in the bounded world of Hollywood props, the oppositional characterization of authentic and inauthentic, original and duplicate, quickly dissolves. As William Mazzarella and Lauren Berlant, as well as Coombe, have noted, when a brand is successful, it acts as a "surrogate identity" and "prosthetic personality," substituting, replicating, and approximating other nonbranded forms of relational and mediated experience (Berlant 1993; Coombe 1998; Mazzarella 2003). If the brand, as Robert Moore suggests, is a means through which producers extend themselves into the domains of their consumers, one might argue that the prop-brand is an extension into the domain of the producers themselves, replicating their own norms of brandedness.

Virtual Rising to Generic

The multidirectional aspects of branding, in that the branded token and type are mutually constitutive, cloud any true distinguishing line between the real and the fictive brand, and highlight a notable space in which the generic is an important social mechanism. But even if, for a moment, we maintain the definitional boundaries of the real and the fictive, we note a number of instances in which the real encroached and legally infringed the fictive, rather than the other way around. Fake beers are a good example. For example, in 1996, the Federal Courts of Australia heard a "brandjacking" case between 20th Century Fox and the South Australian Brewing Company/Lion Nathan Ltd., in which 20th Century Fox sued the Australian brewers for trademark infringement when they began selling the famous fictive brand Duff Beer from *The Simpsons* TV series (G. Scott and Maull 2012). The 20th Century Fox company (and Matt Groening Productions) won, but the courts admitted the difficulty in deciphering the world of fictive brands. As the decision in the case noted:

> An unusual aspect of this case is that it concerns not a fictional "character" as such, but a "make-believe" product, namely the fictional "Duff Beer" which is coupled with a character, a background institution ("Duff Brewery"), and also with the associated advertising signs, posters and images of the beer, which play an important role in the series. These features form part of the fictional "environment" in which the stories are played out. It plays a background role as part of the fictional world which the characters inhabit. No doubt, the assignation of the name "Duff" to the product was designed to achieve a more believable specific fictional effect than to have an anonymous generic "beer" can and it serves to endow the characters with more focused identifiable "human" traits. (*20th Century Fox v. South Australia Brewing Company*, 1996)

Here, the judge described well how the prop-brand works, and the situational force of such fictiveness, in that even the use of "Duff" in *The Simpsons* was less about distinction (as the real brand is) and more about suffusing a broader environment with verisimilitude. It also points to how the fictive universe of the prop is indexically linked to that of the real, and vice versa. Within the play of fictive and real, the role of the proxy and the generic, distinction and avoidance, is core to how "environments," as the decision in the Duff Beer case framed it, get made.

Similarly, ISS has dabbled in the world of the "real" brand. For example, ISS was contracted to create, or better, to re-create vintage Coca-Cola cans for a TV commercial, as well as labels for Subway sandwich shop advertisements. Apparently more agile in its production setup than Coca-Cola itself, ISS was deemed more adept at fashioning the particular vintage "redness" of the original cans. Thus, once again, we see the porous boundary between the ostensible real and fictive, with a prop company being hired by a corporation to create fictive versions of real brands. As mentioned previously, the popularity of Heisler Beer has apparently caused some movie and TV productions to choose other ISS beer "brands," instead. The reasoning, as given by designers I met at ISS, was that Heisler has now become nongeneric, a little too famous, so that it draws attention away from the scene. It has been marked. If the original intent of using Heisler in a scene was not to replicate a particular brand, but rather to provide a proxy for a nonspecific brandedness—a generic form of brand identity—Heisler arguably no longer occupies this position. As Robert Moore (2003) mentioned, and as Rosemary Coombe (1998) describes, genericization of a trademarked name highlights the vulnerability of brands to having their intended indexical (and less commonly their iconic)[12] properties appropriated and redefined. And, significantly, genericide points to the centrality of distinction in brand identity. If genericide is the unintentional loss of distinction, Heisler is an example of the inverse—unintended distinction. But given that Heisler's purpose was to be indistinct, is this then an example of the death of the generic? An unwanted branding ("brandicide")? Where is the boundary here, between brand and nonbrand?

In thinking through, if not the generic, then the appropriation and replication of "real" and fictive, one social theorist whose work appears to be readily applicable is Jean Baudrillard (1994 [1981]). If the prop-nonbrand, in inhabiting the mirror spaces of branding, is embedded in duplicating and reduplicating realness, thinking about simulacra and the act of simulation is critical. The play between real and authentic (and their replications) that Baudrillard highlights is extremely useful in understanding how the prop-nonbrand is enacted and circulates. The importance of Baudrillard here is in his emphasis that the binary of real and fictive is not actually so, but rather a mutually reinforcing act. However, I do not wish to overly bind together the trademarked and the unmarked, as Baudrillard would. Nevertheless, his point about undoing the solidity of the real is well taken. Similarly, with regard to the work of Gilles Deleuze—in particular, virtuality and repetition (and indeed novelty) (1988 [1966]). The very first step in outlining what might constitute virtuality for Deleuze would likely be a denaturalization of the "real" and instead a consideration of how the virtual is manifested through material forms. Indeed, much of poststructuralist thought emphasizes the need to move past the constricting forms of categorical certainty, and instead seek out other conceptual spaces (such as the generic), both for the original and inventive forms that can emerge from them (for example, the nonbrand), and as reflective and refractory space, enabling us to better understand the ground upon which concepts such as the "real" and "authentic" are constituted. However, there is something of a teleology to Baudrillard, and arguably to Deleuze, too, at least in disassembling the real, that I would resist. In focusing here on the nonbrand, I am not seeking to undo the brand itself. Here is not the space to elucidate the complexities of poststructuralist thought on truth and reality, but I suggest at least that a Peircean semiotic does much of the work here that Baudrillard was seeking out. For example, his critique of a Saussurean sign system (2016 [1976]), arguing against any emergence of a settled referent and closed linguistic/semiotic system, is answered by Peirce in his semiotics, in which signs beget signs, and the rolling stones of meaning only ever gather more moss. Even in terms of virtuality, it is worth recalling that Peirce himself defined the virtual in ways that are useful here in thinking about the nonbrand: "a virtual X . . . is something not an X, which has the efficiency of X" (in Baldwin 1902: 763). Put simply, this is how I argue the nonbrand/generic stands in relation to the brand. Ultimately, the vulnerability and instability of branding is not to be confused with vagueness and semiotic underdeterminacy. That the brand is open to be sundered, counterfeited, and appropriated does not suggest that its generic versions are less specific in their mediation of the concept of branding.

If, in the end, the generic nonbrand does indeed have the Peircean "efficiency" of the brand, the result is that in its on-screen forms, it inevitably supplants the brand itself. To this end, inasmuch as the brand does not wish to be generic, neither does the generic wish to be the brand. Or to put it another way, the nonspecific does not necessarily want to be specific. As the work of ISS shows, in cutting out a space for the unmarked generic brand and finding a balance between the real and the fictive, indexical slippages and the instability of branding are taken advantage of. Replicating such structures and normative practices and overarching social categories of brandedness is semiotically precise work. Constituting the outlines of genre, and of type, and occupying the space of the nonspecific, the generic achieves the very specific marking of the nature of the brand without the brand itself. And it does so by highlighting the importance of backdrops and the nonspecific as semiotic shorthands. This is the usefulness of the generic. Within a manufactured world of commodities and brands, and the protection and policing of their integrity, we see how the nonspecific is neither vague nor obscure, but rather can exist as a potent shorthand, semiotically invoking ready-made types and social forms.

I turn now to the question of how the generic emerges out of contested spaces of ownership and authorship. I want to describe how nonspecific backdrops emerge as central facets of contested spaces in which original and copy are crisscrossed with matters of authorship and ownership. For sure, we find legality at play. But I want to scale upward into spaces of ownership and authorship around cityscapes and national identity that often supersede legality. Keeping the tension of token and type in mind, how do we understand the limits and extensions of circulating genericness as definitional of authorship and identity?

CHAPTER 3

Source Mimesis

HOW WE THINK ABOUT THE UNAUTHORED
AND COLLECTIVELY OWNED

Types, tokens, and their circulation have had a resurgence of late in the popular consciousness. The emergence and market boom of digital non-fungible tokens (NFTs) has sought to push back against the open and free circulation of digital media. This has been achieved not by establishing paywalls, or actually limiting the circulation of a particular digital file, but by inscribing origin and authenticity onto them. This is antigeneric work. Digital files (for example, a JPEG photograph or MP3 music file) in many ways democratized the circulation of media and fully did away with the distinction between origin and copy (there is no degradation in copies of an MP3 file) that photography and film had begun a century earlier. Prohibiting access to and circulation of media has essentially been the only way to monetize and profit from digital files. However, in something of a return of Walter Benjamin and his classic understanding of *aura* (1968), nonfungible tokens, using blockchain technology, seek to inscribe originality and authenticity onto the digital file where none existed before. Put simply, an NFT is a digital file that is stamped with originality. That digital stamp cannot be copied, thus replicating an older world in which value was seen to inhere in the original work, distinct from any of its copies. This artificial making of a digital origin is fascinating. By marking a single digital file as the original, a market for such (predicated on a classic sense of scarcity) can be created. This is the re-creation not only of originals, but also of copies, and in doing so affects the nature and value of circulation. Here the (nonfungible) token, and not type, is where value inheres.

In other spaces we find the opposite to be increasingly the case. Take, for example, milk—that is, milk as type. If in chapter 2 we saw how Hollywood prop designers produced generic versions of milk cartons, across the world the term "milk" itself has become increasingly contested. The dairy industry has begun fighting against the generic nature of milk as a category—even if most people believed it already was generic. Though beginning in the 1990s, since 2015 or so the dispute over definitional concerns of animal products has become common. Legal cases revolving around the nature of categories such as "milk" and "burger" have filled up the dockets of courts across the globe, with notable decisions in the European Union and the United States. Such contention and litigation are clearly the result of the dramatic upsurge in popularity of vegan and nondairy products over the last two decades. In the case of milk, it boils down to one simple question: what actually constitutes milk? Can nondairy drinks be classified and sold as milks? In a scaling upward (or outward, depending how one sees it) of the definition, the tensions in brand names and the risk of genericide have expanded to include not only brands but also the very categories of things in the world.

Some cases revolve around false advertising, accusing makers and marketers of plant-based milks or meats of misleading customers by using animal product–related terms. Such cases are obviously slightly absurd, in that it is hard to imagine a person thinking that a "veggie burger" or "soy milk" is animal based. Other cases, however, are more direct and fundamental in their challenge: can plant-based products meet the definitional requirements of a terminology and type associated with animal products? Not only are nouns such as *butter* and *burger* in play, but also adjectives like *creamy* and *milky* or even *meaty*. This latter class of cases has had more success. In 2017, after a complex web of cases running through different EU states, the European Court of Justice finally ruled on a case between a German association, Verband Sozialer Wettbewerb, which identifies itself as promoting fair competition, and TofuTown, a manufacturer and distributor of vegetarian and vegan products. In a dramatic ruling with far-reaching consequences across all of the European Union, the court decided in favor of the dairy industry and unambiguously noted that "the term 'milk' and the designations reserved exclusively for milk products cannot be lawfully used to designate a purely plant-based product" (*Verband Sozialer Wettbewerb v. TofuTown*, ECJ Case C-422/16). The European Parliament went some way in reversing this decision in 2020, creating for a time a difference in how plant-based products could use meat-related terms versus dairy-related terms, allowing one but not the other. Still, such controversies underline the importance of generic types. Moreover, much like genericide, once types leave the stables, it is often difficult to control them. And so, as is the case so often, control appears to be about ownership. In this case, who owns the category of "milk"? Who gets to define it, and of course, who gets to profit from it?

In this chapter, I examine how the generic is often bound up in questions of ownership and rights—in many ways gesturing to the potency of the generic, the need to pursue it, deny it, and otherwise police it. Intersecting such questions, inevitably, are assertions regarding originality and authenticity, as well as public and private concerns. It is not surprising that things that are deemed generic are often thought to be public. It is often not the case, however. For every example of free, open-source software that explicitly aims for universal, generic applicability, there is an equal and opposite example: take Alamy stock photography, a private corporation that aggregates and sells generic photographs. How do we understand the generic when it scales up and outward, circulating in an ostensibly public sphere? Moreover, how do we understand the generic as a *process*, rather than as something static? What does becoming generic look like? I begin with a well-known example in which the nature of ownership disintegrated amid an immense moment of circulation—the Obama "Hope" poster. I then turn to a discussion of genericism in the design of cities and world's fairs, in which circulation has been of equal importance in establishing collective, national forms of identity.

Hope

Disagreements over copyright rarely reach the headlines. Not so with the Obama "Hope" poster. Created by visual artist Shepard Fairey in 2008 for then US presidential candidate Barack Obama, the poster not only became an iconic image of the campaign and of Obama's subsequent presidency, but instigated an almost equally famous copyright infringement dispute the following year.[1] The specifics of the dispute took a winding path through legal definitions of "originality" and "fair use," the "thinness" of copyright protection, and more esoteric questions regarding the relationship between photography, art, and fact—not to mention the nature of political and free speech. The poster itself was designed by Fairey using a photograph of Obama as the basis for the drawing, and quickly achieved remarkable, viral success, circulating globally. Within months of its making, and even before Obama had been inaugurated as president, the Smithsonian Institution had sought the original for purposes of historical significance (Cartwright and Mandiberg 2009).

Putting aside for a moment the involvement of Obama and the prominence of the poster, in many ways the case was seemingly pedestrian. Did Fairey's poster infringe upon the copyright of the photograph, which the Associated Press (AP) owned? Was his image too close to the original photograph? Fairey himself was open regarding how he came across the image: a google search. And although he was initially oblique or perhaps dishonest regarding what exact image he had used, it was quickly revealed to be from 2006, taken at an event at which Obama was sitting on a dais with the actor George Clooney. But in many ways the "Hope" poster controversy is a microcosm of swirling contention and misunderstanding around ownership and originality—and has invited significant commentary by legal scholars, for, as has been noted, while Fairey's case was always seemingly stronger than AP's, the case highlighted in dramatic ways that "increasingly complex intersection of art, technology, and law" (Fisher et al. 2012: 245).

We see in the "Hope" poster controversy how quickly assumptions regarding ownership and authorship can unravel. Ultimately, there were four distinct claims: Fairey, as artist; Associated Press Inc., as owner of the original photograph; Mannie Garcia, as photographer; and Barack Obama, as subject of the photograph. Beyond ownership, we see how the categories of representation—art, news, fact, and the ideologies of visuality and similarity, and of origin and copy—all started to lose their footing with surprising speed. That photography was at play was unsurprising, as it famously blurs the line between mechanized reproduction and authorship, as well as between original and copy. The "Hope" poster case echoed the landmark copyright case, *Burrow-Giles Lithographic Co. v. Sarony* (1884, 111 US 53), in which a photographer, Napoleon Sarony, alleged that the Burrow-Giles Lithographic Company had illegally sold copies of his photograph of Oscar Wilde. Rather than claiming it owned rights to the photograph, Burrow-Giles claimed that no rights could even exist for a photograph, as copyright was limited to "writings and discoveries." The argument rested on the belief that a photograph could not have an author. As a mechanical reproduction, it was outside the remit of an object that could "embody the intellectual conception of its author, in which there is novelty, invention, originality, and therefore comes within the purpose of the constitution in securing its exclusive use or sale to its author" (US 53 [1884], 11). The court disagreed and found that photography could indeed have authorship, existing in the world outside of the limitations of mechanical reproduction. Little was settled in practice, and the fault lines within the world of mimesis and widespread circulation—particularly who owns what, what constitutes originality, and how access to circulation is regulated—are fault lines that still exist more than a century later. For example, the increasing predominance of photography in social media has seen celebrities sued for posting photographs of themselves but taken by others.

That authorship and ownership are combined is in itself worthy of note, and their nature and convention have been questioned in any number of ways, especially through the nature of production and the commodity, and more recently in terms of media reproduction and circulation. Contestation over patent and copyright law unsurprisingly leads into conversations over the nature of intellectual property, public domains, open source, and collective authorship. We see similar slippages and contestations in interrogations into contemporary forms of ownership and participation within online-inflected publics (Barney et al. 2016; Kelty 2008, 2019; Boellstorff 2008). Of course, ideologies, norms, and assumptions of ownership and authorship have been well studied. Foucault's statement that "the coming into being of the notion of 'author' constitutes the privileged moment of individualization in the history of ideas, knowledge, literature, philosophy, and the sciences" (1979) seemingly stood as a neat punctuation to work by thinkers such as Mikhail Bakhtin and Jacques Derrida, and a questioning of the coherence of a single authorial voice. It also served as a prolegomenon to a subsequent focusing of attention on how we should understand the process of mimesis, production and reproduction—and how their location within typologies of agency and self are constituted.[2] But what happens to authorship and ownership after we step past the normative link to object/ product/commodity in which they are seen to cohere? In stripping away authorship and ownership, when we begin to speak of the public domain and of open source, what else might be stripped away? For example, in the Obama "Hope" poster controversy, Fairey and the AP ultimately settled, agreeing to a division of future profits from merchandise sales. But this was a continuation of the misreading of how the poster circulated in the world, its cultural moment having already come and gone, and the poster having become so generalized that everyone involved had all but lost control of the image—to the extent that across the internet and smartphones there is a photo filter known as the "Obama filter," or "Obama effect," allowing one to "obamanize" any photo (figure 10). This is more than the breakdown of the concept of "author"—there is something within the mimetic, and the foregrounding of type, of form over content, that is resolutely unauthored. Whether located within a framing of a zeitgeist of popularity, the affect of political celebrity, or the circulation of copies, we see the generic as a process of becoming, and one that is constituted within communal and collective types of action.

As Lawrence Lessig (2008) has famously described, notably in terms of copyright/trademark law and the internet, the emergence of a "remix culture" (with echoes of Lévi-Strauss's *bricoleur*) does away with the traditional opposition between those who produce and those who con-

FIGURE 10. A generic "Hope" poster generator website. Courtesy of Article
19 Group Inc. Photo of Barack Obama by Pete Souza/White House.

sume. No longer read-only and write-only spaces, points of origin and
authorship collapse. Thus, my interest here is not in an absence of authorship, or indeed of ownership, but within replication and the conflu-
ence of production and consumption, and the emergence of something
more fully, by its nature, unauthored (G. Coleman 2013). That is, one important aspect of what happens when authorship and ownership start to
fragment is the increased attention paid to classification and the types
of things, where the balance between form and content tips in favor of
form, and of media itself. Or to put it another way, can we start to see, not
how contemporary media spaces are highlighting the definitional con-
straints and contestations over ownership and authorship, but rather how
replication and mimesis is the space in which ownership and authorship

emerge? For example, echoing the work of Roman Jakobson and Mikhail Bakhtin, and pushing past the cliché of Marshall McLuhan's "the medium is the message," anthropologists working within the ethnographic spaces of media, such as Patrick Eisenlohr (2018), Birgit Meyer (2015), William Mazzarella (2017, 2013), and Deirdre de la Cruz (2015),[3] have sought to understand how replication itself has influenced the experiential modes of media consumption. As Brian Larkin, for example, has noted in terms of piracy in Nigeria, the practice of reproduction "generates material and sensorial effects on both media and their consumers." Among those he works with, it has been the "cheap tape recorders, old televisions, videos that are the copy of a copy of a copy" that often "shape the ways these media take on cultural value and act on individuals and groups" (2008: 241). Similarly, Zeynep Devrim Gursel (2016) has described how the circulation and replication of contemporary media forms is not in any way automatic, unfolding in an unencumbered manner, but dependent on particular agents consciously pushing and shaping how reproduction occurs. *What is a photo, what is art?* This is well-trodden, clichéd territory, but what I want to highlight here is not only that we have seen outmoded forms of authorship, source and origin, artist and audience, start to fall away. We have also seen that replication and mediated publics have become less a conceptual obstacle in understanding ownership, and more an increasingly useful tool for thinking about how new forms of nonauthorship that are predicated on replication begin to come into frame.

Finding Form

Unsurprisingly, mimesis draws attention to form and type. While we find a growing attention to types of authors within the spaces of media, we also find a growing attention to type *within* media itself. That is, replication intensifies the focus on matters of genre, and a metapragmatics of form. For example, consider contemporary internet memes. Memes are predicated on an explicit recontextualization of artifact (whether photograph, text, or music, and so on), and intentionally draw attention to form and metapragmatic play. Thus, memes occupy a similar space to generic brands, emphasizing the replication of form and type over specificity. Graham Jones (2017, 2011) has explored how things are categorized in terms of concealment or secrecy, and how certain practices (for example, magic) often succeed with such metapragmatics, calling attention to themselves, even if that attention would seem to negate any success. One of Jones's interlocutors, a magician, in discussing misdirection as a form of concealment in magic, noted that "when you explain how misdirection works and then turn around and fool them with it, they begin to appreciate how powerful magic really is" (Jones 2011: 112). Similarly with memes.

If we often find the division between form and content an artificial one, contemporary internet memes surely move beyond the simple interaction between them, or even the co-constitution of both. Predicated on a semiotic core of metapragmatic play on form, the cycles of replication and reproduction of memes inherently challenge the normative spaces of origin, author, and owner. Sources of memes might be traced, but they are inevitably empty of authorship given that it is their very replication that constitutes their meaning. To that end, the ideological spaces of the commons, of open source, of the unowned and collectively accessible gesture to a social space in which the specificity of ownership and authorship is excised. Memes highlight the potency of spaces unmarked by authorship and ownership. The generic may be useful in thinking through the unowned and the unauthored, particularly in terms of how nonspecificity of authorship and ownership enables objects and media to seemingly transcend the spaces and temporalities of production and consumption. For example, those semiotic spaces of mythic origin, archetype, urtext, ubiquity, and universalism. Scrubbed of authorship, of the indexical traces of source, such media and objects are potent in their availability for ascription, similar to what we saw with relation to category and naming in chapter 1. Their generic elements enable them to move between contexts. Such context-hopping depends upon forms of replication.

Returning for a moment to the "Hope" poster, and thinking about form and content, and mimesis, the anticipated—and legal—question is whether the poster was an original or a copy. Such a question clearly reveals its own inadequacy, missing the point of the poster, and of mass media altogether. Fairey maintained his ownership through an argument of fair use, and claimed that his work was "original." But if ever there was an artist who would align themselves with how, for example, Michael Taussig (and by rights, Walter Benjamin) would conceive of the magic of mimesis, it would be Fairey. Never wanting to claim originality in its artificial, truest sense, it is through the power of the copy, achieved in mass circulation, that the "Hope" poster seemingly achieved its goal—capturing, not Obama himself, but his aura and zeitgeist. Michael Taussig's thinking on mimesis in terms of how subjectivity is constituted is useful in understanding media and replication. In describing the sensorial arcadia of vision and contact—those "sensory modalities" shot through with ideological import, one that seemingly privileges vision—he notes that it is not simply replication of objects and matter in the world that is constitutive of subjectivity, but the replication and mimesis inherent in our experiences and sensoria. For example, the repetition of walking the same hallway again and again: this is habit not as the way we learn or absorb, but as repetition. Habit as author. Scraped of the origin and source, the hum of replication enacts itself as source.

If we want to understand how authorship, replication, and form intersect, perhaps the best example is that of urban space. The city is, after all, the exemplar of form and collective subjectivities. The authorship inherent in infrastructural and architectural design is in many ways the great unspoken presence in contemporary urban spaces. Urban planning is predicated on overarching schemas, master plans, and designs for large urban spaces, which in turn determine the habitual ways for being in cities. Architects not only design the places in which people live, but use those places to design how those people *should* live.

This emphasis on replication of form within architecture and urban planning, and its intersection with the generic, has been perhaps best articulated by Rem Koolhaas in his essay "The Generic City," in which he celebrates contemporary forms of homogeneity in urban planning and architecture. Pushing back against a discourse of distinctiveness and celebrating the unique identities of cities, and the "essence" of existing as a cultural, economic center, he argues that the generic city is "liberated from the captivity of center, from the straitjacket of identity" (Koolhaas 1998: 1249–50). If "identity centralizes; it insists on an essence," then the generic, as conceptualized by Koolhaas, is a dilution and thinning of that identity, with the ubiquity of replication and uniformity providing an advantage of blankness. This is something different from the "non-place" of Marc Augé (1995), however, in which spaces are unable to constitute the forms of distinction that are necessary for any legitimate sociality to emerge: for example, the modern airport, indistinct in its architecture, and cold to the particularity of the social. Interestingly, while Koolhaas spins the generic as positive, and Augé (one assumes) as negative, we can see how form begins to have a particular ideological sway simply in its replication—whether through the lens of the individually authored colonial urban plan, or the seemingly unintentional and pilotless craft of globalization.

Of course, designing a city, or even a building, comes with a striking ideological import. The collective forms of action, the minutia of peoples' lives, centrally orchestrated and directed, spoken of in terms of chaos and order, have an inherent strangeness, normalized by textbooks on urban planning. We find tropes of urban disorder and poverty, often glossed as lively and bustling, and of wealth, glossed as quiet and permanent. So where is authorship within these forms of mimesis, where both individual and multiple intent and replication of widely known tropes meet collective subjectivity, experience, and indeed ownership? Should they be assigned authorship and intent at all? Ownership? Or are they simply generic? That is, where do these forms of replication, which are not predicated on normative forms of ownership or authorship, emerge? Or, from a different angle, we might ask: who creates the generic? From whence does *it* come? And how do we locate authorship and ownership in it all? How do we frame this play of genre and form within the process of imitation? This simultaneous attention to both form and content, to genre and its iteration, is notable in how we locate ownership and authorship, and how the markers of self and other circulate in the world.

To return to the Philippines for a moment, Manila, like many other cities, has a deep history of multiple, often competing plans and ideologies of urban space. In accounting for the coexisting and unwieldy types of infrastructural order and disorder in Manila, Neferti Tadiar, for example, has described how an ideology of constant and large-scale urban expansion has resulted in a particular type of replication of "city emulants." This entails a continuous expansion of architecture, labor, and subjectivity (Tadiar 2016). The ideology of reproducing "the city," however, becomes micro and fractal, constituted across Manila's space as multiple and replicated iterations instead of one overarching project. The result is that the design of apartment blocks and shopping malls is always leaning toward making them their own miniature ecosystem. "The globalism of this metropolitan platform," she writes, "converts what would appear to be the model into a component." For Tadiar, such expansion then is best understood as "a fractal enterprise . . . the repetition of certain figurative patterns at smaller and larger, shrinking and expanding scales, where the component reproduces the figurative pattern of the whole of which it is a part" (63). This replication is evident to anyone who has moved in and through Manila, with every middle- and upper-class housing, office, and shopping development promising a complete and encapsulating experience of urban life, albeit one that is in many ways cut off from the rest of the city. Everywhere, then, is its own city, replicated and copied. And for everybody else, often those living in crushing poverty, things are similarly replicated in their relation to the in-betweenness of the connecting infrastructure.

The intentionality in such fractal replication, as Tadiar lays out, is one of a capitalist logic, dispersed across money flows and networks. But even in Manila's own infrastructural history, we find remarkable forms of mimesis and replication, even when located within individual intent and master plans. For example, consider Daniel Burnham, the well-known

American architect and urban planner, who emerged within a US colonial context to take the reins, if only temporarily, of designing Manila
anew. Burnham achieved renown for his design, as director of works, of
the "White City" at the 1893 Columbian Exposition (or Chicago's World's
Fair). As a result, he found himself not only a successful and popular architect, but also the most respected "planner" of his time, moving, as he
did, beyond the remit of single building design, and into a more expansive role in designing urban spaces. Indeed, he was so well regarded that
he was asked to design plans for cities such as Chicago, Washington, DC,
and, in 1905, at the invitation of then secretary of war William H. Taft, for
Manila. The intention was to modernize Manila and remodel the colonial
capital as a cosmopolitan urban center. To that end, Burnham's work in
many ways "became the architectural expression of America's imperialist
thrust" (Hines 1972: 36). In seeking to distinguish Manila from its tropical neighbors, to establish it as a notable global cultural and commercial
center, to set it apart, he did so through a project of comparison, commensurability, and ultimately one of mimesis (figure 11). As Burnham
himself wrote in the submitted appendix to the "Plan for Manila," a plan
that was never fully realized:

> On the point of rapid growth, yet still small in area, possessing the bay
> of Naples, the winding river of Paris, and the canals of Venice, Manila
> has before it an opportunity unique in the history of modern times,
> the opportunity to create a unified city equal to the greatest of the
> Western World with the unparalleled and priceless addition of a tropi-
> cal setting. (C. Moore 1921: 151)

The mix here is of equal and unparalleled, of distinction and uniqueness.
It is also immersed in, indeed emergent from, particular Euro-American
histories and genres of architectural and urban planning, gesturing to the
city's even deeper colonial and indigenous shaping. It emphasizes the
peculiarity in projects of replication. As an unnamed contemporary of
Burnham in the Philippines noted:

> There he had the complicated problem of an old polymorphous city,
> unusual in its way of life, which had developed by the consolidation
> of a number of ancient native villages situated on convenient water
> course landing sites about a wonderful natural harbor. The Spaniards
> had partly solved the problem with an Azcarruga boulevard connect-
> ing the various sections. (*Baguio Midland Courier* 1959: 14)

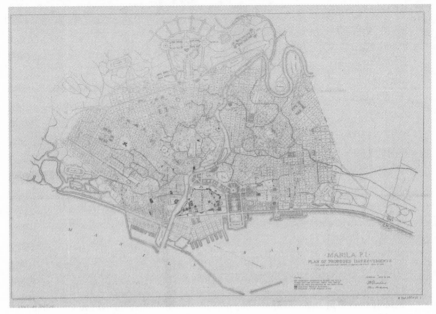

FIGURE 11. Daniel Burnham's "Plan of Manila," 1905. Princeton University Library.

Coming quick on the heels of his work on the design of Washington, DC, his plan for Manila showed striking similarities. His design for Washington, DC, was explicitly influenced by European cities, as Burnham grappled with a city that had a river running through its center. A journalist writing in the *Philippine Herald* in 1968 noted this:

> It is hard to avoid the conjecture that when he planned modern Manila, Burnham had the Washington layout either consciously or unconsciously in mind. Take the rectangle containing the Potomac, the Mall and Union Station, lay it on a north-south axis and remarkably enough it looks like that part of Manila with the Pasig on the north, the Sunken Gardens, Wallace Field, the government buildings, the UP [University of the Philippines] Grounds below it and Paco Station off to the bottom right. (Lachica 1968)

This combination of authorship and intention, with widespread forms of replication, is worth noting. Burnham espoused a plan for Manila that would be shamelessly cosmopolitan along Euro-American lines, while retaining the surface affects of local "flavor." Not only was a space for the Americanized "Manila Hotel" established, but public parks and boulevards were emphasized, replicating a Euro-American urban space. However, such plans came with an emphasis on local aspects also. For example, Burnham described an unobstructed boulevard running along Manila Bay:

> This boulevard, about two hundred and fifty feet in width with roadways, tramways, bridle path, rich plantations and broad sidewalks, should be available for all classes of people in all sorts of conveyances and so well shaded with palms, bamboo, and mangoes as to furnish protection from the elements at all times. (Burnham and Anderson 1905: 628)

The insertion of palms, bamboo, and mangoes within an urban space reminiscent of Naples, Paris, and Venice, and contained within the mimetic design and thinking of a single architect, highlights how form and content, typology and classification are each foregrounded within processes of replication. A "new" Manila, for Burnham and the US colonial administration, was always going to be generic. It was always going to be a token replication of other types. This was part of the US colonial project in the Philippines writ large. Never intended as a remaking of the Philippines (the United States never had any intention of seeing the Philippines as in any way commensurable with America), it nevertheless relied on reproducing a number of generic policies: the institution of English as the official language, contemporary Euro-American ideologies of hygiene and the body (Anderson and Pols 2012; Anderson 2006), and universalist projects of racialization (Rafael 2000). Equally, one might see the colonial design process from the other direction: through such projects as that of Burnham and the United States, it was not Manila that became generic, but rather the boulevards and tramways, the palms and mangoes.

Source Mimesis | Ireland at the World's Fairs

Timothy Mitchell, in his classic work on the orientalist mode of nineteenth-century European exhibitions (1989, also 1991), describes something of a strange cousin to Burnham's Manila plans. Describing an Egyptian delegation's visit to the "Egyptian village" at the 1889 Paris international exhibition (world's fair), constructed for the European visitor, Mitchell writes, the Egyptian exhibit had also been made carefully chaotic. In contrast to the orderliness of the rest of the exhibition, the imitation street was arranged in the haphazard manner of the bazaar. The way was crowded with shops and stalls, where Frenchmen, dressed as Orientals, sold perfumes, pastries, and tarboushes. To complete the effect of the Orient, the French organizers had imported from Cairo fifty Egyptian donkeys, together with their drivers and the requisite number of grooms, farriers, and saddlemakers. (1989: 217)

This exhibitionary mode of seeing by Europeans, as Mitchell notes, was a type of projection onto, and production of, Egyptians that extended far beyond the confines of the exhibition proper. In the reproduction of Cairo's streets, we see the attempts of mimesis, but only in order to replicate an asymmetrical and orientalizing relationship between a European modern cosmopolitanism and the cultural other. It is mimesis as an act not of similarity but of differentiation. I devote the remainder of this chapter to these world's fairs, to see how these mimetic acts of similarity and differentiation were constituted amid a spectacle of modern classificatory order, for which the world's fairs were famous. I also wish to highlight the particular relationship between form and content at play, and how mimesis was put to use in order to constitute generic forms of national identity. In doing so, I focus on a much more tangential, contradictory, and confusing aspect of the genre that was the world's fair, a surprising copier and mimicker of the genre: Ireland and its engagements and appropriation of the genre of world's fairs.

In the relationship and exhibitionary form of representation that Mitchell highlighted, Ireland sought at different times to occupy the positions of both European modern and primitive other. It hosted large exhibitions in Dublin, while having "villages" at other world's fairs. This famous nineteenth-century genre of meaning-making with which Daniel Burnham made his name—the world's fair—is itself useful in understanding how the generic is crucial in the play between form and content, specificity and nonspecificity, and the slippage in authorship in very real ways, enabling (stereo)types and tropes to be manifested. These exhibitions were, as a number of scholars have noted, a petri dish in which a particular type of modernity was cultivated. Notable for their spectacle, classificatory fetish, design, and materiality, these world's fairs in the nineteenth and early twentieth centuries are now known for embodying, indeed constituting, particular forms of modernity and subjectivity, merging a celebratory vision of industrialization with a cosmopolitan one of consumerism, and doing so under a particular rubric (and spectrum) of national and civilizational attainment.[4] Moreover, they were deeply immersed in a teleology of progress and arrival to a moment of modernity, and thus were often the production of origin myths, heritage, and authenticity—providing a necessary narrative arc. The first, and still the best known, was the Crystal Palace Exhibition in London in 1851, followed by other notable examples, such as the Exposition Universelle in Paris in 1889, the Chicago World's Fair (or World's Columbian Exposition) in 1893, and the World's Fair (Louisiana Purchase Exposition) in St. Louis in 1904. These exhibitions competed on a scale of public spectacle hitherto unknown, with each of them inevitably announcing the largest, tallest, or most of something (ranging from buildings, to spectators, to ice cream made in one place). And successful they were, featuring infrastructural and social consequences that are still with us, from the design of urban spaces to monuments such as the Eiffel Tower, to the development of and investment in museums and galleries (Stocking 1987).

Ireland—or more specifically, the city of Dublin—had no real business hosting an international exhibition in the nineteenth and early twentieth centuries, but in fact it held three, in 1853, 1865, and 1907, as well as maintaining a presence at other exhibitions and world's fairs. Neither an economic nor a cultural center to match London or Paris, Dublin nevertheless sought to situate itself, like other major centers, within the exhibitionary mode.[5] For example, the 1853 Irish Industrial Exhibition in many ways defied the realities the country was facing; Ireland was ravaged by famine, and Dublin itself was reverting to the status of a city of an English colony rather than the second city of the empire, as it had styled itself as in the eighteenth century. Essentially failing in the intended form of mimesis—that of performing Ireland as a modern, cosmopolitan center—it achieved astounding success in situating itself as the inverse: the primitive, bucolic, heritage-filled, authentic self; the nonindustrialized, nonmodern periphery. The emergent semiotics of authenticity—temporally situated within a broad, unmarked past, iconically constituted through Celtic and early Christian artifacts—was to fully permeate an Irish nationalism, and indeed a touristic gaze, that continues to the contemporary moment. And yet this "Irishness" was fully predicated on forms of replication and mimesis, of reproduction rather than of production. At its core was a reduced, essentialized form—a generic one, stripped of any indexicality of its own making. The question of authorship and ownership might be seen in this particular light, when expanded beyond the confines of any notion of the individual and situated firmly within a collective experience of large-scale performances and constructed spaces, genres, and ideologies such as nationalism and heritage. Who might own such an identity? Who might author it?[6]

When, on March 14, 1904, interested parties of a planned international exhibition officially met in the Mansion House in Dublin, the meeting was expected to be a friendly if prolonged and unexciting round of committee appointees declaring their ambitious and hyperbolic stratagems to outdo themselves. Most people present would have been acquainted with each other, if not through business interests, then through social connections. However, the meeting, a strange if comfortable fusion of bureaucratic formality and informal socializing, took an unexpected yet telling turn. At the start, Timothy Harrington, the Lord Mayor of Dublin, was called to preside. A requisition, stating formally the intention of the meeting, had been agreed upon, thought Harrington, and was sent out among those in attendance. Harrington, on receiving his own copy, noticed that a number of words had been added. He rose and addressed the crowd. He told them he could not, in face of the altered requisition, preside over or involve himself in the meeting, and walked straight out of the building. The alteration of the requisition had been the addition of nine words: "to be held under the patronage of the King."

A little over a week later a second meeting was held. This meeting was open to the public, ostensibly to allow individuals to voice their opinions, but in reality it was little more than a gesture to a public that by and large had little to do with the exhibition. By this stage, however, the situation appears to have dramatically escalated. Scheduled to begin at three o'clock, the meeting drew a large crowd, many of whom were overtly hostile to the proceedings. As described by the *London Times* (March 25, 1904), some would argue, displaying their allegiances, in "disgraceful scenes of rowdyism," and fighting broke out among some, while others ran to the front and took control of the platform, decrying any exhibition of international character, and any exhibition that was to be held under the patronage of the king. The police were called, and by the time they had pushed the fighting out onto the street, the meeting was abruptly abandoned.

It is unsurprising that the 1907 international exhibition in Dublin, even in its planning, gave rise to divisive nationalist sentiment. Its antecedent, the first Irish international exhibition (the "Great Industrial Exhibition," 1853), while seeking to directly reproduce—both architecturally and symbolically—the Crystal Palace exhibition in London two years previously, became known not for the performance of Ireland as cultural center or industrialized powerhouse, but for its "Antiquities Court." The brainchild of a single person, William Dargan, an engineer and railway magnate, the 1853 exhibition was, as Stephanie Rains has noted, "a self-conscious attempt to stage both Ireland's supposed recovery from the devastation of the Famine and the hoped-for dawning of a new era of industrial progress which would qualify Ireland as an equal economic partner in the Union with the UK" (Rains 2008). Although the 1853 exhibition lost Dargan some money, it was, at the time, the largest international event ever held in Ireland, and attracted more than one million visitors over the six months it was open. It featured exhibitors from around the world, displaying their industrial wares, and sought to present Irish manufacture and industry in a generous light, but its lasting legacy was the exhibiting of Irish historical artifacts.

The nineteenth century had seen a swell of interest in, and professionalism of, archeology and Irish history. Most people had never set eyes on the artifacts that had increasingly become (and continue to be) central not only to Irish history, but also to Irish politics and identity. The 1853 exhibition has drawn scholarly attention, not so much for its success at reproducing the Crystal Palace exhibition of 1851, as for its success in bringing together a substantial and previously disparate collection of Irish artifacts at the very time when these objects were becoming important metonyms with a broad cultural and political resonance (Saris 2000). It is difficult to overstate the role these artifacts played, and continue to play, in how Ireland is constituted, commodified, and otherwise circulated in the world. Although the artifacts were a mixture of pre- and early Christian discoveries, all were conflated, and it was a single nonchronologized past that lay before the visitor. The ambiguity of time-scale, religious significance, and geographical location added to the aura of witnessing Ireland's past, its often referenced "Golden Era," complete and organized within a larger schema of Ireland and the world. The contrast here, within the genre of exhibitionary industrialism of 1853, was apparently compelling. Given that the majority of objects on display were of industrial origin and of everyday quality, from engines to tinned foodstuffs, blocks of granite, and goods produced in prisons, one can easily imagine the effect of standing before clasped bracelets of gold, oaken longboats, Celtic regalia, shrines, and brooches of legendary figures (figure 12).

The full intent—the authorship of William Dargan and the organizers—was to replicate the Crystal Palace, but the inability to attract a dazzling array of foreign presenters, as well as an emergent interest among the middle classes and nationalist movements (of which Dargan was a prominent supporter), pushed the exhibition into becoming something

FIGURE 12. Illustration of the Irish Industrial Exhibition, 1853. Wellcome Collection.

of a spectacle of Celtic nationalism—so much so that it spurred the creation of institutions such as the National Gallery and National Museum, both of which would be established in the following decade, their collections made up primarily of those objects on display in 1853. To this day, a statue of William Dargan stands on the lawn outside the National Gallery in Dublin.

The antiquities on display consisted mostly of collections of jewelry and weapons, along with larger objects such as stone crosses and stone entrances to monasteries, and a number of harps, many of which contained designs that have become the standard insignia of things Celtic. They bridged a considerable time period, from pre-Christian to early Christian, with some exhibits dating to the twelfth century, and very few dating after that time. Of the non-Irish exhibits on display, there was a bronze coating of a shield found in the Thames, some Roman helmets, part of the walls of Herculaneum, an ancient Greek fresco, and interestingly the watch said to have been worn by Charles I on the day of his execution (Sproule 1854). Also, there were some silver ornaments from Tunis, exhibited by the British Museum. The overriding sense of Irishness on display, however, and its opposition to the modernity of manufactures surrounding it, made for a striking vision (Cullen 2017). To this day, these symbols are crucial—to the point of cliché—to how Ireland circulates as a branded form. For example, the first public display of the Brian Boru (Trinity College) Harp was at the 1853 exhibition. It is this harp that became the symbol of the Irish state, currently found on all coinage, passports, and government documents. Guinness Brewery likewise took the harp as its emblem in 1862.

Interestingly, not only was a common narrative of industrialism, one that celebrated mechanization, industrialization, as well as urban, consumerist living, on display, but also its inverse: the nostalgic turn for the simple, rural, and bucolic was already similarly manifest. For example, in the official guide to the 1853 exhibition we find the same author invoking both sides of this narrative. On the one hand, they write, "If we go to the Machinery Court, the attention of the least observant must be arrested by the numerous illustrations of the triumph of mechanical skill there to be seen"; on the other, they note that "with a kind of poetic interest we notice the reed on which the shepherd in a pastoral age piped his rustic lays to while the time away" (*Expositor* 11 [1853]). In fact, the same author combined both in a single sentence, gesturing to the classificatory spectrum upon which objects and ways of living all might be located and compared: "from the needle-making apparatus, wonderful as it is, we are led to a machine which promises ease to weary fingers, and threatens seamstresses with utter extinction" (*Expositor* 12 [1853]).

The 1865 Irish International Exhibition of Arts and Manufactures similarly sought to replicate the Crystal Palace token of exhibitionary type, but without any particular anticolonialism or Irish nationalism seeping through the representational cracks. But this resulted in a muddled message. For example, there was a "colonial department" in which the exhibition organizers attempted to situate Ireland as simply part of the United Kingdom and a colonial power. The Colonial Department contained exhibits from Malta, Jamaica, Lagos, Tasmania, India, Vancouver Island, and Natal, among others. Enacting itself as a colonial power was odd in itself for Ireland, given its position in relation to England, and riven as the country was by anticolonial and nationalist movements. However, in presenting Ireland as civilizationally superior to the "colonies," it was difficult to simultaneously avoid noticing the deteriorating condition of Irish manufactures, mostly caused by English colonialism in Ireland. For example, England had, over the course of the nineteenth century, intentionally diminished Irish woolen manufactures through a series of tariffs in order to aid English wool manufacturing. Thus, when the 1865 exhibition catalogue described Irish lace and embroidery, it was without the expected bombast:

> The young lace-makers fled away from the disease and destitution which followed on the failure of the potato crop in 1846 and sought in America and Australia (where wages were good) to better their condition. The travelers [merchants/traders] ceased to visit the place, and now it contains amongst its inhabitants but a few regular lace-makers, though a slight knowledge of the art is very generally known. Previous to the famine however, the lace manufacture at Headford was on the decline, and for this simple cause, that the patterns were becoming old fashioned, and no one was at the trouble of procuring new ones. The creative power of lace makers in general is very deficient. The patterns are traced and pinholed on parchment, and no scope is allowed for the display of either taste or imagination; and thus the inventive faculties, being never called into exercise, become extinct. (*Illustrative Catalogue* 1865: 273)

With more than a little irony, and unbeknownst to the authors of the 1853 or 1865 catalogues, and indeed to the organizers of both exhibitions, the Irish experience of international exhibitions and world's fairs was only just beginning, but the representational forms Ireland would take would be the inverse of the intended mimesis of the exhibitionary genre. Instead of aping the stance of modernist industrial prowess, it would be this image of the seamstress, of needle-making, of lace and embroidery, increasingly assuming a particular Irish/Catholic/Celtic alchemy, untouched by the modern world, that would constitute an alternative modern Ireland. It was Ireland as arcadian and pure, perhaps not modern in terms of industrialization, but surely modern in its openness to be commodified and to inhabit a generic form of authenticity and heritage.

Ballymaclinton

Skip ahead to 1893, and we find that Ireland's position within the genre of world's fairs had shifted dramatically. All semblance of a cosmopolitan, modern country was gone, replaced by young women handweaving dresses and dancing in an artificial village. By 1891, it was clear that Ireland would be represented at the 1893 World's Columbian Exposition in Chicago. Ishbel Maria Hamilton-Gordon, or Lady Aberdeen, the wife of the highest ranked British politician serving in Ireland and who

expressed an ambiguous support for Irish national causes, set about organizing an "Irish Village." The idea of presenting Ireland as a modern
nation did not appear to enter into any dialogues surrounding the exhibition. The *London Times* noted eight months before the opening of the
Chicago exhibition:

> There is to be a representative Irish Village, with crooked streets and
> alleys, quaint houses and huts, and a central market-place, having a
> large Celtic Cross from Kilkenny, made by the order of Countess of
> Aberdeen. The Princess Louise sends a bust of her Majesty the Queen.
> (*London Times*, October 20, 1892)

The architecture of the Irish Village in 1893 included an entrance that was
a facsimile of a chapel "built by Cormac, the Bishop King of Munster,"
in the twelfth century. Also, there was a two-thirds-scale version of Blarney Castle. With funding entirely by the Irish Industries Association, its
founder, Lady Aberdeen, had gone on a tour of the west of Ireland in 1892,
beginning in Carrikmacross, to find the population for the village. From
bacon factories to convents, she found more than two hundred candi-
dates, mostly female ("colleens"), and shipped them over to the United
States in the months before the exhibition.

The official booklet accompanying the village is oddly heteroglossic,
including a formal description of the Irish Industries Association, a diary-
styled narrative of the tour of Ireland, maps of the village, and finally a
chapter entitled "How the Blarney Stone Got Its Power" (*Guide to the
Irish Industrial Village* 1893). The village included numerous examples
of religious artifacts, lace, and wool and poplin cloth, as well as working cottages where, "by the turf-fire over which the potato-pot is hanging
can be watched the making of many different kinds of lace and crochet-
work which is manufactured in Ireland" (*Ireland at the World's Fair* 1894:
12). And there were women, including Maggie Dennehy "who talks real
Irish." It is easy to perceive how this village was generally construed. Here
was a striking contrast with the majesty and grandeur of modern society
(figure 13). As the author of another pamphlet on the Irish Village remarks, "We believe that, although machinery has wrought many changes,
there are still fields where it cannot compete with the work of the human
hand, and that this fact is now being recognized" (Untitled Pamphlet
1893: 5). While the village was represented as being separate from, even
untouched by, the modern world, it was very much part of it. The same
pamphlet (7) admits as much:

FIGURE 13. Cover of a pamphlet guide to the Irish Industrial Village at the World's Columbian Exposition, Chicago, 1893. Library of Congress.

How can peasants in the wild west of Ireland know what will be wanted during the coming season at London and Paris and New York? And yet this is required if their handiwork is to be saleable, and this applies not only to the fine laces and embroideries, but also to the more homely woolens and knitting and underclothing.

Thus, within a set of distinctions between cultures—and projects of comparability and commensurability—nostalgia, heritage, and tradition were constituted as economically viable in a transnational capitalist context.[7] It was also noted that many visitors to the Chicago world's fair had been misled by a number of "hawkers" who were selling counterfeit Irish lace. This is mentioned in relation to the St. Louis World's Fair in 1904, too, articulating another layer of authenticity in and around this particular form of Irishness.

The Irish Village at St. Louis in 1904 was an expanded version of 1893. There had been some heated debate between the British government and the organizers of the Irish exhibits. Britain found "to be insuperable . . . the proposed separation of Irish exhibits from those in the remainder of the United Kingdom" (*London Times,* September 15, 1904). Finally, it was agreed that the exhibits of Irish industry would be included with the rest of Britain, and the village would be allowed to go ahead. It appears, however, that this fell through, for there is little evidence of Ireland at St. Louis but for the village itself. The relatively new Department of Agriculture and Technical Instruction (DATI) organized the village, copying the format of 1893, and Lady Aberdeen was again involved. The official handbook emphasized, even more than in 1893, the divide between Ireland and modern nations:

> The Art and Industrial section of the Irish exhibition at St. Louis, organized by the Department of Agriculture and Technical Instruction for Ireland and by other bodies, is intended to illustrate, as far as space permits, the industries, resources, arts, education and history of the country. It may be desirable, in a few words, to explain the object and purpose of this national representation of Ireland and its products. In the first place it should be understood that no idea of putting a country so economically undeveloped as is the greater part of Ireland into competition with the advanced arts and industries of America and Europe has been contemplated by the promoters of this project. The object has been to draw attention rather to the possibilities than to the realized actualities of the country. (Ireland DATI 1904: 1)

The history of the textile industry is once again mentioned in these pages, and Britain is accused of "stunting the growth . . . of the Irish Celt." Far larger than the one in Chicago, this Irish village included the same buildings, such as Blarney Castle and Cormac's Chapel, but added a facsimile of the "Exterior of the Irish House of Parliament on College Green": quite a political statement, given how the Parliament had been shut down a century before, in 1801, by the English government in order to rule Ireland directly. There was a replica of the cottage of President McKinley's grandparents who lived in Congher in County Antrim. This replica cottage included the original window frames and doorknobs. Also, there was erected a round tower, based on the one of Clonmacnois. There was an Industrial Hall in the village that appears to have contained the more modern aspects of Irish industry, but it was apparently hidden away and received very little attention. The historical section and the thatched cottages occupied the most space (and the attention of visitors). The artifacts on display were similar to those of 1853, with the Tara Brooch, Cross of Cong, Lismore Crozier, Shrine of St. Patrick's Bell (and ones of his tooth and hand, also), the "Limavaddy collection," and the Ardagh Chalice occupying prominent positions in the collection. Again, within the bounds of a branded heritage, we find a distinct temporal version of Ireland on display. For example, McKinley's Cottage was presented as existing within the same context as the "working" cottages, where "real" Irish people burned turf and cooked. There is a collapsed chronology here. There isn't even a sense of some vague past or present—simply the very modern commodification of heritage itself, where past, present, and future emerge in singular form.

Generic Becoming

By 1904, at the St. Louis World's Fair, the Irish Village had become a traveling roadshow, improved upon, expanded, but with its core buildings and exhibits remaining the same. By 1908, the village had acquired a name: "Ballymaclinton." An international exhibition co-organized by France and Britain, and including the Olympic Games, built at Shepherd's Bush in London, provided its setting. The *London Times*, again, described it thus:

> The Irish village of Ballymaclinton will, undoubtedly, be one of the most frequented spots in the whole exhibition, though it lies at the far end of the grounds. It is not a replica of any actual village, but a composition which includes about 20 buildings representing different existing structures or types in different parts of the country. There are several types of cottage, some new and slated, others old and turfed and thatched; the thatching is going on vigourously now. Among them is an exact replica of the "McKinley Cottage," in which the ancestor of the late President of the United States was born, from Ballymoney in county Antrim. The interior is fitted with the original materials—staircase, doors, windows, dresser, &c. Ancient Ireland is represented by a Galway fisherman's cottage with coracle, a gateway from Glendalough, county Down, a Round Tower of the eighth century, a tiny ruined abbey, a St. Patrick's Cross of the fifth century from Donaghmore,

Tyrone, and some prehistoric stone monuments. Modern Ireland is represented by a village concert room, model cottages, and other buildings in which peasant industries will be carried on by 200 girls, who will be housed in the village. The whole thing is very complete. (May 9, 1908)

This Franco-British Exhibition contained a Court of Honour, Court of progress, Court of Arts, and a Colonial Section, among others (figure 14). It was more an exhibition of empire than a strictly international exhibition, but nonetheless had as its aim that "both countries concerned will be represented at the Exhibition by the most excellent products of their respective industries and Arts, and the Colonies of both nations will assist to a remarkable degree in the great friendly contest of brains and skill" (*London Times*, May 14, 1908). What is most conspicuous in the organization of the exhibition is how the colonies and dominions were represented. Both Australia and Canada had separate buildings, and were similar in style to those of France and Britain. There were Ceylonese, Senegalese, and Indian villages, as well as Algerian, Tunisian, and French East African colonial displays that appear to have been exhibited in a village style. And Ireland as a village—seemingly by choice, constituting the positionality of colonized, but in a world in which that positionality is open to mediation and commodification. Ballymaclinton, named after a soap company,[8] fully inhabited the performance of authenticity within the exhibitionary genre. And yet, it was a generic form of Irishness, one full of intent but without authorship, and owned by no one.

The goal here was arguably one of achieving a certain type of generic fitting-in. It was not so much about the harp or the bucolic idyll, or the Celtic mythic past, as it was about constituting a template of a nation rather than that of a colony. That the harp on display in Dublin in 1853 is now the insignia of the Irish state was sort of always the goal. If other countries have their symbol, we need to have ours. Templates.

To finish, I want to suggest here that the genre of world's fairs enabled generic forms of historical narratives to be procured, indeed generated—a "type" to be filled in with the specificity of artifacts and Celtic designs, merging object and aesthetic. The overarching and essentialized performance of colonial, modern, cosmopolitan forms, located within explicit ideologies of similarity and difference, and of comparison and commensurability, enabled the "Irish Village" to succeed as a modern, commodified form. So, within this quixotic space of copy and original, authorship and ownership, habit and intent, consumption and production, specifics

FIGURE 14. Situating the Irish Village within the cosmopolitan exhibitionary form. Two postcards from the Franco-British Exhibition in 1908. One of the Court of Honour, the other of the Irish Village, "Ballymaclinton."

and universals, genre and form, and of classification: what might the usefulness of thinking generic be? In locating the generic as a guiding practice, enveloping forms of mimesis and replication, there is the often found dialectic, or at times simply irony, that the generic is frequently at the center of projects of distinction. In the world's fairs, and in the case of a US colonial architect seeking to remake Manila as a European capital, we find the specific and nonspecific constantly pulled together within the invocation and circulation of type. And it is in this space—in which generic forms are created and circulated—that we might find a different type of creative space, one in which authorship and ownership collapse and coalesce, one of nonspecific, nonauthorship. That is, arguably, the power of the nonspecific, of the unauthorized: its potency to circulate, to retain, not its origin, but the claim to never have had one. The generic.

PART II

Christian Plurals and a Generic Religious

Given the multiple angles and spaces it can conceptually inhabit, what does a fuller ethnographic engagement with the generic actually look like? In what ways can we both ethnographically account for the generic, and employ it as a conceptual tool to better understand the complexities of social experience? Part II of this book addresses these questions, and undertakes to show what the generic looks like when the so-called conceptual rubber meets the ethnographic road. Over the course of three chapters, I provide what is essentially an ethnographic experiment, in which I tackle the generic, showing how it is critical to the ways in which Christianity circulates in the island province of Mindoro, Philippines.

In sketching out the in situ nature of Christianity, as an anthropological object and at times as a Maussian "social fact," Webb Keane notes how "Christianity may be part of a taken-for-granted background or a fervent frontline concern" (Keane 2007: 29). Here, in part II, I want to take that "taken-for-granted background" itself as a frontline concern, and describe how Christians themselves likewise share and engage that concern. That is, how do we understand generic Christianity? And how do we understand religion more broadly in its generic forms—when it is stripped of specificity, and formatted in ways that enable it to be easily circulated through shorthands and proxies?[1] Christianity is deeply immersed in claims of universality, circulating across much cultural specificity, and historically bound to (post)colonial and capitalist projects of global expansion. Within this milieu exist generic forms of Christianity—predicated on a need for semiotic shorthands and shared knowledge in order to proselytize not only among non-Christians, but also among Christians of other denominations. It is in this space, a striking and emergent one of Christian pluralism in the Philippines, that the following chapters are ethnographically located.

To that end, in chapters 4–6 I describe how Christians in the Philippines are faced with new spaces of religious pluralism with multiple Christian identities and affiliations at play. Not only are people thoroughly attentive to the taken-for-granted backgrounds of their religion, but they also use those backgrounds, depend on them, and otherwise deploy them for crucial ends. I want to show then how the taken-for-granted background is instituted as the generic itself. The question is not only what constitutes such a generic form of Christianity, but also what it actually does in the world. Why do generic forms of Christianity emerge? And what does an ethnographic engagement with the concept of the generic look like? What benefit is there in taking it as an anthropological concern? In order to engage these questions, I suggest Christianity as an ethnographic space of the generic. As I argued in part I, the remit of the generic is expansive, with at least two clear, cross-cutting lines of meaning at play, evaluative and classificatory. Both are readily apparent in Christianity in the Philippines, and even more so in the place where I conducted my fieldwork, on the island of Mindoro, where there has been an influx of Christian denominations in the last two decades (figure 15). Because of improved infrastructure and accessibility, shifts in urban Christianity in Manila, and a general push toward development, the presence of different churches has dramatically increased—from Evangelical born-again churches, Seventh-Day Adventists, and a number of Methodist churches to Baptist, Mormon, Iglesia ni Cristo, and charismatic offshoots of the Catholic Church, to name but some. There has emerged a simultaneously classificatory aspect within Christian forms, with an implicit, shared Christian backdrop—a shared semiotic ground upon which religious difference and commensurability play out.

Protestantism in particular has had a long history of coming together and falling apart. Similarity and difference have suffused Protestant denominational affiliation and identity from its very beginnings, never more so than in how it stands in relation to Catholicism. And of course, Catholicism has both embodied and rejected its own generic forms. At the same time, it is worth noting that Christianity does not always enable its generic forms to circulate, at least not within a space of pluralism. The Orthodox Catholic Church differs from Roman Catholicism in ways through which it acknowledges other strands of Christian affiliation. And in the Philippines, while the Spanish colonial state grudgingly accepted the existence of Muslims in the south of the country, it was illegal for Christian denominations other than the Catholic Church to organize in the rest of the country. This changed upon the beginning of the US colonial administration in the country, which saw the gates open for

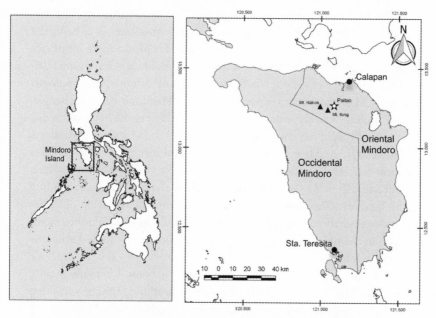

FIGURE 15. Map of Mindoro, Philippines, amended from Villanueva and Buot Jr. 2020. With permission of Elaine Loreen Villanueva, Inocencio E. Buot, and the *Journal of Marine and Island Cultures.*

American missionaries of all denominations. So much so, that the mainline Protestant groups in the United States held meetings and divided up the Philippines among themselves. As a result, even now in different provinces across the Philippines, some Protestant denominations have a stronger presence than others (Doeppers 1976).[2]

Of course, the generic, as the overproduced and culturally devalued, is at work in contemporary Christian Mindoro, too. Like most religious forms and identities, Christianity is open to ongoing appropriation, imitation, and mimesis, as well as attacks on people's sincerity and the "realness" of their faith. In Mindoro, as in much of the Philippines, Christianity is everywhere. From stickers on cars and tricycles, to churches lining the roadsides, to constant invocations of Jesus on television and radio, Christianity runs as an ambient background through much of Filipino life. The geography of Mindoro itself has a certain religious demographic diagrammatic to it—with a population of just under 1.5 million people, the island consists of a large upland mountainous region, inhabited by Indigenous Mangyan communities (about 250,000 people), ringed by lowland, predominantly rice growing and Tagalog-speaking Christian communities. Thus, historically, Mindoro has been a missionary frontier for those seeking to convert Mangyan groups to Christianity. The seventh largest island in the Philippines, it is likely most famous as being the home of Indigenous Mangyan communities, for producing a lot of rice and salt in the lowlands, and not much else. Harold Conklin, whom I discussed briefly in chapter 1, was the first and most famous anthropologist to study Mangyan communities, in particular Hanunoo-speaking people. But Mindoro is rarely remarked upon in Manila or in the national media. The island is split into two provinces, Oriental and Occidental Mindoro, of which Oriental is more developed and wealthier, while Occidental is poorer and less populated, though it does have the largest town, which I call Santa Teresita (about 150,000 people in the town and surrounding countryside).[3] The recent spark of attention from the spectrum of Christian denominations, seeking to convert lowland Catholic Filipinos in addition to the upland Mangyan groups, has dramatically shifted religious norms in many communities.

Thus, over the course of the next three chapters, I explore generic forms of Christianity on the island of Mindoro, ethnographically tracking a conceptual space in which reduced and nonspecific types of Christianity weave in and out of one other, forming something critically different—a communal repository of meaning—enabling shared forms of Christian subjectivity to be enacted across lines of religious difference, at times to emphasize that difference, at other times to overcome it.

CHAPTER 4

Formatting the Religious

"NON-CHRISTIANS" AND THE
NATURALNESS OF LANGUAGE

Like many other towns in the Philippines, Santa Teresita, in Occidental Mindoro, celebrates an annual "Araw ng Katutubo"[1] (Day of the Natives). Unlike most other towns, however, it lies at the base of a large mountain range, famous for being the home of Indigenous Mangyan groups. Very much an exercise in producing a celebratory discourse of acceptance of Indigeneity, the day involves student presentations in schools, free food, speeches, posters, and some singing in the town plaza, as well as an evening performance in the rundown, 1970s Marcos dictatorship–era gymnasium that stands by the side of the plaza next to the Catholic cathedral compound. Even in the events in the plaza, the cracks in the discourse of inclusion are readily apparent. When compared to other public events in Santa Teresita, which are often religious or political, Araw ng Katutubo is pro forma. Local politicians pay lip service to the remarkable tenacity of Mangyan communities, and to their history of being subjected to lowlander discrimination. Incursion into their lands through a century of logging and farming, and more recently large-scale nickel mining, is lamented, often by politicians who themselves have logging and mining interests. The innocence of the Mangyan people is noted, as is their closeness to nature, their vulnerability, and their kindness. Undoubtedly condescending and paternalistic in tone, the day's events are more notable for the general lack of enthusiasm most people have. Locals who bother to attend see it simply as some activity in the plaza, maybe to stand and watch while on their lunch break or if they have nothing else to do, while wondering if they themselves are being condescended to. School-children are sometimes encouraged to attend. The politicians see it is clearly to their benefit to be seen to be supportive of Indigenous rights rather than actually fighting for them. Mangyan leaders are encouraged to dress in Indigenous clothing, and are subsequently shuffled around like quasi-dignitaries, to be shaken hands and have photographs taken with. Politicians and administrative heads give short speeches about the importance of the Mangyan to Mindoro and Filipino culture. For the most part, Mangyan communities themselves do not place much weight on the day. While not viewing it in outright pejorative terms, many see it as nonproductive toward any meaningful end. I describe it here in an ethnographic present, as one year is hardly discernible from another, such is the pro forma nature of the festivities, seemingly empty of meaning but nevertheless organizationally required by the municipality—with true intentionality and authorship located elsewhere, inevitably somewhere in a government office in Manila.

In 2012, the evening performance of Araw na Katutubo was different than in previous years. As people entered the gymnasium, the forty or so Mangyan performers were already inside, but the Mangyan audience—friends and family, tribal leaders, schoolchildren—were parked outside in a large, open-topped livestock truck waiting for the lowlanders (often simply labeled as Christians) to enter first—entering to ostensibly celebrate those same Mangyan people in the truck. The truck was a kind bureaucratic gesture on behalf of the Santa Teresita municipality, to transport Mangyan people to the performance. The performance itself, composed of a multitude of short dances with a Tagalog narration, was more expertly directed than in previous years, with a professional director (from Mindoro but working in Manila) having been brought in to design and guide the affair. Together the dances provided both a narrative and commentary of a Mangyan experience, predominantly concerned with their relationship with lowlander Christian Filipinos. The same themes of closeness to nature (the Tagalog word *katutubo*, meaning "native," is incidentally the same term used for "nature"), encroachment of modernity, and the value of a Mangyan perspective—featured earlier in the day—were repeated. This performance, though, was much more dynamic than the glad-handing and speeches, with the performers acknowledging that as Mangyans, they often saw "modern" Filipino culture as a corrupting force and yet nevertheless sometimes wanted to emulate it. Through dance and song, the lure and repulsion of the lowland were woven together. Each part of the performance evidently had different authors, with some enacting the overarching nature of the Araw ng Katutubo, as required by the organizers. The trajectory of the performance concentrated on the experiences of loss—notably of their land—to the lowlanders, having their natural resources stolen, and experiencing mistreatment at the hands of Filipino Mindoreños. As the performance moved toward its conclusion, with the Mangyan performers, mostly teenagers, dressed in native attire, the narrator summarized the hardships and exploitation of Mangyan people. And then, three Mangyan teenagers appeared on stage, dressed as Franciscan Missionaries of Mary (FMM), a Catholic missionary group that has long worked in the mountains among Mangyan communities, particularly among Hanunoo and Buhid Mangyan. These Mangyan performers wore the famous FMM white-and-blue habits, and as they appeared, standing over crouching Mangyan, the narrator changed tack to a fawning appreciation instead, erasing the previous hour of critique. The narrator described how the Catholic missionaries had helped raise the Mangyan people from their own limitations and protected them from the dangers of the lowlanders. If it was strange that Mangyan teenagers were dressed up as FMM sisters, stranger still was that the FMM sisters were themselves seated in the front row, watching themselves help raise the Mangyan from their torment (figure 16). Questions abounded: *Were the Mangyan performers wearing the sisters' spare habits, or did they make them themselves? How did they feel dressing up as Catholic missionaries? Did performing in front of the missionaries make them nervous? Did they get to choose the theme of the performance? How did it feel for the sisters to watch themselves enacted by those they had saved, replaying the very act of salvation? And afterward, later that evening, how did it feel for the missionary sisters watching the performers climb up into a livestock truck outside the gymnasium to be shuttled back*

FIGURE 16. In a video from the 2012 Araw na Katutubo celebration, three Mangyan performers dressed in Franciscan Missionary of Mary (FMM) religious clothing (habits) help the Mangyan rise from their torment.

to their villages in the mountains? The following week, one of the sisters curtly noted to me that "we were just helping them out, that's all."

I begin part II here, in a classic moment of mimesis. Scales of mimesis proliferate. In a formal sense, the FMM sisters substitute themselves in a formal mimetic fashion to the Virgin Mary in their missionary work—they are doing the work of Mary, embodying her, replicating her. The clothes—the habits—worn by the Mangyan performers are there to imitate the FMM sisters, but FMM sisters wear those habits themselves to imitate the shawls worn by the Virgin Mary. The arrangement of the image, the physical stance of the missionary and the Mangyan, is itself mired in mimesis. On stage, in 2012, the Mangyan performers enacted the FMM sisters and the moment of salvation had them stand at center with a Mangyan person on each side. This spatial organization is not new. For example, in the 1950s, the Catholic Church in Mindoro was engaging for the first time, and against its will, in a project of Christian pluralism. Long the sole missionary groups to work among Mangyan communities, after World War II, Catholic missionaries witnessed an influx of Protestant missionaries to Mindoro. Put on the back foot, and watching the Protestants work more closely with Mangyan people, learning their languages and circulating Bibles in native languages, the Catholic Church attempted to respond in kind, by publishing a catechism in the "Mangyan" language (actually Hanunoo Mangyan). Written in 1953, it is diglot in form, with Hanunoo on the left and Tagalog on the right, and numbers seventy-five points, including prayers, Bible verses, and teaching questions and prompts, such as "Who is God?" "What is sin? Sin is an infraction against God," and so forth. Notable for our interest here is the cover of the catechism (figure 17), enacting the same Christian-to-Mangyan stance as in the Araw na Katutubo performance.

Echoing Taussig's Cuna figurines (1993), with a simultaneous fetish of the mimic, and the mimic of the fetish, with the replication of self and other, *through* self and other, the Christian missionary message of salvation is alive and well in Mindoro, but not as it once was. Here, when framed through a narrative of Mangyan history and the Araw ng Katutubo, it is embedded in a generic modernist discourse of Indigenous rights. Of course, such a discourse is generally highly critical of such Christian triumphalism. But for the FMM missionaries, their work aligns well with a broad ethos of Indigenous rights. They espouse a "contextual theology," whereby conversion and formal teaching of Christian doctrine are secondary to locating similar forms of Christian belief and worship within local, native forms of meaning. It is easy enough to view this as a Christian appropriation of the more fashionable, and globally circulated,

FIGURE 17. Cover of a Catholic Mangyan Mission catechism,
1953. Courtesy of the Mangyan Heritage Center.

discourse of Indigenous rights that challenges the creaky and paternalistic Christian one of old. But the FMM, and other Christian missionaries in Mindoro, continue to recirculate a Christian/non-Christian opposition, and appear to be unable to escape it, even when they explicitly try to do so. This opposition falls within a classic marked/unmarked frame. More than that, however, what becomes of the marked—in this case, the non-Christian—is a generic formatting of what falls into the category. Missionary strategies, goals, and attitudes might change, but in a fundamental way, the Mangyan people remain the same, shunted into a category of the "non-." Who has authorship and ownership within these settings? If we find mimesis and reproduction wherever we look in the Araw ng Katutubo performance, who has ownership—discursive, representational authority—over that mimesis? Who is inhabiting what? And what might generic forms have to do with it all? How do the generic and mimetic interact, reproducing unauthored, nonspecific, universalized forms? Even within a context in which ownership is contested, and in which actors are navigating well-known and accepted definitions of ownership and authorship, can we see how processes of mimesis give rise to new *types* and *kinds* of ownership and authorship?

Mangyan Codified

"This is a study of contrasts and parallels." So wrote the anatomist, evolutionist, and sometime ethnologist Robert Bennett Bean in a 1913 article on the physiology of the Indigenous and upland "Mangyan"[2] people, in which he aligned the Mangyan physical character to that of the Ilongot of Luzon and the lowland Tagalogs. Coming at the tail end of an initial flurry of scientific and colonial interest in Mangyan communities, which began with the arrival of the US administrative apparatus in the Philippines after the country was ceded to the United States in 1898, Bean's piece, a racial and physiognomic ordering of Mangyan and Negrito groups in the Philippines, was very much in keeping with representations of the "primitive" current in anthropological and ethnological thought at the time.[3] This would not be the last time Mangyan people would be shunted into racialized taxonomic categories—something that current discourses and categories of Indigeneity in the Philippines continue to be laced with—and it continued a context in which Mangyan people would exist for the state primarily through a lens of similarity and difference. Indeed, such categorical difference is still the primary means through which Mangyan people are discursively constituted in Mindoro. What this difference is, however, and what categories are employed in articulating difference have shifted over the course of the last century, and earlier typifications predicated on physiognomy and primitiveness notably have coalesced with religious categories of difference. It has been—surprisingly or unsurprisingly, depending on how one views the *longue durée* of the Philippines—the role of Christianity that has come to mark and unmark Mangyan groups as well as Indigeneity writ large in the Philippines. On the one hand, one might argue that this is simply an inherited term, a placeholder, with little religious intent—something the early twentieth-century courts argued. But that would be to mistake the valences of Christianity, the semiotically charged tacitness of the unmarked, and how religious universals circulate in the world.

Categorized for centuries as the primary Other for Spanish and American colonists, as well as for Filipino lowlanders, Mangyan people have cycled through appellations of "wild," "primitive," "indigenous," and prominently, "non-Christian." For in Mindoro, people speak less of lowland and highland, of primitive and civilized, than of Christians and non-Christians.[4] It is this question of how Mangyan groups have at once been constituted as a generic form of the other, and the obverse, how this constitution references an equally generic "Christian," that I turn to in this chapter. The dialectic of "Christian" and "non-Christian" has informed a fierce dynamic that has defined categories of personhood in Mindoro since at least the turn of the twentieth century. As a number of scholars have noted, colonialism as an ideological project has often constituted such self-defining oppositions. Talal Asad, for example, has underscored how the category "European" was consolidated through an exercise of comparison and contrast with those peoples who were colonized (Asad 2003). I will briefly describe here a setting that highlights some of the nuances of how the Mangyan and Christianity are constituted as generic forms, particularly within a politics of naming and unnaming. I examine how the term "non-Christian" not only became common parlance for Mangyan people, but was legally instituted in 1919 as the proper referent for Mangyan groups—and declared by the US-administered Philippine Supreme Court to be a generic term referring to Indigenous groups. Oddly similar to the practice of genericization of branding, the Court decided that "Christian" in this context had nothing to do with Christianity, but rather was a nonreligious marker of a baseline civilizational status—one that, in the end, was more important than citizenship in attaining legal rights from the state. Reflecting back on its other in the "non-Christian" Mangyan, we might see another type of generic project at work, not just within the remit of appellations, but within the pluralization of Christianity, away from the predominant Catholicism—forming a "natural" baseline of Christianity. I take up this matter of a "generic Christianity" later in this chapter and describe how Jehovah's Witnesses in Mindoro, proselytizing among deaf and hard-of-hearing people, engage with a shared form of Christianity, against which they define themselves. I discuss how an ideology of "naturalness" they imbue in sign language merges with a similar one of Christianity.

What Is in a Term? Rubi et al. v. Provincial Board of Mindoro

For the most part, historical records pertaining to Mangyan people rely on minimal details recorded by Spanish colonialists and Jesuit missionaries over the course of the eighteenth and nineteenth centuries. Throughout this time, the island of Mindoro itself was lightly populated, primarily by different Mangyan groups. It was not until the twentieth century that internal lowland Filipino immigration from other islands began in earnest on Mindoro. Given that missionary reports from this time consistently articulate exasperation in approximating the population of Mangyan communities, census figures are untrustworthy at best. Nevertheless, Spanish-conducted censuses in 1878 and 1887 noted the entire population of Mindoro (without a breakdown of Mangyan groups and Tagalog-speaking lowlanders) to be 19,728 and 25,154 persons, respectively. The

first US-administered census, taken in 1903, recorded the population to
be 39,582 persons overall, with 32,318 "civilized" and 7,264 "wild." Some
later analysts have estimated that the number of "wild" persons, or Mangyan, was far higher, perhaps even three times that listed in successive censuses (Gibson 1983; López 1976).

My concern here is not so much to unpack the discourse on "primitiveness," a topic that has been widely dealt with, and substantially in anthropology (within the development of the discipline, see Stocking 1968,
1991; and in the Philippines, Rafael 2000; Brody 2010; R. Rosaldo 1993),
as it is to locate ideologies, and classifications of Christianity and primitiveness, as part of the genericization of self and other. The classification
of Mangyan as "non-Christian" has reached beyond a practical engagement between the two, and the figmental presence of the Mangyan, as a
nonreligious other, has been enough to establish shared, generic forms
of Christianity in the lowland regions of the island. It is not simply an inherited, anachronistic, and representationally loaded term, but one that
defines the borders of Indigeneity and Christianity. If in previous chapters I looked to how the generic is dependent on unmarked forms, I focus
here on how the unmarked is forcefully constituted through the marked.

What is in a term such as "non-Christian"? Having controversially
gained a new colony as part of the spoils of the Spanish-American War in
1898, the United States quickly set about redesigning the forms of governance in the country. The term "non-Christian" quickly achieved prominence within the US administration of the Philippines.[5] It first attained
official usage through the establishment of the Bureau of Non-Christian
Tribes in 1901 by the US Philippine Commission. Designed to mirror
(indeed, to be affiliated with) the Bureau of Indian Affairs in the United
States (Darnell 1998, particularly chaps. 3 and 7; Fixico 2012) the bureau
had a dual mandate to anthropologically study the non-Christian tribes
and to improve their status of civilization.

> Its objects are the investigation of the little known pagan and Moham-
> medan tribes of the Archipelago, the conduct of systematic work in the
> anthropology of the Philippines, and the recommendation of legisla-
> tion on behalf of these uncivilized peoples . . . but the practical duties
> also entrusted to it of investigating the material condition of these wild
> peoples, and of assisting in the measures adopted for their material
> progress. (Barrows 1901: 3)

The bureau administered and financed many studies of Indigenous groups
in the first decade of the twentieth century. As Renato Rosaldo has noted

of the bureau of this period, policies toward these non-Christian people "reached a peak of explicit conceptualization and systematic application" (R. Rosaldo 1982: 313).[6] In a 1901 handbook for volunteers, the bureau outlined two sets of points of interest and importance when studying the non-Christian tribes of the Philippines, including physical type, dress, social organization, tattoos and hair styles, ornaments, religious beliefs, language (including a list of fifty focal terms), warlike nature, disease, and economic exchange (see R. Rosaldo's [1982] appendix for full list). Dean Worcester, chief architect of the bureau, noted in a letter to the governor of Mindoro, L. J. Van Schaick: "If I were as young and as light on my feet as you are . . . there is nothing I can think of which I should enjoy more than to fill in the blank places on the map of Mindoro" (Worcester Correspondence in Beyer 1918: 151).

The Mangyan, like other Indigenous groups, received much attention from the bureau, but, as with missionaries in the nineteenth century, the bureau's interest in them gradually fizzled somewhat due to inaccessibility and disease—Mindoro was known among US administrators and missionaries as the "white man's grave" (Beyer 1918). Thus, the Mangyan communities were never studied to the same extent as those in Northern Luzon, such as the Ilongot and Ifugao, or Negrito communities in the central part of the country. Anthropological studies began to taper off by 1910, and did not reappear in any substantial way until professional anthropologists, such as Harold Conklin, began working on the island after World War II (Conklin 1949, 1955a, 1959).

Yet, while the scholarly aspect of the bureau never attained the measure of its US affiliate, the Bureau of Indian Affairs, the bureau's role in the practical regulation of Mangyan communitites certainly did. There had been a continuous effort on the part of Worcester, as secretary of the interior (for all intents, this position governed the country), and the US administration to more fully engage with Mangyan people, in order to "better their lot" and to civilize them. As archival records show, aside from questionable matters related to the design of the US intent, their administration of Mangyan groups was fraught with corruption and mismanagement.

For example, in the same letter to Van Schaick in which Worcester wrote of "filling in the blanks" of Mindoro's map, he criticized the governor and his predecessor for not doing enough, either in studying or in helping Mangyan groups:

The one feature of Governor Offley's work with which I was dissatisfied was his failure to do more for these people, and I am afraid that I must say to you that it seems to me that you have done considerably less than he did . . . it is high time that we began to know something about the interior of Mindoro, and that we begin to do something substantial for the people which inhabit it. (Worcester [1910], in Beyer 1918)

As early as 1901, anthropologists, missionaries, and US officials were noting that Mangyan people were often taken advantage of by lowland Filipinos, who with impunity would often contract them to work for lowlanders and subsequently refuse to pay them wages (Beyer 1918). Governor Offley himself wrote in 1902 to Worcester that "these people, known as the 'Manguianes,' are, in my opinion, a desirable acquision [sic] and I shall do everything in my power to win them over; first by passing such laws as will protect them from the Filipino, who rob them on every occasion" (Offley Correspondence in Beyer 1918: 179).

By 1914, with little movement in their civilizing mission, and deciding that if you cannot go to the mountain, the mountain must come to you, Worcester and his successors began to implement policies of tribal relocation to lowland regions in Mindoro, particularly in the northeast of the island, outside Calapan. These attempts to civilize Mangyan groups (and the lowland Filipinos to a lesser degree) were viewed as a rejection of the previous Spanish colonial administration that had focused almost solely on Christian missionization. As Offley noted in a report to the newly established census office in Manila: "It should be borne in mind that Mindoro was used as a penal colony by Spain, and that nothing other than the erection of immense churches and convents was done to improve the condition of the people" (Beyer 1918: 186). The relocation project that began in earnest in 1914 arose from a belief that Mangyan communities would be best served by integrating them with lowland Tagalog Filipinos, as well as settling them in one circumscribed area as opposed to their scattered, inaccessible villages. From letters from the governor's office in Mindoro, it appeared that the US administration believed the settlements would benefit Mangyan people. They would protect them from lowland abuse, while also facilitating a relationship of trust between Mangyan groups and the US administrators. Indeed, it was believed that after the success of the first settlement outside of Calapan, by Lake Naujan, the Mangyan communities themselves would want to establish other lowland settlements (Beyer 1918).

Nothing of the sort occurred, however, and the settlement resulted in a famous Philippine Supreme Court case that saw the US regulation of Mangyan people officially coalesce with the relationship of Christianity in the civilizing process. The case *Rubi et al. v. Provincial Board of Mindoro* (1919), which revolved around the constitutional validity of forced settlements, was a direct result of the Mangyan settlement in Lake Nau-jan, established five years prior. One man, named Dabalos, escaped the settlement and was caught, arrested, and imprisoned in Calapan. A lo-cal Calapan lawyer applied on his behalf and that of another man named Rubi for habeas corpus. As the decision describes the case:

> this is an application for habeas corpus in favor of Rubi and other Manguianes of the Province Mindoro. It is alleged that the Manguia-nes are being illegally deprived of their liberty by the provincial offi-cials of that province. Rubi and his companions are said to be held on the reservation established at Tigbao, Mindoro, against their will, and one Dabalos is said to be held under the custody of the provincial sher-iff in the prison at Calapan for having run away from the reservation.

While the official reports and letters that discussed the planning of the settlement unsurprisingly promoted the settlement in terms that were seen to benefit and protect Mangyan people, there was no discussion of the *forced* nature of settlement. However, by 1917, the provincial governor of Mindoro, Juan Morente, had submitted for approval under the Admin-istration Code (essentially the US constitution for the Philippines) a pas-sage that stated:

> Whereas several attempts and schemes have been made for the ad-vancement of the non-Christian people of Mindoro, which were all a failure. Whereas it has been found out and proved that unless some other measure is taken for the Mangyan work of this province, no successful result will be obtained toward educating these people. Whereas it is deemed necessary to oblige them to live in one place in order to make a permanent settlement. Whereas the provincial gover-nor of any province in which non-Christian inhabitants are found is authorized, when such a course is deemed necessary in the interest of law and order, to direct such inhabitants to take up their habitation on sites on unoccupied public lands to be selected by him and approved by the provincial board. Whereas the provincial governor is of the opinion that the *sitio* of Tigbao on Lake Naujan is a place most con-venient for the Mangyanes to live on. (*Rubi v. Provincial Board* 1919 [G.R. No. L-14078])

From the Supreme Court ruling, it is clear that a number of Mangyan peo-ple were opposed to the idea, and balked at the regulation of their move-ment. In a remarkable seventy-nine-page ruling that ultimately attempted to align Philippine law with US law regarding Indigenous First Nation Americans—which begins by invoking US Chief Justice John Marshall, followed by a discussion of Daniel Webster's view of due process, the trial of Standing Bear in Omaha in 1879, a history of Spanish colonialism and its treatment of the *indios*, and the Catholic Church—the Supreme Court of the Philippines not only decided in favor of the constitutional basis for forced reservations of Indigenous groups, but also presented a history of the civilizing process of "wild" peoples and, interestingly, offered an in-depth etymology and defense of the term "non-Christian."

There was evidently an unease with the term "non-Christian," and eight pages are devoted to the adequacy of the term as the correct appel-lation for the "primitive" peoples of the Philippines. After listing the US administration's laws that used the term "non-Christian people," "non-Christian inhabitants," or "non-Christian Filipinos," the decision notes that the Administrative Code, introduced in 1917, explicitly states that the term includes "Mohammedans and pagans." Engaging the term directly, the section on "Meaning of the Term 'Non-Christian'" begins by noting that "if we were to follow the literal meaning of the word 'non-Christian,' it would of course result in giving to it a religious signification. Literally, Christians would be those who profess the Christian religion, and non-Christians, would be those who do not profess the Christian religion." It goes on to cite a number of ethnological studies of the Philippines to give credence to the usefulness of religious distinction. The decision quickly dispenses with the religious view, quoting a widely circulated letter by the secretary of the interior, written in 1906, that raised the question "as to whether people who were originally non-Christian but have recently been baptized or who are children of persons who have recently been baptized are . . . to be considered Christians or non-Christians." Within this line of questioning there is clear admission that, contrary to the Christian teachings, not all Christians are created equal, and that the racialized, civilizational classification of wildness and primitiveness was not about to be jettisoned because of some conversions.

The decision then moves to considering "non-Christian" as a geo-graphical designation, on the basis that many of its legal uses in the de-cade preceding the forced movement of the Mangyan related to "non-Christian" territories, rather than to any particular group of people. It is noted, however, that the geographical meaning is likewise inconsistent, due to the movement of people, and that the political rights afforded dif-ferent provinces and territories did not map easily onto the lines of divi-sion the court was seeking.

After winding through these different avenues of epithetic thought, the decision ultimately discards religious, as well as geographic, reasoning and admits to the "awkwardness" of the term, highlighting how it was often preceded by "the so-called" as a means of diluting its religious connotation. The court pushed on, however, forcing a square peg into a round hole, and made another admission—that it was not really all that concerned with religious, geographic, or political organization, but rather wished to simply shunt Mangyan, as well as other Indigenous groups, into a category made up of the uncivilized, wild, and primitive.

> If the religious conception is not satisfactory, so against the geographical conception is likewise inadequate. The reason is that the motive of the law relates not to a particular people, because of their religion, or to a particular province because of its location, but the whole intent of the law is predicated on the civilization or lack of civilization of the inhabitant . . . the idea that the term "non-Christian" is intended to relate to degree of civilization, is substantiated by reference to legislative, judicial, and executive authority. (*Rubi v. Provincial Board* 1919 [G.R. No. L-14078])

At the same time, the justices were clearly aware of the risk of religious discrimination in the use of the term, but they nevertheless concluded:

> We do not feel free to discard the long continued meaning given to a common expression, especially as classification of inhabitants according to religious belief leads the court to what it should avoid, the nullification of legislative action. We hold that the term "non-Christian" refers to natives of the Philippines Islands of a low grade of civilization . . . [and later in the decision] the mere act of baptism does not, of course, in itself change the degree of civilization to which the person baptized has attained at the time the act of baptism is performed. (*Rubi v. Provincial Board* 1919 [G.R. No. L-14078])

This thinking was the basis for the court ruling in favor of forced resettlement for Mangyan communities:

> Theoretically, one may assert that all men are created free and equal. Practically, we know that the axiom is not precisely accurate. The Manguianes, for instance, are not free, as civilized men are free . . . If all are created equal before the law, all must be approximately equal in intelligence. If the Philippines is to be a rich and powerful country, Mindoro must be populated and its fertile regions must be developed . . .

The Manguianes, in order to fulfil this governmental policy, must be confined for a time, as we have said, for their own good and the good of the country . . . Segregation really constitutes protection for the Manguianes. (*Rubi v. Provincial Board* 1919 [G.R. No. L-14078])

While the deep concern with matters of appellation running throughout the ruling stands in contrast to its remarkably untroubled object—Indigenous groups of the Philippines—one can see in it the genericization of Christianity.[7] Indeed, the discussion in the court's decision echoes any number of court cases deciding in favor of generic trademarks, whereby the court decides that a brand name (or mark) no longer has the type of distinction or specificity it originally had (such as Kleenex, or linoleum, or Q-Tip—all legally declared generic trademarks).

One can argue that this ruling—which had a dramatic effect on the policing and regulation of Indigenous communities for decades (and arguably informs in more nuanced ways the Philippine state's current attitudes toward Indigeneity)—was not actually about a civilizing intent, but rather, as Volker Shult argues, was simply a land grab of Mangyan property by lowland Filipinos under the cover of protecting and educating Mangyan people. In describing the Mindoro provincial government's policies of resettlement that led to the Supreme Court case, Shult notes not only that the land that Mangyan communities occupied was extremely fertile and desired by Filipino immigrants to the island, but also that this part of the island (the northeast, around present-day Calapan) was marked as being the future economic center of the island, and thus they wanted to move the Mangyan groups inhabiting this space (Schult 1997: 484).

There is, I would suggest, another motivation, or at least an admission, within the court's decision—and that is concerning the nature of "Christian." The term itself arrived mostly with the United States, as before 1898 the Catholic Church was the only Christian denomination legally allowed by the Spanish state in the Philippines. With a touch of etymological irony, given the universalist connotation of "Catholic," it was the term "Christian" that for the United States signified a pluralist form of Christian practice (and for others a determinedly anti-Catholic stance), as missionaries from a whole range of American denominations flooded the country in the early years of the twentieth century (Clymer 1986). Although, due to issues of access, missionary in-fighting, and sparse populations, Mindoro did not attract any substantial Protestant attention until after World War II, the popularizing of the term "Christian" was very much part of a project to remake the Philippines in the image of the United States, that is as a pluralized Christian nation (Doeppers 1976).

Thus, while it seemed that the uncertainty of language expressed by the Supreme Court betrayed a remarkably rigid and fixed view of the "non-Christian" as primitive and uncivilized, the category of "Christian" was much more fluid, and existed within a project of intended change, from a monopolizing Catholicism to free-market Christian pluralism. Thus, the ostensible deracination of the religious from the terms "Christian" and "non-Christian" by the Supreme Court was at once a reaffirmation of a universal but closed system of civilizational classification, and the opening up of religious categories, away from a Catholic universal. The path was created for the establishment of a generic Christianity, one that, though it had officially been decoupled from its explicit religious identity, in the end was only reinforced by doing so, enabling it to circulate even more widely and easily as a descriptor of people.

Sign Language, Jehovah's Witnesses, and a Christian Baseline

But what of the wide-ranging consequences of such universalizing categories—of an unmarked Christianity that was instituted as a legal norm? In the following chapters, we will see the contemporary engagement between Christian missionaries and Mangyan converts through the practice of Bible translation, and how a generic Christianity enables particular types of silence, unspokenness, and erasure. But I turn now to describe how this unmarked form of "Christianity," a century after the *Rubi* case, circulates in contemporary Mindoro. I do so by describing how a deaf and hard-of-hearing community identifies with a remarkably generic form of Christianity. By way of a number of intersecting causes—notably, the special needs education system in Mindoro and low rates of familial fluency in sign language—members of this community, from a young age, are educated not so much in a nondenominational form of Christianity, as in a free-flowing aggregation of none and all. This generic Christianity is foregrounded when we come face to face with the proselytizing work of Jehovah's Witnesses in the town of Santa Teresita. For the Jehovah's Witnesses, the merging of sign language and Christianity (both viewed as "universal") enables them to critically enact marked and unmarked categories of Christianity as well as its alterities for their own purposes of conversion.[8]

Jehovah's Witnesses in Mindoro, as elsewhere, are in many ways self-isolating from other Christian communities, doctrinally and socially, and are hugely committed to drawing stark lines of difference between themselves and other faiths and denominations. When I first visited Santa Teresita in 2009 for preliminary fieldwork, I began to attend Jehovah's

Witnesses meetings both during the week and on Sundays. At the time I was also attending a range of other services, from Pentecostal to Catholic, and the Witnesses' Kingdom Hall meetings were always striking in their difference: less a space of active worship, and more a combination of a local school-board meeting, Sunday school, and evangelical workshop. Each week, people would take turns practicing their door-to-door preaching, with a volunteer member standing in for a nonmember. By practicing all forms of interaction one might expect from a stranger answering their door—from minimal curiosity, to frustration, to eager interest—the Jehovah's Witnesses honed their proselytizing skills in front of one another.

My research interest in the Jehovah's Witnesses at this time circled in on how the reputation, indeed stereotype, of their door-to-door evangelism engendered forms of self-reflexivity,[9] and how such a globally centralized and organizational focus on evangelism led to a particular view of Christian pluralism. The Kingdom Hall in Santa Teresita, like most other Kingdom Halls, is stripped of the iconography of a Catholic church, as most Protestant churches are, and the very notion of a church is eradicated. Instead, on the simple dais, to the side, are two chairs and a table, in a mock-up of a (generic?) kitchen. It was here that, week in and week out, members would take turns pretending to knock on a door and approach another member sitting at the small table, acting as if they were entering the other's home. Other members would chime in on how to approach the person more easily, or how to better express their views. "Don't spend so much time on Catholicism," one member once said to another, "talk about our beliefs first." Another disagreed, wondering aloud if it was better to situate themselves in terms of Catholicism, given that the vast majority of people in the two provinces were Catholic. They talked about whether one should remain standing for a time, or if they should move to sit down quickly. Should one immediately begin discussing religion, or engage in some general conversation first? Should one act differently with older people? How soon should one include media, such as pamphlets or magazines, or use a digital tablet? This was all notable. While this type of teaching and rehearsal were commonly found in many Christian missionary volunteer and outreach workshops, no other Christian group I knew had so openly embedded the actual nature of evangelical work into their weekly worship services, moving past the language of saving souls and finding Jesus, and attending to the interactional specificities of missionary work.

However, after regularly attending meetings in 2009, and becoming friends with some members, I suspected that some of the elders of the church, while initially friendly, were not altogether comfortable with my presence, especially if I had no intention of becoming a Jehovah's Witness. So when I returned for my long-term fieldwork in 2011, I did not set out to study the Jehovah's Witnesses. Instead, I focused on other emerging Christian networks in the town and across the island. One such network was a special needs school, what I call here the CHESC school in Santa Teresita, run by a born-again Evangelical couple, Pastor and Mam Arnel, who had established it in the 1970s. Quite quickly, I became interested in how the school was run by born-again Evangelicals, but was nondenominational and open to all. There were Catholics and Seventh-day Adventists, and children of many different born-again churches. At the same time, the school was Christian, and had prayer meetings and Bible reading for students each day. Aside from its religious aspect, the school itself was a bureaucratically interesting anomaly in Occidental Mindoro. While the public school system in the Philippines claims to provide special needs education, or SPED (SPecial EDucation), where it is necessary, in practice this is not always the case. In Santa Teresita, there were SPED teachers in two of the public schools, but their attention was often divided between special needs students and the general student population. There were on average five or six special needs students in each of these public schools. The CHESC school, in contrast, was entirely devoted to special needs with and had more than a hundred students. However, while the school was accredited by the Department of Education, it was not financially supported by the government, and thus always struggled for funding and depended on a Dutch NGO for the majority of its income. Catering to students with all types of physical and intellectual disabilities and special needs, CHESC unintentionally specialized in teaching deaf and hard-of-hearing students. When I first began my research at CHESC, there were nineteen deaf students. This might not sound like many, but given that the public school might have one or two deaf students, CHESC was central to the teaching of most deaf and hard-of-hearing students in the province. Moreover, students who had graduated from CHESC would often return to socialize or help out in some manner. In this way, CHESC was the center of a deaf network in Santa Teresita, with the vast majority of deaf and hard-of-hearing children in Occidental Mindoro educated there. Because of CHESC, the type of Christianity that the deaf and hard-of-hearing community in Santa Teresita align with is fundamentally a generic one, not simply a nondenominational or ecumenical Christianity. These children and young adults receive instruction in a Christianity that not only is accessible across denominational divides, but also can circulate with minimal forms of complexity, and without text and specific visual representations.

In this way, the focus is often on the person of Jesus alone, as this was seen to be the point of convergence among churches.

Early on, I was talking to Pastor Arnel about sign language. He said that he could teach me. There were one or two other people who were interested, too: a young woman thinking of training to become a teacher in special needs education, and a man who worked at a local Coca-Cola bottling factory and was simply fascinated by the language. We began to meet on Saturday afternoons at the school, when the children who stayed in the small dormitory behind the school would watch cartoons in the television room, or play music, if it was too hot to play outside. Over the next couple of months, some new people came to this free and informal sign class, while others fell off, or attended only intermittently.

On one of these Saturday afternoons, after our class, and as I was talking to some of the students, I was surprised when I saw two members of the Jehovah's Witnesses walk into the school. I hadn't seen them in more than a year. They remembered me, and we began talking. They had heard I was back in town and asked why I had not attended a meeting. Perhaps, I wondered, I had exaggerated some aloofness I had sensed with the elders and some of the Jehovah's Witnesses community when I had first come to Santa Teresita. We talked briefly, and I asked what they were doing here at a nondenominational, but born-again Evangelical school? They replied they were just handing out some literature and teaching Bible stories to the children. They said goodbye, and I promised I would visit them, and soon attend a meeting at the Kingdom Hall.

The interaction intrigued me, as it was rare to come across such relaxed ecumenism in the town. But when I discussed this with the pastor and his wife later, I learned they were actually troubled by the Jehovah's Witnesses' visit to the school. They had been here before, said Mam Arnel, the principal of the school. The Jehovah's Witnesses had first come into the school without seeking permission. But there was no big fight, said Mam Arnel. She and the pastor had told the Witnesses that if they did come into CHESC and talk to the children, there was to be "no doctrine." I said that they had told me they just wanted to tell Bible stories to the children. Mam Arnel waved at me in dismay, "They drop in doctrine! They believe Jesus is a little god!"

Natural Language/Natural God

So what were the Jehovah's Witnesses doing at CHESC? It turned out that, as I was beginning to learn sign language in late 2011, the Jehovah's Witnesses were doing the exact same thing across town. As I was to find out later, there had been a decision at the top level of leadership in the Jehovah's Witnesses in New York that, beginning in 2012, there should be a global push to convert deaf and hard-of-hearing students. With videos and literature in sign produced and distributed to all countries and posted online, classes in sign language began in Kingdom Halls across the globe, and it was no different in Sta. Teresita. There were two Jehovah's Witnesses in the north of Mindoro, in the town of Mamburao, about a six-hour drive from Santa Teresita, who could already sign, and they showed a number of members in Santa Teresita the basics. Additionally, the central administration of the Jehovah's Witnesses at the Branch Office in Manila forwarded books and DVDs. When the two members walked into CHESC, they were beginning this project of converting deaf students.

Soon after I had met the two members at the school, sharp words were apparently exchanged between them and Mam Arnel, and they did not return to CHESC. This did not hamper their enthusiasm, however. Aside from taking classes in sign, I was becoming increasingly interested in the pedagogy of sign in Santa Teresita. What was most interesting to me was that students at CHESC were learning Signed Exact English (SEE). This variant of sign is somewhat controversial in itself, as it mimics the grammar of English, unlike most forms of sign. Proponents of SEE argue that it helps students learn how to read, while others suggest that this is untrue and that it hampers students' development of "spoken" sign, which becomes slow and cumbersome when trying to ape the grammatical constructions of English. Further, opponents of SEE argue that it is simply an ideological bias of spoken over sign languages. While personally I was more likely to side with opponents of SEE, students themselves never appeared to give it much thought, and were quick to change SEE to their own needs. To this end, their SEE came to be very similar to American Sign Language, or ASL (which at any rate is what their SEE was based on).

But I was interested in an altogether different aspect of the children's sign language at this time: that in addition to sign language, they were learning English. None of them could read, or lip-read, Tagalog/Filipino—the language of their families and community. In Santa Teresita, while most people have some English, knowledge of English most definitely skews upward in terms of class; poorer people might have no English beyond a couple of words or phrases. These children, mostly from such backgrounds, thus did not share the language of their family. Again, this language bubble was also why CHESC became a social hub of deaf people, and indeed a religious one as well.

I began to accompany the Jehovah's Witnesses who used sign language in conducting Bible studies and preaching among deaf and hard-of-hearing people. At this time, as their work among the deaf was only beginning, six members would combine Bible studies with prospective converts in their homes with a continued search for new deaf individuals (figure 18). It was a peculiar enough practice. They would find out, for example, that there was a young deaf girl living on a certain street, and we would go and try to track her down. The door-to-door knocking, in this manner, was less about introducing Jehovah's Witnesses to those who opened the door, and instead about inquiring, "Do you know any deaf people living near here?" or "There is a young man who is deaf that lives near here, right?" On one such occasion, a Witness woman and her young daughter, both dressed formally in full-length skirts and buttoned-up shirts, and I went to find a young deaf woman, who lived in one of the densely populated squatter neighborhoods of the town. We knocked at the door, and the girl's mother answered, while the girl herself went out the back of the house, apparently trying to avoid the unwanted attention. The Witnesses eagerly followed her. To be running through alleyways and busy narrow streets with Jehovah's Witnesses, in pursuit of a deaf woman trying to escape us, was an odd and troubling experience, to be sure. Such tenacity in proselytizing was matched by the Witnesses in terms of their approach to language. Not many religious groups that I knew in Occidental Mindoro attended to the matter of language in such an institutional manner. As is well known, the Jehovah's Witnesses make a considerable effort in translating all their literature, the Bible included, into as many languages as possible. Their relationship to sign language was no different.[10]

Nature and the Icon

The Bible studies that Witnesses conducted with deaf and hard-of-hearing people were structurally similar to those conducted with hearing people, although different literature, such as drawings and sometimes a tablet with sign language and images, was used in deaf Bible studies. Using text and pictorial images, usually from the *Listen to God* magazine (not designed with deaf and hard-of-hearing people in mind), a usual Bible study would begin by having the proselyte look at and describe what they liked about a particular image, and say whether they would like to live in such a place. These images are ubiquitous within Jehovah's Witnesses literatures, and are near uniform in their aesthetic. Portraying images of paradise, such artworks mix romanticism and realism, and are dramatically utopian, with panoramic and deep perspectives of bucolic wonder, blue skies, and smiling people. Subsequent to this the Witness

FIGURE 18. Two Jehovah's Witnesses conducting door-to-door missionary work, here inquiring about the presence of deaf and hard-of-hearing people in the neighborhood. Occidental Mindoro, 2013. Photo by the author.

member would delve into more theological matters, specifically the difference between the beliefs of Witnesses and other Christians. By "other Christians," they were inevitably referring to Trinitarian forms of Christian belief, and thus the difference between Jesus and Jehovah would be keenly emphasized. They would also sometimes include a tablet with messages in sign language (ASL and later Filipino Sign Language [FSL], although I never knew anyone in Santa Teresita who signed FSL). I mention this because the Witnesses discussed the unmediated nature of sign language, and framed it in terms of being more "natural" than spoken language. However, during their Bible studies, their use of sign language was always embedded within other representational, and notably visual, practices.

In my conversations with the Witnesses who worked on establishing a deaf Witness community, the issue of language, and sign language in particular, was often foregrounded, and included in a broader process of engaging with Jehovah. As I was sitting at a plastic folding table in my apartment one afternoon with four members, drinking sweetened coffee and talking about the Bible, one member, Brother Bobby, talked earnestly of how faith was a process of discovery, not necessarily a moment of revelation. To this end, faith was something that might have obstacles inherent in it. One needed to traverse matters of this world in order to find the divine. This issue of obstacles is an important one for Witnesses and is embedded in a Witness view of language. For example, in our discussions of the Bible, the word of Jehovah was seen to be divine, although the language itself was not. The Bible was sacred—as the collection of Jehovah's words—but the word could be delimited from specific linguistic instantiations of it. Language, and specifically translation, is thus seen as a problem to be solved. It is a problem of mediation. Brother Bobby talked much of the Tower of Babel,[11] understanding its meaning in the Book of Genesis as relating not only to the biblical entropy of languages in the world, but also to language diversity, again in terms of "obstacles."

Interestingly, however, for the Witnesses, sign language was somewhat set apart from other languages. When we talked about sign language, and how we were all learning it simultaneously, the Witness members often spoke of how "natural" sign language was. One example they gave, and one undoubtedly common to students of sign language, was that the sign for "up" or "upward" was just to point up. For them, there was no linguistic mediation in this. Recalling the Tower of Babel and linguistic obstacles, sign language stood apart, somehow devoid of the specificity of spoken languages. But for the Witnesses, such naturalness was not limited to deictic gestures; they saw an assuredness—a naturalness—in the iconicity throughout the language. Of course, for them, such naturalness stands in contrast to the arbitrariness and specificity of most spoken linguistic signs. This is by no means an unusual take on sign languages, and as Douglas Baynton has written, the oppositional character of sign language to spoken language has a long history (1996: 108–12), and the perceived connection between "natural" sign language and "arbitrary" spoken language was historically central to disagreements between oralist and manualist approaches to teaching sign language. Similarly, while many people believe the gestural components or additions to spoken language exist in a point-to-point iconic relationship to the world, and as such are unmediated by formalized structures of language, this is not necessarily linguistically the case (Haviland 1999).[12] This, of course, relates to conceptions, on the part of Witnesses, that iconicity is itself often unmediated, or indeed conventionalized, as are linguistic signs. Or, put more bluntly, sign languages are more natural than spoken ones.

For Witnesses, this can be seen to be the motivating factor of gestural techniques as signs in the world in a way that linguistic signs are not. The naturalness of sign language relied upon an understanding of their shared ubiquity. However, the interaction of sign language with Christian proselytization enabled them to frame sign language as natural in ways that moved beyond more straightforward language ideologies. While Witnesses assuredly opposed other forms of Christian practice, more so than other denominations, disaffirming any inadvertent sense of ecumenism in Santa Teresita, they nevertheless relied upon a ubiquitous backdrop of Christianity in order to proselytize. In all of their Bible studies with deaf people, the focus was on clarifying the difference of a Jehovah's Witnesses' view of God, heaven and hell, and particularly the relationship between Jesus and God. But this was a clarification, set against an assumed knowledge of Christianity at large. There was no denial on the part of the Witnesses of the presence of Catholicism and other forms of Christianity. They tackled the matter head on. Thus, in figure 19 (an example of the supplemental drawings used by Witnesses in Santa Teresita in Bible studies with deaf people), Catholicism (and Islam) is explicitly represented—so much so, that the entire Bible study often tended to be built around the scaffold of negating other forms of Christianity. The Bible study was thus dependent on a shared understanding between proselytizer and proselyte, of what a generalized Christianity entails. A generic

FIGURE 19. Teaching aid used by Jehovah's Witnesses conducting deaf and hard-of-hearing Bible lessons. Note the sash on the figure of Jesus. The sign used for Jesus/Lord by the Jehovah's Witnesses incorporates the signing of a sash. Courtesy of Kingdom Hall, Santa Teresita, Occidental Mindoro.

understanding, if you will. A shared background—the ubiquitous against which one sets oneself apart.

Those from CHESC who engaged with the Jehovah's Witnesses' proselytism found that their version of Christianity intersected well with Jehovah's Witnesses' teachings, with easily intelligible forms of Christian commensurability and alterity. The minimalist forms of Christianity they learned at CHESC never meant nominal. Much attention was paid to Christian instruction, with no child spending less than an hour a day studying biblical verses and learning about Christianity. Pastor and Mam Arnel often joked with me about the inadvertent way that the children melded their limited experiences of their family's denominational Christian specificity and CHESC's teachings into a Jesus-centered Christianity that looked very similar to a born-again Evangelical outlook. In some ways it was, but in other ways it was not. It was Jesus-centered, for sure, but with none of the forms of continuous renewal, embodiment, or social forms of evangelicalism that are common in born-again communities. For the deaf students at CHESC, there were daily prayer meetings after classes. Mam Arnel (or one of the teachers or older students) would write a Bible verse on a blackboard. Everyone—maybe ten to fifteen students ranging from six years old to thirty—would then sign the verse. Individual students would then step up to sign it from memory without looking at the blackboard. This prayer meeting was always very warm and informal. Often Mam Arnel would extrapolate on the verse, perhaps about how much God loved us, or how we can best understand Jesus's sacrifice in our daily lives.

Parents of the students never seemed to be perturbed over any denominational divide, or pushed by the school in any direction, and appeared happy that their children were at least being educated in a Christian manner. The outcome of all this was that the Witnesses were essentially attempting to convert deaf people who had a view of Christianity that was surprisingly generic—one that was designed to be baseline, universal, open to circulation, appropriation, and transformation into denominational specificity (as the Jehovah's Witnesses hoped for). Thus, because of the daily teachings in Christianity that the deaf students at CHESC had, the Witnesses had little or no work to do in articulating the basics of Christianity. Rather than having to teach the Bible, or who Jesus was, they only needed to specify a Witness view of Jesus and the question of whether he and God were one and the same. This reliance on a shared backdrop of Christianity animated their view of sign language. If we return to the use of spatial deixis, such as pointing upward, a Witness view of the sign as being naturally iconic found a similar resonance for them in terms of Christianity. When referring to "heaven," they didn't necessarily need to use the ASL sign for "heaven," but rather, when discussing Jesus or Jehovah, could simply point upward. The ASL sign for "heaven" does not actually include pointing upward; it involves placing one's palms over one another in a step-like formation before flattening out the palms horizontally and forming a sign similar to that meaning "ceiling." That the Witnesses could point upward when referring to heaven depended on the proselytes' understanding of the concepts of heaven and of God. Similarly, the sign for Jesus is to draw a clasped right hand diagonally from the left shoulder to the hip, referring to the sash Jesus is artistically represented as wearing in most of the Witnesses' literature (see figure 19, for example). But in my discussions with Witness members and in these Bible studies, they saw the ease of sign language—what they glossed as its naturalness—in terms of the ease of articulating a Christian message. The perceived naturalness of sign language was deeply implicated in the supposed naturalness, and indeed universalism, of Christianity itself. For these Witnesses, whether working with deaf or hearing people in Santa Teresita and Occidental Mindoro, they were constantly working with and against other forms of Christianity, and yet it was the shared understanding of these forms of Christianity that reinforced its naturalness. Thus, as with sign language, for these Witnesses, Christianity itself did not need to be a highly mediated experience.[13] It could be natural. It could be universal. It could be generic.

CHAPTER 5

Divine/Generic | Olive/Mango

For then will I turn to the people a pure language, that they may all call
upon the name of the lord, to serve him with one consent.

—*Zeph. 3:9 (KJV)*

It is no surprise that in recent decades, anthropologists studying Christianity have consistently found themselves working with language. So
significant is the role of language in Christianity that in many ways it is
woven into its very fabric. Many of the ideologies that are at play in language practices—truth; intentionality; divisions between interiority and
agency, and the external, material world; the arbitrariness of signs—are
similarly key to Christian experience. Christianity has always been concerned with language, notably in terms of representation and presence,
between God and the self, knowledge and experience. Language as text
has, of course, been at the heart of the Christian experience. Indeed, the
creative forcefulness of Christianity often rests on navigating the fric-
tions of similarity and difference in and between language and materiality, words and things. The Bible inhabits this division, circulating in the
world as both (Engelke 2013; Keane 2013; Harkness 2017a). Of course, the
centrality of the Bible in Christianity is due to its matching of its singular
divine authorship and authority, and its (post-Reformational) universal
access (universal, that is, in traversing all contexts and cultures).

In many ways, this chapter is a mirror to chapter 2, focusing as it does
on how people explicitly work to constitute generic forms; here it is
Christian translators translating the Bible into a number of Mangyan languages, seeking to achieve a translation stripped of figurative language,
one that would be universally understood, outside of the specificities of
a cultural milieu, in this case a Mangyan one.[1] Just as we saw how the

design artists in Los Angeles worked to produce generic brands, I turn now to how the generic emerged as a goal of Christian translators working in Mindoro, and how in practice they achieved it. In the last chapter, we saw how Jehovah Witnesses saw sign language as being in some sense generic, coalescing as it did with an abbreviated proxy for the shared backdrop of Christianity; in this chapter I ask, what does it look like when Christians explicitly set out to actively create a Christian generic?

The "olive and mango" problem, as one Philippine Bible translator described it to me, is the old but enduring problematic of language equivalency within Bible translation. How does one translate the olive, mentioned throughout the Bible, into cultural settings in which there are no olives? Does one leave the term untranslated and maintain linguistic fidelity to the original biblical texts, or does one find a similar object, or concept, in the target language that one is translating into, but one that is unmentioned in the source texts? For the Indigenous Mangyan communities on the island of Mindoro in the Philippines, unsurprisingly the lexical item "olive" and the tree itself have little in the way of denotational or connotational value, unlike their material and symbolic role in biblical societies.[2] Should one then view the Bible not as a text bound by the specificities of its language, but rather as a repository of sacred meaning that reaches beyond language?

This dilemma *in perpetuum* for translators has long assumed an oppositional nature and has been variously designated as the difference between literalism and context, form and meaning, faithfulness and interpretation, and, for Philippine SIL International translators, formal and dynamic equivalence (Nida 1964; Carson 2009).[3] While a number of translation theories have sought to undo such an oppositional framing (such as Skopos theory and relevance theory), the dilemma nevertheless stubbornly remains. Whether one's fidelity should be to the most literal rendering of the source text into the target language, or whether one should try to capture a more contextualized linguistic form and "meaning," is an ever-present tension in translation. Of course, an attempt at a denotational correspondence comes with the underlying expectation of a certain symmetry between the source and target languages, and stands in contrast to translation projects that attend to the complex and multiple indexical modalities that form a broader semiotic rendering of the text. Unsurprisingly, for Christians translating the Bible, the matter of maintaining fidelity to the source text while producing a translation that meaningfully resonates with the reader entails a larger responsibility than is usual. Because of the sacredness accorded to the Bible, its meaningfulness is not always judged to exist solely in the intelligibility of the text itself. As a result, the relationship among author, text, and meaning is duly complicated. Which approach to translation should be privileged depends, therefore, on nothing less than the role one assigns to the underlying relationship between language and God. For Christian translators the question then becomes, does God have a language, or is he forever mediated by it?

In this chapter, I discuss the practices of SIL International Bible translators, working on the eastern side of Mindoro island, in Oriental Mindoro. SIL International (formerly the Summer Institute of Linguistics) and its US-based sister organization, Wycliffe Bible Translators, together form the world's largest nonprofit Christian NGO that translates Christian literature, particularly the Bible, into languages that have little or no history of such literature. It is their stated intention to aid Christian missions by providing a Bible in all spoken languages. Twice a year, approximately ten Christian members of three ethnolinguistically distinct Mangyan communities travel from the mountains to the lowlands of Mindoro, where for a month they work with an equal number of SIL and Wycliffe Christian linguists, translators, and missionaries to translate the Bible into the Hanunoo, Western Taubuid, and Eastern Taubuid languages.[4] In the first part of this chapter I want to examine the struggles Christian translators face in their work and discuss how the practice of translation reveals underlying sets of Christian ideologies regarding the commensurability of linguistic forms that move far beyond claims of vernacular and grammatical correctness. I describe how the source-to-target directionality in Bible translation is complicated both by the day-to-day practices of translation and by the underlying questions concerning the authorship of the Bible itself. The theopneustic aspect of the Bible as source-text and the determinations of the degree to which the actual linguistic forms in the scriptures are divinely inspired often play out as an insolvable problem for translators. I discuss the means through which the Holy Spirit is taken as an essential mediator between the fallible work of Christian translators and the Bible as a language-instantiated form of God's presence. This role that the Holy Spirit occupies as language mediator reconstitutes how language is seen to communicate the universality of the Holy Word.

In the second part of the chapter, I take up these engagements with the universality of divine meaning and the discrete nature of language difference through a discussion of "generic" language. In particular, I focus on the use of denotationally generic terms as a translational and ideological tool. Rather than viewing claims of generic language as presupposing that there exists language merely stripped of specificity, the generic can instead be seen as a site in which multiple and often conflicting claims of universality and purity are at play. Moreover, the concept of generic language may be seen as implicated in ideas of text circulation and conversion. I describe how for Christians the unique form of divine (co)authorship of the Bible leads to an intertextual and semiotic break between the translational process as evidenced by the workshop and how that text is subsequently taken up by the intended readers, in this case by Mangyan Christians. Although translators often express their goal as one of recension and of rendering a text that is linguistically and socially embedded within the "target" (or receptor) culture, their translation work is also an attempt to purify and dislocate the biblical text from any and all cultural specificity, thus enabling it to exist and circulate as a universal text. Ultimately, I describe how the use of generic language by translators is an earthly attempt to mirror, and indeed enable, the universality and circulation of the Holy Spirit's inspiration in language. We can see how, more broadly, the concept of generic language has been neglected by language analysts as an ideological site of interest as well as its role in how people conceptualize the scaling of specificity in meaning.

Translating Christianity

Anthropologists have long sought to locate projects of translation in a wider set of social and intertextual practices, with the work of Benjamin (1968) and Bakhtin (1981, 1986) serving as important cornerstones of the literature. Additionally, there have been moves both toward and away from viewing social forms and practices of sociality in terms of translation itself (Clifford 1982; Asad 1986; Callon 1986; Latour 1993, 1987). Because the work of Bible translation has so often taken place within settings of Christian missionization and colonialism, it has been to those settings that scholars have looked in order to elucidate the broader complexities of translation practices (Jolly 1996; Keane 2007; Hanks 2010). While we may view these translation practices intrinsic to Christian missionary work as embedded in large-scale projects of social and religious change, perhaps the most fruitful aspect of this literature has been a focus on how translation practices themselves have effected change in the target languages and cultures (Handman 2014; Rafael 1988; Brodwin 2003; Schieffelin 2007). For example, Tomlinson has shown how Methodist translators were responsible for shifts in the meaning of *mana*: "Besides nominalizing 'mana' in the Bible, Methodist missionaries reconfigured people's imaginations about the invisible world, placing Jehovah atop the pantheon of gods and displacing ancestral spirits into the realm of 'devils' and 'demons.' In doing so, they rendered the invisible sources of earthly power both more remote and potentially more dangerous. Missionaries, in short, reshaped ideas about the potential for effective human action" (2006: 179). Likewise, Schieffelin has argued that, unlike the structured and fixed nature of certain missionary-dictated Christian practices in Bosavi, the practices of Bible translation were instead "unstable [and] heteroglossic" and resulted in "hybridized, translocated, and dislocated language forms and practices" that substantially transformed local vernaculars (2007: 140, 145). As this literature shows, whatever the specific theories of translation at play, Christian translation practices engage ideologies of language as both prescription and proscription (Rafael 1988; Keane 1997). Additionally, there is the important though understudied facet of how the practice, or the event, of Bible translation itself is taken up in the intended communities (Rutherford 2006; Handman 2010).

Throughout this literature we find the irresolution between ideas of universality intrinsic to Christian doctrine and the missionary need to work through vernaculars foregrounded in the work of Bible translation. For example, as Matthew Engelke has described in his work on the Friday Masowe apostolics of Zimbabwe, Bible translation was an inherently fraught affair, and the history of missionary translation has led to many viewing the Bible as increasingly nonuniversal and corrupted—by the very practices of translation and circulation that were intended to achieve the universal essence of the Bible (2007). In describing British missionaries (in particular the work of the nineteenth-century Church Missionary Society) and their view of Bible translation and vernacular language, Engelke highlights a surprising lacuna in their thinking—that they "failed to account for an important fact: Africans might read the Bible differently" (62). In this tension between the vernacular and the universals of Christianity, we see emerging a distinct discourse related to the purity of language.

The Workshop

The Bible translation workshop in Calapan, Oriental Mindoro, was funded primarily by SIL International and Wycliffe Translations, and took place in this town because the Overseas Missionary Fellowship (OMF), a nondenominational Protestant missionary organization, is located there. The headquarters of the Philippine (and Southeast Asian) OMF was established in Calapan in the 1950s, in a large American-style house built on a hill overlooking the ocean. Although the OMF is now considerably smaller than in its heyday in the late 1960s, the house in Calapan remains the primary center of the organization's work in Mindoro. Moreover, the earlier success of the OMF is evident, as a large number of Mangyan people living in the mountains on the north side of the island (where Calapan is located) have been Christianized along Baptist and Evangelical lines. The OMF missionaries were some of the first to begin translations of a Christian literature into Mangyan languages (Davis 1998), and by the 1970s New Testament translations had begun.

With Western-style gardens, a fully staffed kitchen serving Euro-American food (freshly baked whole wheat bread, milk, butter, honey, and black tea—items difficult to find in many parts of the Philippines), and a library whose books range from Christian literature and linguistic work on Filipino languages to John Grisham novels, there is a colonial, missionary feel to the OMF grounds. Aside from being the OMF headquarters, the house is something of a bed and breakfast for Christian pastors and missionaries traveling across the island. The OMF provided housing for translators in the main house and in a smaller house on the grounds; the workshop was held in a nearby Mangyan school (whose dormitory housed the Mangyan translators) built by the OMF in the 1970s and 1980s.[5]

The Bible workshop was headed by a Wycliffe translator named Samuel. Hailing from Minnesota and now in his sixties, Samuel was remarkably energetic in every activity he engaged in and over the course of a day would spend time sitting with each translation group. Having lived in the Philippines for more than thirty years, he had worked his entire adult life as a Bible translator with SIL and Wycliffe. Married to a Filipina, Marianne (also a translator), Samuel spoke at least six Philippine languages and was the only translator at the workshop who had near fluent Hebrew and Greek. He directed all three translations (Hanunoo, and Eastern and Western Taubuid), both ideologically and practically (he often cast the final decision on word choice, for instance). An American couple in their fifties, Louis and Annie (who both held doctorates in linguistics and were professional Bible translators, although not officially affiliated with SIL or Wycliffe), worked on the Eastern Taubuid and Hanunoo translations. Arthur, an English missionary (formerly with the OMF) who had lived for more than a decade among the Taubuid communities in Occidental Mindoro, also joined the workshop. Though no longer a missionary, Arthur was the only English speaker fluent in Western Taubuid.

A typical day began with a group breakfast in the OMF house, after which everyone proceeded to the workshop at the Mangyan school, some walking, some cycling, and some riding in tricycles. Those in tricycles would carry the eight large SIL laptops. The laptops were laid out along the three long tables and benches that each group huddled about, shaded by a concrete awning. Before any translation would begin, the group would say some prayers and sing some Christian songs. Prayers and songs would switch between Tagalog and Mangyan languages. During these prayers, the Holy Spirit would be called upon for guidance in the day's work, to lead them in translating best the word of God. Translation would begin at eight o'clock sharp, with a break for lunch, and finish at five. This was the routine six days a week; on Saturdays, translation finished at one o'clock.

Mediating Fidelity

I want to focus on some typical aspects of the translation practices that took place while working on the Hanunoo texts, to show how the problem of fidelity was ever present. Although SIL translators in general aim for dynamic or functional rather than literal or formal translations, matters of fidelity consistently arise. During the workshop, Annie, one of the American translators, worked with Cora, a young Hanunoo woman in her early twenties. While Cora grew up in a Hanunoo village, she received her schooling in the lowlands of Oriental Mindoro, was fluent in Tagalog and Hanunoo, and had a reasonable grasp of English. As was the case with the other languages, the New Testament in Hanunoo had been completed, and the translators were working on the Old Testament. Over the course of four years, five people had drafted twenty-eight of the Old Testament books. Ten books had been drafted in the late 1980s, but it was agreed by all that these were so badly done that they needed to be entirely redrafted. Annie herself was competent in Tagalog but had little, if any, Hanunoo.

Annie and Cora sat together at one of the long tables, each using a laptop running the SIL Paratext software. This software enables one to simultaneously view a verse in numerous Bible editions, as well as displaying the original Hebrew and Greek together with a gloss in English. Nearly all of the translators in Calapan would have eight or so translations open on the screen at any one time, but would closely read two or three. The actual Hanunoo draft contained notes and suggested revisions by different translators who had previously worked on the text. Each translator had their own favorite translation to which they often referred. Annie favored the New Living Translation (NLT), although she noted that it is far from literal, and its use for her was limited to broadly informing her translation work rather than providing any semantic specificities.

Annie had the Hanunoo verses organized vertically on the screen, along with two Tagalog translations, the Ilonggo, three literal English translations (formal equivalence) and three meaning-based (dynamic or functional equivalence) translations, and some explanatory notes, but no Hebrew or Greek. Cora's screen had a similar setup, although the Tagalog translations were understandably more prominent than the English. Everyone at the workshop agreed that the Hanunoo was by far the easiest to translate (after the Tagalog). The draft was good, and the Hanunoo translators were more practiced, and as a result they often sped through a book of the Bible in perhaps one or two days. The Eastern Taubuid men working as translators were not nearly as proficient with English or Tagalog as their Hanunoo counterparts, nor were they comfortable with the process of translation overall. As a result, the Eastern Taubuid translation process was much slower: even with five people working together, it could take up to an entire month to complete some basic edits to a book, sometimes with as few as six or seven verses taking up an entire day.

On this day, Annie and Cora began with Proverbs 21 and looked at the Hanunoo draft already entered into Paratext software:

The king's heart is in the hand of the Lord like channels of water; he turns it wherever he wants. (Prov. 21:1, NET)

Hanunoo draft:[6]

Ti kaisipan manga hari parihu sa sapa pag-amparahun PANGINUUN kay
The mind of [a] king same to river of control LORD to
pagbulus inda.
flow it.

Pag-amparahun niya inda angay sa kay kagustahan.
Control his flow now to his wanting.

Annie looked to Cora, who read it silently and then read the English and Tagalog versions (AMB and ASND).[7] Cora looked back to the Hanunoo and nodded that it was good and that there was no need for any changes. Prov. 21:1 was easy, with Cora making no suggestions to alter the draft. If Annie was unsure, she would usually ask Cora to translate the verse into Tagalog, and if Annie agreed that the Tagalog aligned with her view of the verse, they would move on to the next. Neither Annie nor Cora was a native Tagalog speaker. However, if Annie saw that Cora was entirely certain of the Hanunoo, she would often move on to the next verse without asking for a rendering in Tagalog. Interestingly, while Cora had good conversational English, she tended to look to the Tagalog translations on the screen without paying too much attention to the English versions, unlike Annie, who would do the opposite:

> All of a person's ways seem right in his own opinion, but the Lord evaluates the motives. (Prov. 21:2, NET)

Hanunoo draft:[8]

Mahimu mag-isip kita   hustu   yi   gid   ti   tanan nita
Owner   think   you(pl.) correct already very the every we
pagbuwatan, dapat ti   PANGINUUN
actions,   but   the LORD

lang ti   makahatul   nu unu   gid   kanta
only the to judge upstanding if   what very our
pag-isipun.
thoughts/contemplation.

When Cora translated this into Tagalog for Annie, Annie was unhappy with *pag-isipun*. Annie would easily have recognized the root *isip* from Tagalog, and she would have understood it as being close to *pagisipan* (contemplation) and *pag-iisip* (the mind). She stopped Cora, and they began looking to the English, Hilagaynon (Ilonggo), and Tagalog translations. Cora recalled that the verse was very similar to Prov. 16:2, and they looked back to that also: "Mahimu mag-isip kita hustu yi gid ti tanan nita pagbuwatan, dapat ti panginuun lang ti makahatul nu unu gid kanta pagkaibgan." Here *pag-isipun* was not used for what was the same Hebrew term, but instead *pagkaibgan*, again very similar to the Tagalog word for "friendship," *pagkakaibigan* (however, in older Tagalog, the root *kaibigan* was also connected to meanings associated with "inclination"). The Hiligaynon (Ilonggo) translation previously completed by Samuel and his team used *motibo*, which could be more easily glossed as "motivation." *Heart* in English and the Tagalog equivalent *puso* are commonly used. But as Hanunoo people see no metaphorical connection between heart and moral integrity, they chose to take a more "literal" stance in this case. But Annie did not view this simply in matters literal and figurative. She also viewed the stripping away of the *heart* trope as moving toward a position of the generic. That is, the trope in this context was understood as added specificity. I will return to this later, but one can see even here how the concept of generic is at play, and for purposes other than ones of (non)specificity. In this instance the generic became synonymous with "literal." In the end Cora and Annie decided on *pagkaibgan* (friendship).

Some thirty minutes later, Annie found herself frustrated with a passage and had difficulty explaining to Cora her issue with the subject/object perspective.

> The appetite of the wicked desires evil; his neighbor is shown no favor in his eyes. (Prov. 21:10, NET)

Hanunoo draft:[9]

> Ti   manga daut   pag tawu   magkaibug lang   gid
> The of(a) bad/evil of   person want/desire only/just very
> pirmi   magbuwat daut
> always actions   bad
>
> unman sida   magkaawa   sa kanda kaparihu.
> no   them pity/pitiful to them   both/each other/neighbor.

The problem here for Annie was the difference in perspective between different translations. This was important to her. For her, there was an essential difference between, for example, the CEV ("Evil people want to do wrong, even to their friends") and the KJV ("The soul of the wicked desireth evil: his neighbour findeth no favour in his eyes"). Was the verse to be understood from the perspective of the wicked/evil people, or from the neighbor? Annie wanted the verse to emphasize the point that the neighbor shall receive, in a general manner, no pity from the evil person, and not that the evil person, as in the CEV, desires to do evil upon his neighbor. However, Cora was not sure what she meant. Annie admitted that the English translations were somewhat evenly split on the matter of perspective here, but warned of the appearance of an equal ratio. Often, she noted, even new translations will follow older versions, so the decision might only have been made once. In this sense, she said, there is an element of the game "telephone" or "herd mentality" about Bible translation. Thus, it can often look like there are more versions than there really are. After Annie tried explaining to Cora the differences in her opinions of the various texts, Cora suggested:

Ti daut tawu unman   may   miawat   sa kay
The evil person not/does not there exists no help/favor to toward
kapirihin.
the other.

But Annie again found problematic the direction inherent to *sa kay ka-pirihin*, which locates the evil person (*daut tawu*) as the subject. Cora again had trouble understanding her.

On a note pad Annie drew *K*s (for *kapwa* [neighbor/other]) and an *X* (for the evildoer), explaining to Cora the directionality she wanted in the sentence. One can see in figure 20 that at the top is written "Ang Kan-yang Kapwa," which is itself a difficult term to translate, as the common term for "neighbor" in Tagalog, *kapitbahay*, is more literal in its meaning, signifying "next-house." "Walang aasahan (sa ati)" might best be glossed as "not to expect (they)." Again, one can see Annie's attempt to shift the perspective. Likewise, Annie wrote out "Kay [she inserted kanya later but subsequently removed it] kaparihu tawu unman _____ kaawa sa kanya." Annie then suggested *tanggap* (to receive) for the blank space, to which Cora replied that it was the same. Annie disagreed, but to no avail, and Cora once again repeated, "ti daut tawu unman may miawat sa kay kapiri-hin," maintaining the evildoer as the subject focus. And thus, after twenty minutes, the original draft suggestion remained in place, and they moved on to the next verse.

We can see in the interaction between Annie and Cora how there is an opposition in translational fidelity: Annie's fidelity to the biblical text, and Cora's fidelity to the Hanunoo language. This opposition is repeated again and again throughout all the translations at the workshop. While this maps easily enough onto a source-to-target type of translational mediation, these fidelities (to biblical text exegesis and language)—and indeed source and target themselves—instead are arguably a cover for a far more complex and competing set of ideas concerning translation. Among these are universal, generic, and pure forms of language; com-mensurability of linguistic forms (in these cases lexical and semantic, but also grammatical forms such as parallelism); and perhaps the more over-arching issue of biblical authorship and inspiration. Cora was concerned throughout with an idea of "natural" Hanunoo language. Of course, this is unsurprising; her participation in the workshop was an attempt to make sure that the text read and sounded right.

Yet even when the overarching goal was to achieve a vernacular Bible, the translation practices often presented conflicting ideologies of fidelity and naturalness. Cora's sense of "natural" language was applicable only to

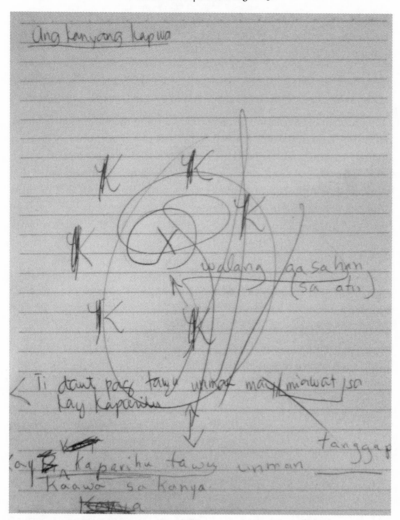

FIGURE 20. Bible translation notes, between Annie and Cora. Photo by the author.

the extent that it did not contradict fidelity to the biblical text. In Annie's discussions concerning fidelity to the original intention of the scriptures, she would often speak of the universality of a biblical language, even as she sought to transform that universality into specific vernaculars. On one level, this was obviously a conflict. But it also speaks to the nature of the divinely inspired word and to the view of the Bible as having a communicative universality outside of its specific vernacular instantiations (Rutherford 2006; Handman 2010). That is, the biblical meaning is universal in that it transcends cultural specificity. While this line of thought is most often pursued by Christians in terms of the universality of Christian practice, it is also an issue that shines a light on the translational nature of biblical language itself.

Purity of Language

One problem of translation often revolves around the nature of the "original" biblical texts, the autographa. If these were (co)authored by God, or divinely inspired, are translations similarly so? This raises a central concern of the biblical text, and indeed it is this role of a divine presence that separates the author-to-text relationship of the Bible from that of most other texts. If the Bible is a sacred and divine text, can that sacredness be lost in translation across different languages, or does the divine inspiration remain intact? In addressing this problematic, the Chicago Statement on Biblical Inerrancy (International Council on Biblical Inerrancy 1978) has become a foundational document for North American Evangelical Christian views on the role of divine inspiration in the writing of the Bible (Allert 1999), one that many Philippine Protestant groups, including those working as translators in Mindoro, also accept. Emanating from heated debates and discord among Evangelical Christians in the 1960s and 1970s, the Chicago Statement was designed to be the preeminent and unifying expression among Christians believing in the inerrancy of the Bible. However, the document itself, in discussing the inerrancy of the scriptures, tackles the matter of language and form in an interesting manner:

> So history must be treated as history, poetry as poetry, hyperbole and metaphor as hyperbole and metaphor, generalization and approximation as what they are, and so forth. Differences between literary conventions in Bible times and in ours must also be observed . . . Scripture is inerrant, not in the sense of being absolutely precise by modern standards, but in the sense of making good its claims and achieving that measure of focused truth at which its authors aimed . . . Although Holy Scripture is nowhere culture-bound in the sense that its teaching lacks universal validity, it is sometimes culturally conditioned by the customs and conventional views of a particular period, so that the application of its principles today calls for a different sort of action. (International Council on Biblical Inerrancy 1978: 295)

This "different sort of action" for the translators in Mindoro is in keeping with their view of "dynamic equivalence," a theory of translation most famously associated with Eugene Nida (1964, 2002). In this theory of translation, they view their work as applying scriptural meaning into another language, which no doubt muddies the view of what scriptural language itself entails. Indeed, while viewed in the context of the debates concerning biblical inerrancy in the 1970s, the Chicago Statement clarifies much, but it is another matter entirely when one tackles the actual practice of translation. The Chicago Statement notes that "no translation is or can be perfect, and all translations are an additional step away from the autographa," but also notes that "no serious translation of Holy Scripture will so destroy its meaning as to render it unable to make its reader 'wise for salvation through faith in Christ Jesus' (2 Tim. 3:15)" (International Council on Biblical Inerrancy 1978: 296). Are we then to assume that every translation destroys at least some meaning? This is a matter that many Christians, including the translators in Mindoro, feel ambivalent about. While many Christians agree that translations are not inerrant, at the same time they do not view a translated Bible as a mistranslation. Rather, Bible translation is viewed as an ongoing project that attempts to align language most closely with God's inspiration, or indeed God's language. In this manner it is always a project in becoming, never achieving. The language of translation approaches but never becomes God.

While the problem of equivalency between languages applies to all translation projects (thus the ubiquity of statements such as, "Well, one really ought to read Thomas Mann in the original German"), the issue of equivalency, and commensurability, of linguistic forms becomes an altogether different matter when the author-to-text relationship is divinely inspired. For what emerged during the Bible translation in Mindoro was not only the search for equivalency between languages, or indeed meaning, but also the attempt to find equivalency of the authorial relationship to the text. How does one carry over the indexical relationship (both of contiguity and causation) of the Holy Spirit's divine inspiration or (co)authorship into the translated text? The relationship between meaning and the language of the divinely inspired text, in this case the autographa, can never be fully transposed into another linguistic context. It is much more than a problem of denotational or connotational equivalency.

For the Bible translators in Calapan, there was a difference in what was determined to be equivalency and in what might be described as commensurability. While they aimed for equivalency of translation between source and target languages, this was not to say that they saw the original biblical language in the texts as commensurable to the Mangyan languages (or English, or French, and so on), as that was the inerrant language of God. The original languages of the autographa were inspired, while the Mangyan Bible texts were not, nor could any translation be. In this sense, as we have seen, equivalency entails something of a decoupling of the idea of language from meaning, in this case of scriptural language from scriptural meaning. At the same time, however, the translators, as Christians, saw their work as being led by the Holy Spirit. To have and to pray to the Holy Spirit to guide them in their work was more particular than looking for divine guidance in one's daily activities. To translate the Bible was taken to be not only the "work of God" in a general sense but specifically the actual work of God. There were no qualms of whether one should translate the Bible, only qualms regarding the efficacy of the correct translational choices. Unlike in missionary work, where any number of questions regarding the very nature of evangelism may arise—Should one be working to convert this particular person or group? How should one describe God and one's own faith? What evangelistic strategies might best succeed to convert a potential proselyte? Indeed, what does true conversion mean?—there were far fewer contingencies to face in translation. In Calapan, there was a certain clarity at hand. There was no doubt that they should be translating the Bible. The Holy Spirit was called upon not so much to care for the translators as to explicitly direct the linguistic choices they made.

Thus, in ways not dissimilar to the writing of the original texts, the Holy Spirit was present in the translation, guiding them in their rendering of the Bible into Mangyan languages. At the same time, the actual rendered language was not, as noted, inerrant. The work of translation itself was inspired, even if the language was not. This bifurcation between the divine inspiration involved in the work of translation and the result of that work in many ways replicates the division between the universality of biblical meaning and the specificity of language. For Arthur and the other Mindoro translators, ultimately the predicament of Bible translation lay in this dependence on the inherent limitations and specificity of language to elicit the universality of the Holy Spirit and to communicate the divine (meaning) through the earthly (language). The presence of the Holy Spirit in the work of translation aided the production and circulation of the transcendent meaning of the Bible, but at the same time highlighted the confines and particularity of language. It is in this space between linguistic specificity and the universality of divine meaning that the generic and concerns of circulation come to prominence.

Searching for Equivalence

Ten years earlier, a translation committee had been formed to agree on the approach to the Old Testament translation. This committee, consist-

ing of the publishers, the translators, and the Christian elders from Hanunoo tribes, agreed on the tone and style as well as on some explicit issues that inevitably arise in each translation, such as the use of "Yahweh,"
"Jehovah," and the word "Lord" (capitalized); the inclusion or exclusion
of the Deuterocanonical for Catholic worship (excluded in these translations); and whether to attempt a more poetic and rhyming rendition of
the Psalms. For these versions of the Bible, they chose a more vernacular
rendering. All of this was consistent with SIL approaches to Bible translation. While dynamic and formal equivalency were the terms most often
discussed by Arthur, the head translator, and the other translators, the
cornerstone of the SIL translation methodology, as Courtney Handman
has noted, is the concept of "heart language" (2007). This concept captures well both the approach to translation and the desired end product.
"Heart language" refers not only to the native first language of a person
but also to the manner in which the Bible and God's word should be
communicated to a person. However, as Handman notes, SIL prioritizes
language groups over speakers, an interesting alignment of the Christian
emphasis on individual salvation and relationship to the Bible with a
translator's emphasis on groups and populations (173–77). Over lunch
one afternoon, Arthur spoke to the translators of wanting the Bible to be
for the Mangyan what the Bible was for its original readers. In effect, this
was his argument for moving away from a formal or literal translation. He
was "pro-mango," as it were, and saw little point in producing a translation that was in a native language but still not meaningful in that native
culture. At the same time, he was wary of diluting the inspired word of
God and felt constrained in how far he could shift such indexical modalities across languages.

While it had been agreed by the committee that these translations
(Hanunoo, and Eastern and Western Taubuid) should be original translations (that is, made from the original Hebrew and Greek), in practice
they aimed to have a text, in terms of form and style, that fell somewhere
between the New International Version (NIV) and Today's English Version (TEV), otherwise known as the Good News Bible. However, there
was some confusion over the original nature of the translations. Some
translators at the workshop claimed they were undertaking original
translations, while others informed me that the first drafts were translated
from Tagalog (for Eastern and Western Taubuid) or from Hiligaynon or
Ilonggo (for Hanunoo). The difference in thinking here, I suspect, was
a difference in definition of what an "original" or "new" translation entailed. It seems that a number of the translators, particularly Samuel, had
been involved in a new translation into Hiligaynon and Tagalog, and that

these were the bases for the Mangyan translations. Thus, Samuel saw the Mangyan translations as a continuation of those first translations. This mediation between multiple languages, both in terms of this issue concerning originality and the SIL Paratext software, complicates not only the directionality that underlies the translation process from source to target but also how the languages of the autographa are comparable to the language of translation.

Commensurability and Meaning

As noted, for SIL and the other translators at the Calapan translation workshop, the work of Eugene Nida (1966 [1959], 1964, 1975, 2002) and his theory of "dynamic equivalence" were important; Nida's theory, however, was not one to which they felt obliged to adhere. Throughout their work in Calapan, the translators articulated a view of texts as objects that attain meaning fundamentally through their relationship to the broader culture and language in which they exist; they would have agreed with Nida's view that "translating consists in producing in the receptor language the closest natural equivalent to the message of the source language, first in meaning and secondly in style" (1975). Indeed, Nida actually used Hiligaynon as an example for the preference of a dynamic equivalent translation:

> It is assumed by many people that the repetition of a word will make the meaning more emphatic, but this is not always the case. For example, in Hiligaynon (and a number of other Philippine languages), the very opposite is true. Accordingly, one cannot translate "Truly, truly, I say to you," for to say "truly, truly" in Hiligaynon would really mean "perhaps," while saying "truly" once is actually the Bible equivalent. (1966 [1959]: 12)

At the same time, the translators felt a deep reluctance to stray too far from the scriptures. In Nida's formulation, instead of a formal lexical and semantic mapping of texts from source-to-target languages, translators seek to focus on the reception of the meaning in the target language. Underlying this view of language and translation is an assumption of some communicative universality of the biblical message. Nida himself wrote often of the universality of biblical meaning, in particular paying attention to, in his view, universal concepts such as "God," "prayer," "saint," "patience," "forgiveness," and so forth, which he believed could cut across linguistic divides if pursued through the right semantic and indexical domains (1966 [1959], 1982). It is the problematic of language and its inherent nonuniversality, and not one necessarily of message, that in this theory of translation assumes prominence. Similar to the view of the Chicago Statement, this problematic is dealt with as well as possible, producing translations that are viewed as faithful (to meaning/message) if nevertheless ultimately errant (or at least not inerrant). As Birgit Meyer has pointed out, "Although [Nida] is aware of the fact that meaning might be changed through translation, his purpose is to achieve translations that mirror the original meaning as closely as possible. For him, transformation of meaning is a problem that should be reduced to a minimum, rather than an unavoidable to be studied" (1999: 80).

This approach to translation entailed the mapping of concepts (or of meaning rather than form) (Nida 2002) that are intrinsically extractable from the source texts and communicable across cultures. But, as the translators were the first to admit, such a project is inordinately difficult to achieve. This is visible even on a lexical plane. For example, in the Tagalog draft (ASND) Ps. 71:3, the issue arose as to how to translate *commandment*. The draft contained *niloob*, but *ipag-utos* and *ginusto* were also suggested. While the terms might very well be glossed as "commanded" or "commandment," the difficulty was that *ipag-utos* has connotations of a more military-style order, whereas the translators preferred a broader view of "command" and "commandment" that they believed was the intention in the Hebrew. Or, for Ps. 71:10, the matter of "whispering" was discussed and proved problematic. The draft contained *nag- uusap-usap*, which may be glossed as "to talk or discuss." As one of the translators noted, "We should use whisper [*nagbubulungan*] but in Tagalog it doesn't have . . . whispering in English can be associated with being poetic and secretive, but not in Tagalog."

In the Eastern Taubuid translation, it is possible to see that even single lexical items raise much broader issues of a semiotic nature concerning not only translation but also the indexical properties of lexical items as related to basic religious stances. In this reckoning of translation, the translators remained oddly neutral in their stance toward their own language and the target language. Not only were source and target languages taken to be necessarily equivalent (admittedly with problems), but the translational process was seen to be inherently intermediate and productive of no new semiotic form. But this was not necessarily the case. For example, in the translation of Ps. 34:7 in Eastern Taubuid, the term for "fear" became a somewhat problematic term. The lexical item for "fear" in Eastern Taubuid is *limu*, but Arthur did not wish to use this word because it has been commonly employed in the broad sense of fear (as we would understand it in English), and was also used to mean "fear of spirits" prior to the people's conversion to Christianity. Arthur did not want the same term that had been applied to animistic spirits to now be applied to God, and so they searched for another term. In the end, Arthur argued for *fagsugun*, which would be better glossed as "respect." But the three native speakers from the Taubuid village that were also working on the text with Arthur had no problem with *limu*. Here, there was more than the matter of language equivalency at play. It was the production of a religious stance, in this case, the desire to make Christianity distinct, even in its language, from other religious spheres. Arthur's concern here was not only how the Bible would be read, in terms of a reader-text relationship, but also how the Bible as text/religious artifact would be situated within a broader social milieu. This, then, is also a matter of circulation and of the translators' conceptualizing of the social domains through which the Bible would travel. The concern for circulation, and what Lee and LiPuma (2002: 192) have called the "interpretive communities" that define the boundaries and nature of such domains of circulation, is deeply connected to the goal of replicating the universality of the divine biblical message.

If the specificity of language difference, coupled with the possible errancy of a translated text, ultimately works against the goal of biblical universality, the translators at times looked to counter these obstacles through two interconnected means: (1) the employment of generic language; and (2) the effacement of the translator/translation in the text. This goal of having the translator exist as a neutral and ultimately effaced intermediate in translation corresponds to the matter of circulation. While the translators were well aware of the narrowness of readership that these translations would garner, the ability of circulation and the universality of the text they were producing were ever-present concerns. It was often for this reason that the translators turned to the concept of generic language.

The Specific Generic

The one who wanders from the way of wisdom will end up in the company of the departed. (Prov. 21:16 [NET])

Hanunoo draft:[10]

Kamatayan ti   patabgan tawu   mag-aman sa kadunungan.
To die   the destiny person refuse   to wisdom.

Here is an example of where the metaphor was stripped away and replaced by what many of the translators termed a more "generic" language.
So where, for example, the KJV ("The man that wandereth out of the
way of understanding") and the NET ("The one who wanders from the
way of wisdom") include the trope of wandering away from wisdom, this
was not included in the Hanunoo (though Samuel's Tagalog translation
[ASND] did include the figurative use of wandering). As Arthur, a translator for the Western Taubuid text, noted when discussing the translation
of Ps. 32:6: "To be faithful to King David, or to be faithful to Taubuid,
it's always a tension. If I'm fully faithful to King David, I'll just give them
the Hebrew, but if it reads like a newspaper it's probably missing something that King David wanted to convey . . . it's neverending, that tension." Examples abound, for instance, in the Tagalog translation of Prov.
107:9, where "hungry" was replaced with "desire." This was also framed
by Samuel as making explicit what was implicit in the text. Thus, for the
famous "camel through the eye of a needle" passage (Matt. 19:24), they
used the term for "animal." Here, then, the generic is aligned with the explicit, rather than with the literal. Nida himself (1966 [1959]) argued for
replacing metaphors (and specifically this instance with the camel) with
similes, not the generic, as Arthur would have it.

With regard to the Mindoro Bible translation, the generic was employed for purposes beyond nonspecificity. As already noted, the generic
was viewed in terms of both literalness and explicitness (for example,
"removing a metaphor"). At the same time, however, the translators
often spoke of the generic in terms of the breadth of specificity, in that
they viewed the generic as encompassing a wide range of interpretations
rather than excluding them. The generic was viewed less as a compromise
between different exegetical renderings than as a form that enabled the
reader to interpret God's words themselves. In this manner, the generic
does not exclude specificity but encourages multiple specificities and
points to a translation that is inclusive.

Instead of the generic being an overarching set, including all specificities of type, or the negation of specificity, I suggest here that for the translators the generic assumes a correlation with the concept of universality. For it is often specificity that hinders both the linguistic and material
circulation of the Bible. Without specificity, the generic Bible is viewed
by the translators as purified of potential problems of meaning and as rendering the biblical message in the target heart language. And, importantly
for potential circulation, the use of generic language in the Bible miti-
gates the risk of multiple interpretations, as such a Bible will not stand
in positions of contrast to other possible translations. For example, one

concern for the translators in Mindoro was that, while their Bible would be the only translation available in each Mangyan language, a Mangyan pastor who read Tagalog might find discrepancies between the two. They wished to avoid any contradiction with other versions, especially in settings where Christians were unacquainted with a world of multiple and differing Bibles. While it is true that "mango" or some other local fruit might correlate better to the biblical meaning they intended to impart to the reader, it would be limited in both its circulation and its intertextual position relative to other biblical translations. In the end, the translators did not actually choose a generic term to replace "olive" but rather the loanword *ulibu*, closely related to the Tagalog term *oliba*. In a somewhat similar manner to such intertextuality, and aligning the generic with matters of circulation, Cory Hayden (2007), discussing generic pharmaceuticals in Mexico, notes how projects of circulation are inevitably married to concepts of the domains through which they are intended to move. In terms of conceptualizing the generic, Hayden's emphasis on similarity and copying in the debranding of patents likewise shares in many ways the Bible translators' conceptualizing of the generic as reaching (or replicating) a "universal" meaning, or at least a domain in which the universal may be semiotically located.

Circulating Commensurability

Through this process, the generic was at times seen to enable better circulation of the Bible. It is of note that the translational process, while always directed toward an in-practice reading of the text, relates to matters of language mediation differently than the presumed reader of the final text. For in its most common uses in Mindoro, the Bible itself is rarely seen to be a translation at all. It is simply the material instantiation of the Bible. In a similar manner, when one places one's hand on a Bible in a US courtroom and swears upon it, one is swearing not on an intrinsically erring translation, but simply on the word of God. Matters of mediation are not included in the semiotic relationship established between the translated word and God; rather, the relationship is collapsed, and a single instantiation remains. Thus, we may view the work of the translators as a project that is dependent on certain ideologies of the mediation of language, but one of which the reader experiences little. Of course, this is by no means a ubiquitous outcome. As Handman (2010) has argued, among the Guhu-Samane in Papua New Guinea, not only was the work of SIL translators there foregrounded in religious practice, but it was taken up and often continues to be viewed as a transformative event in their experience of

Christianity. Similarly, Danilyn Rutherford has noted how the translated Bible has been foregrounded in Biak social practices, becoming a material site in which concepts of foreignness are mediated, and how "imported words [of the translated Bible] seemingly could serve as 'proof,' the mark of a confrontation in an alien realm" (2006). However, for Mangyan communities, the target readership of these Bibles, there appeared to be no such transformative purpose placed on the translations of the New Testament that were already in circulation. Rather the translational process was effaced in the anticipated domains of circulation. As a result, the Bible produced in Mindoro tends to avoid in-text details of other translations, such as cross-references, exegesis, or concordances.

In practices of Bible hermeneutics and exegesis (Radmacher and Preus 1984; McLean 2012) common to the Christian translators and on display in the workshop, the generic (especially as related to vernacular forms), is seen to be less mediated through linguistic specificity. It is enacted as a gloss for universality, thus aligning with the intentionality of the Holy Spirit. The generic, in its circulation, achieves in an earthly form what the Holy Spirit does divinely: a universality of meaning that reaches beyond the specificities of particular languages. In other words, the transduction of a semiotic modality does not carry with it the traces of that transduction (Silverstein 2003b; Keane 2013).[11] Rather, it becomes an instantiation of the original. We can see a break between the rendering of the Bible in Mangyan languages and the circulation and use of those texts.[12] Due in large part to the unique authorship of the Bible, the target language in this context becomes for all intents and purposes the source language, as the translation is inherently the objectified and instantiated word of God. A straight line, in denotational and exegetical terms, links the reader to the inspired word of God. In this scenario, the source text and the ideologies contained within it (divine authorship) cannot be translated without God's guidance.

It is a matter not simply of materiality overwhelming the practices of production but rather of the claims to universality intrinsic to the practice of translation itself; it is the effacement of translation aided by the employment of generics. Unlike the case with other texts, the process of translating the Bible is not one of clear semiotic transduction, the mapping of one language (within certain forms of cultural and semiotic modalities) onto another (with commensurable but different forms of cultural and semiotic modalities). Within the pursuit of dynamic and functional equivalent translations, we see that the idea of "language as a repository of culture" is rampant; however, it is only truly ever seen to be the case on the side of the target language. The relationship between the original biblical texts and their original contexts (the source) is unique when viewed through the Christian lens of authorship-to-text. For many Christians, the Bible is distinct from the cultural milieu in which it was written. The Bible, as Word, might be instantiated in language, but there is nothing cultural about it. It is God's word. Somewhat paradoxically, while "language as repository of culture" might exist as a stated goal of translation, the employment of generic language is as much about the purification of the biblical text as it is about transducing entire semiotic modalities. For Christian translators, such as Cora and Annie, the Bible is located differently as a translated text artifact. While the translation of the Bible into Mangyan languages is produced through ideologies of denotational explication (even with an eye to other in-context semiotic modalities), these translators also assume a certain author-to-text relationship that is unique, one that is concerned instead with the purification of language. In this sense, the employment of generic forms of language achieves both. It may be seen as the purification of language, removing from God's word local and cultural specificity. For in the end, the generic is seen by the translators to enable the translation and circulation of semiotic modalities while at the same time achieving a divinely universal text, even if it is generic.

So how does the generic—generic Christianity—circulate outside of the strict confines of textual authority, existing as the unspoken, unmarked, yet nevertheless potent element of religious identity? In the next chapter, I take up how the generic is employed as means of opening up new religious spaces, but equally of contesting them. I do so by describing the birth of a small born-again Christian church in a predominantly Catholic community just outside of Santa Teresita.

CHAPTER 6

Big Faith

CHRISTIAN PLURALS AND THE
AMBIENCE OF CATHOLICISM

Everyone in Kulaman[1] used to be Catholic. There were some rumors that two people near the main road had become Mormons, but no one seemed to be sure. And there was one family whose members were Iglesia ni Cristo. But that was before. Before a small bamboo-hut church was erected by Pastor Sazon, a born-again Evangelical, in 2012. This new church, the Jesus Is Lord Church, began with some informal house visits by the pastor, who could be seen arriving in his tricycle and wandering in around the houses that sparsely dotted the edges of the rice fields, and then, some months later, with evening Bible studies for the community. Within a year he had a congregation of more than thirty people. He never mentioned Catholicism in his sermons, and his church was never mentioned by any Catholic priests during their masses, and yet they were in constant, unspoken confrontation.

A central facet of the concept of the generic as taken here is how it not only relies on forms of templates, copies, and reproducibility, but also enables particular shorthands in sociality. That is, we may ask, in what ways do people rely on particular types of shared forms of knowing as accelerants in getting along in the world? If the shorthand—in its essence, the ability to quicken the nature of communication—depends on the taken-for-granted discursive resources about what is shared and already known, what does that do in the world? The term "shorthand" is of course most closely associated with a specific form of writing, used by journalists and court reporters, and by people in a multitude of settings who, temporally squeezed, are required to be semiotically reductive. Speedy and concise, a shorthand is sometimes classically both symbolic and indexical, in that it provides a system of communicating that points to another system of communication (the journalist's shorthand system points to a standardized written/spoken language). The ability to squeeze language, indeed meaning, into more concise forms is in itself a fascinating thing in the world. In such squeezing, the semiotic practices become ever more central, with multiple orders of indexicality and iconicity at work. The work of Constantine Nakassis on *citationality* (2013) is a good example here, in which the indexical forms that are at play are foregrounded. Citations make explicit their own forms of indexical relationships by referencing and inserting the existence of different texts/speech (that is, entextualization), but Benjamin Lee, playing off Derrida, has noted how "citation highlights a fundamental structuring principle of language: the inter-substitutability of equivalent (paradigmatic) elements in specific (syntagmatic) places of combination" (B. Lee 1997: 43).

Similarly, the popularity of certain internet memes is configured on such forms of citationality and substitution. Not only can memes move through multiple contexts, but they do so explicitly, constituting themselves out of citation and substitution. This commingling of citation and substitution produces the shorthand. And arguably the most potent of shorthands is not the ability to say something quickly or pithily, but the freedom of not having to say it at all. In its communicative forcefulness and resilience, how are silence and the unspoken predicated on genericness? That is what I explore in this chapter. How do certain spaces of tacitness, implicitness, and of unspokenness succeed? The assumption that things are known by others—so fully known that they need only be gestured to indirectly—is arguably the inverse of distinction, and yet somehow unsatisfactorily contained by the appellative forces of convention and the normative. How do we understand the consequences of a semiotics of the unspoken, the sociality of silence, and the overwhelmingly shared knowledge upon which they are dependent?

This chapter is about one such silence—that of producing the religious other as unmentionable, as practiced by Sazon and his church. But first, I want to fast-forward to the end of the story, to the moment of recognition within a Catholic setting of the Jesus Is Lord Church, indeed, a moment of recognition of a Christian plural itself. Kulaman, a small rural area on the outskirts of the main town in Occidental Mindoro, Santa Teresita, is located at the foot of the mountains. In 2013, Kulaman didn't have electricity or paved roads, or even smooth unpaved roads. It technically has a plaza, but this is just a 20-by-20-foot slab of cracked concrete with a bent basketball ring. Most houses are made of bamboo, sometimes with one concrete wall, but more often than not without. Homes are spread out, by the edge of people's rice fields. There are two full concrete buildings in Kulaman—the small Catholic church and the elementary school. It was here, in the school, on Wednesday afternoons that the six- and seven-year-old children of Kulaman had religious class. Ate Reyes, a catechist and a local Catholic lay leader from Talisay, a twenty-minute drive from Kulaman, would arrive each week, unfurl some posters and visual aids, pin them to the blackboard, and spend an hour teaching the basics of Catholicism to about thirty children. For over a year, as more and more of the community joined the Jesus Is Lord Church (JIL), and as the Catholic community debated among themselves in private the role of Sazon and JIL, Reyes never mentioned it once. On this day, she changed tack, and finally did:

We should make the sign of the cross before our prayer, that prayer [pointing to a poster with the words of Ama Namin (Our Father) pinned to the blackboard]. That's right, Ama Namin. And before sleeping, who here prays before they sleep? Oh! Nobody raised their hand except Kevin! OK, remember you should always do the signing of the cross before praying. Anyway, in the other sect there is no signing of the cross. Who among you are attending meetings at the Born Again, there at Pastor Sazon's? In ours, in Roman Catholic, we sign the cross. As you can see in the picture the child is doing the sign of the cross before he prays. So, let's go back to Ama Namin. What is Ama Namin? That's right, it's a prayer. Who taught us the prayer? Jesus. Jesus was the first who taught . . .

And minutes later:

That's why you should be silent and not be noisy. But Sirley, you should attend meetings. In your church. I know that because I've been talking to Pastor Sazon. And even for you kids it must be your attitude to go to the church every Sunday. Very good. But the others are in the field [pointing to the pictures], what do you think is happening? Why in the field, instead of attending the church . . .

This was a remarkable moment in the religious community in Kulaman. If Catholicism was the generic baseline, then the common, indeed, universal form of Christianity was appearing to change. In this chapter, I engage a particular aspect of the generic—its tacitness. If in chapter 1 we saw how certain anthropologists viewed the generic as covert categories, and in that way unspoken, I address here the issue of how people navigate such silences and unspokenness. Moreover, I show how the generic—in this case the *generic Christianity* described in the last two chapters— changes. How people change it. I do so by looking to an ethnographic context in which Pastor Sazon, a born-again Evangelical, employed a peculiar conversion strategy with Catholics: never mention Catholicism. In his yearlong attempt to build an alternative born-again community among Catholics, Sazon never, in his Sunday worship services, house visits, or Bible studies, once mentioned Catholicism—the religious affiliation of everyone around him, and the religious affiliation he was trying to change. Indeed, even when potential converts would mention the Catholic Church to him, he would eschew any direct reference in response. I say "direct" here, for, as I describe, while Catholicism was not mentioned explicitly by Sazon, a determined critique of Catholicism was nevertheless often apparent. After all, he was trying to convert as many people as he could.

By 2013, the Jesus Is Lord Church was a success, and had become the first Protestant church to make any real inroads into this Catholic-dominated community. Although JIL is a large Philippine and transnationally affiliated born-again Evangelical church, it was Sazon alone who represented and was responsible for establishing JIL in Kulaman, and who evangelized less in the name of JIL, and more as a generic form of evangelical Christianity. With the arrival of his church and the beginning of conversions, the community had begun to engage in a larger narrative of religious and Christian pluralism that has been playing out across the Philippines, contesting the ubiquity and singular universalism of Catholicism, and ultimately leading to new projects of religious commensurability.

One common theme within an anthropology of Christianity, and of religious conversion more generally, is that of rupture. Anthropology has, of course, long situated religious conversion in terms of a discourse on social and religious continuity, or as is more often the case, discontinuity (for example, Comaroff and Comaroff 1991b; Coleman and Collins 2004; Daswani 2013; Engelke 2004; Keane 2007; Meyer 2004; Sanneh 1989). As many have argued (Asad 1993; Hefner 1993; Saunders 1988), religious conversion is always about change, thus there are nearly always aspects of rupture, religious or otherwise, inherent in it. At a minimum, Christianity, in its varying forms, may necessitate engagements with any number of distinct socialities of temporality, personhood, economics, governance, and so forth, as well as an engagement with a more expected but nevertheless overlapping set of thematics revolving around belief, faith, and an outward Christian identity.[2] In some cases, as has been well noted (Cannell 2005), conversion to Christianity, particularly for those coming from a non-Christian background, may entail either elements of disruption or wholesale dislocation from the cultural worlds in which people live.[3]

However, the context of conversion in Kulaman and JIL is one that has been less conspicuous in the anthropological canon, in which conversion entails moving from one Christian faith to another (although see, for example, S. Coleman 2003; Csordas 1997). The dislocation in this type of conversion produces a different set of anxieties and difficulties than what we often see occurring in a move from non-Christian to Christian, but nonetheless carries with it fundamental issues regarding religious and social rupture. I look at a context in which conversion occurs from Catholicism to a born-again faith (the Jesus Is Lord Church, in particular), focusing on how such matters of discontinuity are explicitly avoided. That is, I discuss a setting in which it is the risk of rupture, rather than rupture itself, that is the preeminent factor in determining how people talk about religion.

I suggest that while there might very well be fundamental discontinuities embedded in the forms of Christianity that Catholics convert to, in this case, any existence of such is downplayed, while the language strategies employed to avoid anything in the form of disharmony or rupture shape the nature of conversion itself. Both proselytizers and proselytes engage in a series of language practices that seek to avoid any overt ideological or social clash. But avoidance of rupture does not negate religious critique, instead pushing it into a more indirect and implicit territory. This is undoubtedly due to the nature of Catholicism in the Philippines.

In this context, critique becomes wholly dependent on a backdrop of shared and unspoken views of Catholicism—what might be called the ambient aspect of Catholicism (Engelke 2013), which has been the historically dominant form of religion (and indeed governance) throughout most of the country. As I will argue, not only does Catholicism exist as the unmarked and ubiquitous form of religious practice in Mindoro (as in many other parts of the Philippines), but its synonymy with the category of religion itself leads to Catholicism playing out as the religious generic. This position that Catholicism occupies in Mindoro has allowed people to engage with it as an objectified religious type in linguistically interesting ways, notably in the omission of any direct reference to it, while at the same time maintaining a critical engagement. It is this issue of discursive omission[4] and tacitness that I will explore here.

How to engage with the emergence and consolidation of this Christian pluralism—the new religious backdrop, the new generic (Kirsch 2004; S. Coleman 2003)?[5] In particular, the role of religious critique that is essential to new denominations establishing their viability and challenging the status quo within religious communities? In this setting, in Kulaman in Occidental Mindoro, where the pastor of JIL was contesting the hegemony of Catholicism, the wholesale avoidance of any direct criticism of a Catholic faith was central to his attempts to change what was included within a generic form of Christianity—the one that Jehovah's Witnesses relied upon (see chapter 4). One cannot overstate the unstated here. Sazon's topic avoidance was less about the actual conversion of people, and more about constituting a space in which the possibility of conversion could even exist. In my conversations with Sazon over the course of a year, he was very much aware of the mistakes others had made before him, both in Kulaman and elsewhere. Pushing too hard, presenting born-again Christianity as too sudden a shift away from Catholicism, and as something altogether too pointedly antagonistic to accepted norms and backdrops of religious practice, risked achieving a universal frame of religious identity. As I will describe, in Sazon's conceptualization of a "big faith," he located different denominations along a spectrum of religious devoutness (with Catholicism less devout than born-again Evangelicalism), and erased any particular dividing line in terms of doctrine or belief. In this way, he was trying to constitute a generic religious backdrop that now included born-again Christianity. While Sazon was trying here to explicitly shift what constituted a generic religious, or generic Christian backdrop, he was doing so in less than explicit ways. Moreover, we can begin to see, in the multiform practices of tacitness, indirectness, and avoidance, the simple dealing with the assumed nature of things, how the generic exists, and how it is referenced and semiotically constituted. We see in Sazon's strategy of religiously pluralizing Kulaman the centrality of genericness and of backgrounds, and of the unmarked, to how people orient themselves in the world. And we see how the generic can and cannot be referred to.

Jesus Is Lord in Kulaman

In Talisay, the nearest town to Kulaman, there are any number of denominations to be found, including a new large Mormon church, Iglesia ni Cristo, United Methodist, Jehovah's Witnesses, Catholic, Seventh-day Adventist, and at least ten born-again Evangelical churches, including Pastor Sazon's own main JIL church,[6] next to his house. His church there had approximately sixty members. During my research I got to know Pastor Sazon through his son-in-law, himself a pastor at an Evangelical church in Santa Teresita. I was initially interested in his work in Kulaman as he was working mostly alone and without any institutional support or funds, and in a community that was far less accustomed to a multidenominational Christian milieu. I was fascinated at how Sazon had attained the right to work as a JIL pastor, and establish churches in the JIL name, without, it seemed, any support from the JIL organization in Manila. What sort of brand did JIL have, I wondered. Did it help Sazon in his church-building to have the name of a well-known church, or were there downsides and assumptions people made on the basis of the JIL name? Who owned the church then, Sazon or JIL? Was it a legal corporation? And why didn't he get financial support? While these were my questions when beginning to study Sazon and his work, I was viewing him through the frame of conversion, rather than seeing him as someone trying to bring about new forms of Christian pluralism. I had thought it was simply all about getting numbers in the church—attendance, conversion, baptism, membership. But while that was important, over time, it became apparent that most of Sazon's work was oriented toward gaining a certain acceptance among those whom he knew had no interest in converting to born-again Evangelical Christianity. It was their acceptance, even if nominal, that would enable others to feel more comfortable in joining. Thus, the general community, the backdrop against which he would set JIL, was always his focus.

Throughout the first year of the church, the weekly service at JIL was essentially a stripped-down version of most Evangelical born-again services in Santa Teresita. It consisted of three to five songs sung collectively (about fifteen minutes), an opening prayer by the pastor (ten minutes), an open floor for people's testimonies (fifteen minutes), a Bible reading or extended testimony by one of the pastor's aides or ministers (twenty minutes), the pastor's sermon (forty to sixty minutes), one or two more songs while offerings were given, and finally a closing prayer by the pastor (ten minutes). All told, an average service would last approximately two hours. While the service in Kulaman began at six o'clock each Sunday evening, Pastor Sazon would always make sure to arrive at least an hour earlier. Riding his tricycle up the bumpy road, he would dismount outside the church, and accompanied by two or three members from his church in Talisay, he would, without fail, remove a beat-up guitar, an amplifier, a microphone, a rolled-up set of sheets of song lyrics, a light fitting (that he would swing up over the rafter), a small 12-volt battery, and of course his Bible. After briefly setting up, he would leave the church and walk in and among the houses grouped nearby. He would then proceed to systematically wander, making sure to call at every house, but the casual and impromptu appearance of his actions, as he would later tell me, belied the conscious and planned nature of his effort.

At first glance, there appeared to be a certain aimlessness to the pastor's movements, as he engaged with whoever was sitting outside their house, or walking by. Some houses he would enter, at others he would stand outside or in the doorway. At times he would take a coffee and some sweet bread if offered to him. But after I had spent some weeks attending and talking to Pastor Sazon, the evangelistic aspect of all this became clear. And far from it being inconsequential or supplementary to the service, Sazon viewed this time as central to his work. It was his evangelical project in practice. At the core of this project, however, was a subtlety of action and a consistent downplaying of the purpose at hand. When viewed in light of other missionary work that the people of Kulaman and Santa Teresita were generally accustomed to, there was a clear circumlocution of standard evangelistic practices at work. For example, compared to the work of Jehovah's Witnesses or Mormon proselytizing, where the missionary is conspicuous in dress, speech, and occasion, and where an explicit attempt at proselytism is acknowledged, Sazon's approach often countered the expectations of what evangelism looked like.

For most people in Kulaman and Santa Teresita, a basic assumption of proselytism was that it was presented as just that—proselytism. Arguably, a foundational feature of most missionary encounters is that the composite aspects of the social dynamic involved in evangelism may be easily read by participants as iconic markers of evangelism itself. The ability to distinguish and discursively locate what falls within or outside the realm of evangelism has more generally been taken to be a cornerstone of missionary practice (Bialecki and del Pinal 2011; S. Coleman 2000; and see Susan Harding's [2000] discussion of evangelical rhetoric). For the would-be proselyte, the ability to read evangelism as evangelism, on the most basic level, allows one to choose whether to engage as a willing participant or to opt out. And for the evangelist, being able to locate evangelistic work outside of normal acts of sociality, enables them to conduct and assess their fulfillment of a primary Christian responsibility, to spread and give witness to the Lord's word.

Sazon's avoidance of explicit critique of Catholicism was very much reliant on this mode of evangelistic strategy. In downplaying his role of evangelist, he simultaneously downplayed an apparent antagonistic relationship between born-again Evangelicalism and Catholicism. Unsurprisingly, as he noted himself, he was attempting in large part to avoid a clash of opinion, or the collision of faiths—that is, to pit born-again against Catholic. Thus, these evangelistic instances manifested the avoidance of a fundamental competition of faiths. In a sense, then, there was no articulation of an antagonism between two faiths, and their existence as fundamentally objectifiable entities was drastically lessened through Sazon's evangelistic strategy.

Week in, week out, it would play out the same way: Sazon would greet people, perhaps engage in some small talk about the weather or crops. Sometimes, he would not mention the church or religion at all, and just talk about rice prices. When he did, he would, smiling and laughing, sometimes shift the subject matter to attending church. "You should attend the church," he would say. "You're very welcome to join us." More often, he would not mention the church, but talk to them about believing in God. He would ask people if they believed in God. The almost obligatory response of "yes, of course"[7] would lead him to his next question of whether they had attended church that morning. If a person told him they had not, he would offer his church service as an evening alternative to morning mass. Never quite accepting their disinterest or refusal, he would after some time move on if they still refused or their discomfort grew all too apparent. Much of the time, they would say that they were busy, but perhaps they would attend the following week. It would be rare that he would be met with an outright refusal, although this did happen, and was usually the result of an explicit anti–born-again sentiment that a minority of people were always happy to express.[8] But for the most part everyone involved avoided any discord whatsoever, and many people clearly felt pressured into telling him they would attend, if simply out of politeness. And, as noted, he would always stress the lack of religious difference between Catholicism and born-again Evangelicalism. "One Christ," he would say, "it's all the same," when a person might reply to him that they were Catholic. Again, this statement, "One Christ, it's all the same," was both the drawing of equivalency, and the avoidance of it, but strictly along the lines of a born-again faith, in that the focus was already on a personal relationship with Jesus Christ, as distinct from institutional forms of Catholic practice. He was not arguing that Catholicism and born-again Evangelicalism were commensurate with one another, although this was surely his ultimate goal. But rather, in this first instance of the evangelistic process, his aim was to do away with, or at least diminish, religious boundaries altogether.

This attempt to furtively position born-again Christianity within a generic formulation of Christianity, by eschewing a direct distinction and comparison between Catholic and born-again faiths, while at the same time tacitly arguing for their comparability, continued in Sazon's sermons. For almost a year, as I attended services, talked and traveled with Sazon, and got to know a number of families in Kulaman, Sazon worked hard to attract Catholics into the church, to retain them as congregants, and to normalize the church to the broader community (figure 21). He was well aware that affiliation to Catholicism was an ever-present aspect

FIGURE 21. Pastor Sazon standing in front of the Jesus Is
Lord Church in Kulaman. Photo by the author.

to how he was seen by people. For those who attended his services on
Sunday evenings, he was likewise aware that everyone was Catholic, and
likely thinking about how they were at that very moment in a church that
was not Catholic. And yet for such an amount of time, to have been actively trying to convert a roomful of Catholics without ever mentioning
it was rather striking.

Big Faith as Generic Faith

Perhaps the fundamental means through which Sazon established the
commensurability of Catholicism and JIL (as token of born again) was
through establishing a spectrum or, better, a continuum of faith (figure 22). Rather than presenting Catholicism as incorrect or false, or pos-
iting JIL as the true faith, as the months passed he began to talk in terms
of more and less faith, or "big faith," and of growing closer to God. He
did so both in and outside of his church. In both his sermons and small
talk, he would also minimize his reference to born-again or Evangelical
practices. Rather than criticize or even mention Catholicism, he would

instead talk of "shallow faith" (*mababaw panampalataya*) and of "deeper understanding" (*malalim na pagkilala*). He would ask: "Do you want to accept that you are lacking of faith and you want to fill your lives with honesty?" "Do you want to come closer to God?" "Do you want to know God more fully?" He would say: "If your understanding is just a little, if your understanding is just the Lord who you should not be afraid of . . . you will not serve the Lord."

In one sense, such statements are unremarkable enough, and in almost all strands of Christianity, particularly those associated with born-again and Evangelical churches, ideas converging on the ability to grow in one's faith and attain a personal relationship with Christ are standard utterances. However, in this context, what normally would be taken to be at best universally expressed sentiments, at worst platitudes, took on a more pointed and combative meaning, and essentially were a means to engage Catholicism as generic religion, albeit in a tacit manner. Also, it may be noted that in Occidental Mindoro, and in the Philippines more broadly, there is not such an apparent discourse on some religious groups being more or less religious. When religious difference is voiced, outside of the conversion setting, most likely it is through claims of falsity and inaccuracy, and

FIGURE 22. A Catholic woman attends a Jesus Is Lord service. Photo by the author.

of corruption of faith and belief (for example, the continuous and bitter debates between the leaders of Ang Dating Daan and Iglesia ni Cristo).

When approaching people, Sazon emphasized a pointed form of ecumenism, foregrounding a shared nature of Christianity beyond Catholicism, dismissing denominational divides as the doings of man rather than God. One God, one Christ. Same. Depending on how one sees it, he was striving here for a project of wholesale commensurability of Christian faiths, or else the inability to even begin such a project. He would implore people to resist becoming overburdened with definitional and theological issues, and instead to focus on Christ alone—an interesting and simultaneous negation and affirmation of religious divide, favoring as it does the born-again worldview, with its classic Protestant stripping away of institutionality and reverence of Christ over all else.

With this practice of discursively erasing the forms of specificity within Christian worship, when people would begin to regularly attend worship services at JIL, Sazon would begin ever so slowly to mention differences. From time to time, for example, when visiting a house before service, he might very gently suggest that their Catholic statues (a multitude of which are found in most homes) inhibit their faith, or entreat them to read their Bible. Religious "things," whether composed of talk or material, all got in the way, he would say. The only intermediary they needed between them and God was the Bible. Likewise, he would start to advocate for refraining from drinking and smoking (permitted in Catholicism, but not in most other Christian faiths in Mindoro). But again, no mention of Catholicism would ever be made, nor indeed any mention of Catholic leaders in the community, such as priests, catechists, and organizers.

In the context of his sermons and prayers, Sazon increasingly underscored the concept of "togetherness." But interestingly, time and again, he blended the idea of togetherness with the Lord, and the idea of togetherness as a congregation. Thus, slowly and obliquely, the notion of a born-again faith (one emphasizing the link between the individual and Christ) commingled with the notion of a Jesus Is Lord congregation, without either explicitly questioning or disparaging the Catholic congregation of which they were members.

For all of Sazon's discursive omission of Catholicism, most congregants were quite aware that integral to his sermons was a critique of the theological orientations associated with the Catholic Church. Thus, although there is an element of concealment here with relation to conversion strategies, congregants were cognizant of Sazon's nonconfrontational and noncategorical approach to church-building and conversion.

I choose here, as an example, perhaps the most frequent and effective means through which Sazon critiqued Catholicism—his sermon. On one particular evening, as the sun descended, the small JIL church was crowded with congregants, with many people standing at the back and in the doorway. As local children jumped and played outside, and in turn were shushed by adults, Sazon centered his sermon on Daniel 3, an Old Testament story concerned with the erection of a 90-foot golden statue on the plain of Dura in Babylon by King Nebuchadnezzar (one assumes a statue of himself, but perhaps of his father [Collins 1984]), his demand that all worship it, and finding only three young men, Shadrach, Meschach, and Abednego, who refuse to do so.[9] Burned alive for their defiance, they did not die and they did not burn. As Pastor Sazon, with a buzzing microphone in one hand and a small torch in the other to better read his Bible, related the story to his congregants:

The King was a mighty person, and he had the statue built for him. And they adored the statue, and it was said that he invited all the leaders in the town. And he told them, "I am commanding all the people in all countries, wherever they have come from, whatever their languages and dialects, to lie down before this statue when they hear the trumpet and flute and all other musical instruments. And whoever does not follow this commandment will be thrown into the fire." And when the musical instruments rang out, everybody who heard this sound kneeled down and adored the statue; this statue that was built by King Nebuchadnezzar. That is, except for three men, three friends. These three friends: Shadrach, Meschach, and Abednago. These three young people were captured in Jerusalem. The Jews surrendered to their enemies. Why did they do so? Because, like all others, they too learned to adore the statue. They learned to marry people who adored the statue as well. And they were convinced to adore the god and goddesses. The Lord got angry with them. The Lord gave Israel to her enemies. Jerusalem was destroyed. The temples were destroyed. The people were captured, especially the young people, and they were sent to Babylon as slaves. And with them were the three friends, Shadrach, Meschach, and Abednego. The people said to King Nebuchadnezzar, "Long live the King! You have commanded us to kneel down before the statue and adore it, whoever among us who has heard the sounds of the instruments, and you have said also that whoever will not follow this commandment will be sent to the fire." So, what do you think? Why did these young people not follow the commandments of the King? Because they knew who they are adoring and who is their God. If you know Jesus Christ and you have strong faith, if you know Jesus Christ you will have strong faith. And you will not be like a wave, dancing in the wind. He is just following the law of the wind, whatever the direction of the wind is. But if you know Jesus Christ, you will be consistent in your faith. You will be firm in your faith. But if you just have a little understanding of your God, you will be like a wave. You will be a slave. Shadrach, Meschach, and Abednago, they knew their God. Thus, they did not adore the golden statue.[10]

While at first glance, this excerpt might not read as in any way particularly remarkable, it and other similar sermonic techniques were central to Sazon's strategy and avoidance of conversion rupture. It was clear to everyone in the church that this story, as related by Sazon, was directed toward the subject of Catholicism and idolatry. And by no means was this infrequent. Sazon would regularly employ biblical stories in analogical form that were aimed toward discussing Catholicism, without flagging its subject matter. He would often read from the Bible or paraphrase a story or verse, and leave it standing alone, without comment and without context (for example, Isaiah 40, Jeremiah 13, Exodus 20). Sometimes there would be a slight smile, perhaps a hint of recognition, but as often not. It should be noted, these were asides to the main thrust of his sermons, which for all intents and purposes were similar in manner to many other born-again Evangelical services, wherein the Bible is read, reported or summarized, and subsequently contextualized for the congregation. I quote at length his rendering of Daniel 3 in part because he did provide commentary afterward, while maintaining an omissive stance with regard to Catholicism. I want to draw attention here, not to the fact that biblical narratives may be appropriated for different purposes in specific contexts, or that the incorporation of biblical passages in a service might include some analogical component, but rather to the importance of the analogical form as a means of simultaneously engaging and avoiding. That is, Catholicism, and thus the generic, was semiotically indexed without any explicit reference to it—something I suggest is critical to how the generic exists as a type of shared, obvious backdrop.

But in what ways are the denotational norms of religious critique employed and circumvented here? How is Sazon achieving an engagement with generic forms of Christianity? If the generic, in one of its many guises, appears as the unspoken, unmarked, and indeed obvious—the water in which fishes swim—in this context for Sazon, it demanded a form of engagement that was likewise oblique. He did so here, if not by subverting, then by pushing to an extreme, an acknowledged form of interlocution with the Bible, an interlocution that is arguably at the center of all conversion practices in born-again Evangelical Christianity—that is, an appropriation of biblical authority and/or divine presence. Sazon not only employs biblical authority outright but plays with the relational stance therein between him and the text. The merging of both pastor and Bible as authoritative voice within a service setting is the norm, with all manner of entextualizing practices at play (Silverstein and Urban 1996), usually with a pastor employing the Bible as singular textual authority, but providing an in-context supportive mode of authority, not unlike more widespread and general relationships between talk and text that incur an ideational asymmetry ("It is true! It says it right here in black and white . . ."). At the very least, Sazon himself becomes associated with the authority of the Bible.[11] Moreover, the form of authority, or critique, aligns with the generic. It is there, but cannot be pinned down. It is Sazon's voice, the Bible's voice, God's voice—all merged into one. Thus, we begin to see elements of the generic—universal, unmarked, there and everywhere—and yet without a seeming point of origin.

In what is perhaps the most common example of entextualization, reported speech, in this case the Bible, carries with it elements of a language ideology that forefronts the value of clarity, denotational reference, and truthfulness, perhaps best collectively termed "transparency" (for example, Keane 2002; Haviland 2003, and for the role of ambiguity in sacred text exegesis, see Trawick 1988). Yet, there is an amplification of the normative positioning of biblical reporting here in sermonic speech. Normatively, where the Bible is implicated as source authority and ground for a pastor's articulation, instead the biblical text, in reference to Catholicism, is here enacted as and substituted for Sazon's own voice. This is achieved by leaving his rendering of Daniel 3 open-ended and untouched by further commentary on idolatry.

This is not to say that all manner of genre assortment (Briggs and Baumann 1992), heteroglossic voices (Bakhtin 1981), and differing forms of addressivity (Harkness 2010; Keane 1997) are not likely to be found in any other Christian service, yet in this instance, Sazon, while paraphrasing the Bible, does not clarify or make explicit his point in ways one would expect; indeed, he does not assume the role of authoritative mediator of the Bible, which again is the norm in born-again services in the Philippines. Most common, in fact, is a reading/rendering of a biblical verse or passage, followed by exegesis that contextualizes biblical meaning. There is a tendency to produce a scale of directionality here, moving from the biblical text as universal meaning to pastoral exegesis as in-context meaning. The mode of addressivity and genre function in the context of a service usually follows this form of directionality. Most congregants in JIL have not read the Bible in detail, nor until recently have they had one,[12] and for the most part they find Sazon's contextualization more useful than an actual reading of the Bible. Somewhat ironically, given the conversion here of Catholics to born-again Christianity, there is the expectation of biblical mediation. What Sazon does is contextualize Daniel 3 in terms of stronger faith, while leaving Catholicism unmentioned. Thus, on the matter of Catholicism (and idolatry), Sazon seeks to attenuate his presence, taking full advantage of the role of addressivity embedded in practices of reportage that efface one's role in the message (that is, don't shoot the messenger).

As I have already noted, Sazon is making a fundamental categorical play throughout his evangelistic practice more broadly, and specifically here in his retelling of Daniel 3; Catholicism is presented as an inferior faith to born-again Evangelicalism, but notably one of the same type. Thus, the continuum of faith that Sazon invokes in his retelling of Daniel 3 (to not be like a wave, to be strong in faith, to really know Jesus, and so on) works hard at avoiding any difference in category or type when it comes to religious differentiation. There is a vulnerability in taking this line in relation to conversion and religious difference. Does one create a religious "other"? Or does one avoid doing so at all costs? For Sazon, the most important part of such a continuum is that the two faiths do not exist in opposition. He struggled hard to maintain that position. In house visits with potential congregants, when he would find them more than willing to criticize Catholicism, he would avoid making any similar assertions himself. Yet in my conversations with him, he could become quite passionate in his advocacy for a born-again approach to faith, and in his criticisms of the Catholic Church. He truly believed that Catholicism was a corruption of Christianity. As with many other born-again pastors, he was far more comfortable with praising Islam than Catholicism. But then, as a friend in Santa Teresita once remarked, Muslims have never claimed to be Christians.

The Tacitness of Religious Backdrops

In framing Pastor Sazon's actions in terms of religious critique and the avoidance of explicit reference, I suggest that his strategy was not simply to avoid offense or to openly attack the beliefs and practices of Catholics; instead, he was engaging in the formation of Christian pluralism that produces, and at the same time contests, Catholicism as the religious generic of the community. While he was avoiding a framework of oppositions of

Catholic versus born again, he was also thoroughly engaged in a discourse in which Catholicism is acknowledged to be the fundamental and ubiquitous category of religious experience. This often worked to his advantage, so that a proselyte was able to turn away from Catholicism without it being an explicit "conversion" with the necessary sense of rupture that such an event connotes. For Sazon, the ultimate conversion, it seemed, was for a person to arrive at a born-again religious identity without, as it were, ever really leaving a Catholic one. This was, of course, in stark contrast to many of his missionary counterparts, who happily emphasized such rupture in conversion, by marking the time, date, and place of someone's acceptance of Jesus as their savior.

Unlike other born-again pastors, who not only proclaim Catholicism as oppositional to born-again Evangelicalism, but assume that the two are not even of categorically similar type, with Catholicism excluded altogether from the moniker of "Christian," Sazon took a different tack. However, for the different strategies at play, all were engaged in producing Catholicism as the generic form of religious practice. Again and again, in a multitude of conversations with born-again practitioners, this formation of Catholicism as the generic was evident. Indeed, it was through talk that this formation primarily played out. A wide range of linguistic, primarily semantic, practices were employed, through which the issue of Catholicism (and more broadly religious difference) was indirectly broached, including a consistent use of the subject pronoun *sila* (they) as the unnoted Catholic, constant references to institutionalization in a pejorative frame, and, perhaps most interestingly, the use of the term "religion" itself to denote the failures of Catholicism. This was captured most precisely in the continually repeated born-again phrase "Christ, not religion."

These utterances are semiotically indexing Catholicism, drawing in a wide range of ideological stances that depend on a universally shared understanding of Catholicism's role as religious archetype. Of interest here is the general reliance on implicitness and indirectness. This inclusion of a discursive technique of indirectness is calling upon a shared knowledge, and a shared expertise, of a specific, context-bound meaning. It is thus reliant, not on any particular view or opinion of Catholicism, but on a shared knowledge of its position as religious form with respect to a broader social context in which religious practice occurs.

Although I have suggested that the role Catholicism plays as a generic religious backdrop depends upon linguistic indirectness, a number of scholars have argued that "indirectness" is a troubling analytic (Philips 2010; Silverstein 2010).[13] As Michael Lempert has noted, "perceived 'indirect'-ness may just be an artifact of an ideological commitment to denotational explicitness" (Lempert 2012; see also Irvine 1993; Banfield 1973). While indirectness may be taken to be performed against, or stand in contrast to, implicit assumptions concerning communicative norms (as per Grice, one "flouts" norms), "direct" speech, conversely, is often stripped of more context-bound contingencies. As can be seen in Sazon's employment of forms of indirect speech, he was as dependent upon such shared norms as any denotationally explicit rendering of a critique of Catholicism would be. His "indirectness" here did allow him, however, to attenuate or efface full authorship of the critique. This deflection of authorship, in taking up indirect aspects of addressivity and muddling the voices of speaker and text (pastor and Bible), deflected accusations of overt denunciation of the congregants' faith and religious affiliation. At the same time, his condemnation was bolstered by encoding it within biblical authority.

At best it seems that "indirectness" here is, as Michael Silverstein suggested, a "cover term" for a range of discursive practices that are universally in place already (Silverstein 2010: 338). Essentially then, all categories of "direct" and "indirect" speech are very much folk (or native) categories. I suggest that the metapragmatics of indirectness at work here specifically involves the shared conceptualization of Catholicism, and the avoidance of rupture in conversion. For all the problems associated with "indirectness" as a linguistic and pragmatic category, and as an analytic tool, that "deep, if not fathomless category," to quote Lempert again, there is a need for something approaching it, as marker for the sets of discursive practices embedded in evangelistic strategies.

While it is tempting to locate the explanatory weight of Sazon's strategy in terms of politeness,[14] or even verbal taboo, I would argue that it simply does not account for the manner in which Catholicism and the risk of religious rupture are treated. This is particularly the case because, as I noted previously, in Kulaman, as in the rest of Occidental Mindoro, and indeed the Philippines, people are commonly willing to openly criticize Catholicism. No matter what one's religious affiliation might be, the Catholic Church has long been implicated in social, political, and national discourses. There is little in the way of taboo of such critique of Catholicism in the Philippines. Also, and perhaps most important, such a strategy of tacitness, such avoidance of rupture, was not all the doing of Pastor Sazon. The congregation involved aligned themselves with the tacitness that was at play. It was not simply his strategy of proselytism, but collectively theirs.

Whether understood as topic avoidance of religious and social rupture/discontinuity or evangelistic strategy, the means through which this type of tacitness, of circumlocution of Catholicism in particular, can succeed is in large part due to the role of Catholicism as the generic form of religious practice—not only the religious prime, but ubiquitous to the extent that it exists in an ambient manner, suffusing religious space and discourse, pervading and occupying the category of religion itself. It is the knowledge and practice of Catholicism, shared by all, that enables such born-again Evangelical conversion strategies. The forms of omission and silence around Catholicism that we see at play here—successfully so, it might be added—are wholly dependent on universally acknowledged social baselines, and ones that are seen as having no particular author, viewed instead as collectively articulated. In the Philippines, Catholicism and religion coalesce as token and type. For Pastor Sazon, to contest Catholicism was indeed a dangerous game, for in many ways it was to contest the fundamentals of religion.

Ate Reyes 2

And so, to finish, back to Ate Reyes, and her explicit reference of Sazon and JIL—evidence of Sazon's success in shifting the religious backdrop of the Kulaman to include born-again Evangelical Christianity. As discussed in the introduction, there are evidently scales of the generic, and also structural forms of the generic, organizational and infrastructural, such as the MIFARE chip. This is true also of Ate Reyes and her catechism in a fundamental sense—her actual presence in the school. While her teachings were constitutive of Catholicism as ubiquitous and generic, promoting a Catholic doctrine to all the children present, her presence in that classroom was perhaps of even more import. Although approximately 20 percent of people living in Occidental Mindoro were non-Catholic, throughout the province, the majority of students of different faiths took part in weekly religious classes in the public schools. Most people I have ever talked to were under the impression that religious instruction was required, simply as part of the public school curriculum. In these religious classes, everyone, whatever their religious faith, was expected to recite Catholic prayers, make the sign of the cross, and otherwise enact Catholic doctrine. As a result, whether one was born again, Mormon, Iglesia ni Cristo, or Muslim, almost everyone in Mindoro knew the prominent Catholic prayers, such as the Hail Mary and the Rosary, as well as the basic theology of Catholicism. Against such ubiquity, one can see the challenge that was set before Sazon.

In one sense, these were just weekly religious classes, as mundane as could be in a predominantly Catholic country like the Philippines. Surprisingly, however, and unknown to the majority of people, these classes were in no way part of the Philippine state curriculum. They were not even classes per se. More akin to sports clubs being allowed by schools to use their gyms, these religious classes were entirely voluntary and solely organized by the Catholic Church. At the same time, the vast majority of parents assumed otherwise. Indeed, I have known school principals and administrators who have likewise believed these religious classes to be part of a national curriculum, even as they were the ones who authorized the classes. The generic scales up and down, and is constituted in language, in organizational structures, in religious beliefs, and in the thousands of small assumptions we make every day. Within a Philippine context of Christianity, the generic is in Jehovah's Witnesses pointing up to heaven when speaking to deaf and hard-of-hearing children, early twentieth-century jurists unpacking the meaning of "non-Christian," in the history of Spanish colonialism and the ubiquity of Catholicism, in Sazon's oblique critiques of Catholicism, and in the assumptions people have regarding the Catholic nature of religious instruction in public schools.

House of Generics Pro Forma

During a research trip in 2019 on death and killing in Manila, I traveled to Santa Teresita in Mindoro, where I had conducted my dissertation research. I noticed a new shop on the street that I had lived on for two years: "HJJ House of Generics." A pharmacy, House of Generics sells perhaps the best-known generic, off-brand pharmaceuticals (figure 23). With a similarly generic diagrammatic of a house on the shop sign, the caption *"mura! de kalidad! maaasahan!"* (cheap! quality! reliable!) established their attempt to break into the consumer drug market so famously dominated in the Philippines by the duopoly of Mercury Drug and South Star Drug. If the town plaza is the predominant inheritance of Spanish colonial urban design, with every town across the Philippines, big and small, replicating this same urban template, the contemporary urban replication must surely be the ubiquity of either Mercury or South Star Drug, often both, similarly found in nearly every urban space across the country. These drugstores are ubiquitous across provinces—they pull people in, are continuously humming with customers, and are open for much longer than most other shops. They act as small economic and social hubs, with the red colors of Mercury and the blue of South Star instantly recognizable from a distance, and together form a doubled archetype of Filipino pharmaceutical distribution. In Santa Teresita, South Star is differentiated from Mercury Drug by having air conditioning, while Mercury Drug is without doors, and instead has an open-air counter. South Star also sells condoms, while Mercury Drug maintains a stricter Catholic ethos, to the extent of having erected a 3-foot-tall statue of the Virgin Mary in a glass case next to the counter in 2017.

House of Generics does not wholly replicate Mercury or South Star—for example, it does not stock any food, alcohol, or baby formula (a hugely important stock for the drugstores), but it does have refrigerators

FIGURE 23. HJJ House of Generics, Santa Teresita, Occidental
Mindoro, 2020. Photo by Karina Thyra Novio-Cordova.

with bottled water and soft drinks. Its main market niche is selling generic versions of prescription drugs, as it leaves the selling of health and
beauty products to its competitors. It must be said that House of Generics does not threaten the omnipresence of Mercury or South Star. It just
exists there in the background, seemingly eking out an existence, generically so, within the ecosystem of pharmaceuticals. There is a strange play
here, contesting the ubiquity of Mercury and South Star through another
form of ubiquity—ubiquity of form, pro forma, universals versus universals, but of different type, differentiation of self through sameness, nonspecificity as the marked, a semiotics of mimesis and alterity combined,
and so on.

In many ways, in this book, I have sought, not to settle an issue in anthropology, but to highlight one—that is, the way that normative, background forms of social practice are theoretically and ethnographically situated. While anthropologists are in constant ethnographic engagement
with the normative, there has been, as one might frame it, either a theoretical aporia or flat-footedness regarding how we understand the repetitive and normative. As I mentioned at the beginning of this book, given
the theoretical high-wire acts we see in the discipline regarding change

and innovation within the social, the descriptors for the inverse, when we find them, arguably rely on staid representational forms: lived experience, the everyday, the ordinary, the taken-for-granted, the background, and so forth. Relied upon, rather than theoretically explored, this ethnographic space is universal and ubiquitous, and is evidently at the beating heart of a greater anthropological project. And yet, there is a hesitancy in engaging it. It beats, Poe-like, beneath the floorboards. In one way, this makes sense and follows on from the breach social theorists made with the concept of culture as far back as the 1970s. With a shift away from culture as a containing and motivating descriptor of all, so too went those subordinate concepts fastened to it, such as tradition. And rightly so. In some ways as problematic as culture, perhaps less so when defined narrowly, the concept, indeed the very term, of "tradition" recalls more than a whiff of a derogatory and externally imposed designation, with a particular lack of coevalness of time, its history as a concept one of repeated and consistent use to dispossess people of agency. At the same time, nothing really has replaced it in pointing to one aspect of tradition, that is, its less notable aspect, the repetitive, ordinary, and shared practices of people. Some notable exceptions here are praxis and habitus, which mine the nature of action and routinization. And yet, they are notably inward-looking and located within the individual, thus famously reflecting back, outward, to structures of being. Similarly, doxa, while situated fundamentally within the social and collective, again is more about the (non)realizations of structure, with awareness and assumption looming large as individuated forms.

By conceptualizing the generic in this book, I don't wish to locate it as a replacement for a concept such as tradition or habitus; rather, I want to chip away at the assumptions and aporia around the simply repetitive spaces of the social—especially in the vast and quickening circulation of media. In these media spaces, form, type, and genre are increasingly foregrounded as practices of classifying and sorting the vast deluges of information. What surrounds particularity and distinction? The generic is part of all of this. It is part of replication and of sorting, and of finding quintessence. It is also the template of the social.

Acknowledgments

In a book that is concerned with the backdrops of the social, it would be absurd not to take this space to note my own backdrops, which essentially constituted remarkable forms of support in the research and writing of this book.

My teachers at the University of Michigan have been, to a person, generous and intellectual ports of call. Krisztina Fehérváry, Matthew Hull, Stuart Kirsch, Michael Lempert, and Bruce Mannheim have all guided my thinking in different ways. I owe a particular gratitude to Deirdre de la Cruz, Judith Irvine, and Andrew Shryock, who guided me in my graduate studies. To Webb Keane, who has supported me intellectually, emotionally, seemingly at times almost spiritually, I am thankful.

Before my time at the University of Michigan, Steve Coleman and Jamie Saris taught and inspired me in anthropology and semiotics at Maynooth University in Ireland, and indeed my time there also crisscrossed with Rob Moore, whose own work on the generic was perhaps the origin point for this book, even if I did not know it at the time.

Many eyes have been set on drafts of parts of this book, or have contributed in conversation or to different instantiations of my work on the generic, including Patrick Eisenlohr, Ilana Gershon, Courtney Handman, Graham Jones, Elisa Lanari, Richard Parmentier, Kelly Fagan Robinson, Farhan Samanani, and Greg Urban. My sincere thanks and appreciation to them. Colin Hoag and James Meador were beyond generous with their time and thoughts, and read full drafts of the manuscript. The two anonymous reviewers provided critical eyes and thoughtful insights, and have made this book better than it otherwise would have been. A special note of thanks to Kyle Wagner at the University of Chicago Press, for his wisdom, his insights, and support.

At the University of Michigan, I have benefited from innumerable conversations with colleagues and friends that contributed to the ideas in this book, even if they themselves would never think so, including Meghanne Barker, William Benton, Nick Emlen, Erica Peltman Feldman, Geoffrey Hughes, Jieun Kim, Jane Lynch, Elana Resnick, Josh Shapero, Nishita Trisal, and Andrea Wright. Ismail Fajrie Alatas, Craig Colligan, Gabi Koch, Michael Prentice, Perry Sherouse, and Stuart Strange, as well as Chip Zuckerman (something of a fellow traveler in the generic), have all been wonderful friends and have helped me in so many ways, intellectually and otherwise, over the years. I am forever grateful to Letty Pagkalinawan, who first tried to teach me Filipino/Tagalog at the University of Michigan. My sincere gratitude to the Forum for Interdisciplinary Religious Studies, University of Göttingen. I owe a special thanks also to Independent Studio Services, and to Melissa Dale, James Zarsadiaz, and the Yuchengco Philippine Studies Program and the Center for Asia Pacific Studies at the University of San Francisco for their support.

My time at the Max Planck Institute for the Study of Religious and Ethnic Diversity and the Max Planck Society–Cambridge Centre for Ethics, Economy, and Social Change allowed me to write substantial parts of this book. I am wholly indebted to Peter van der Veer and his guidance; he gave me time, space, and support, as well as pushing me, in the most generous way possible, to intellectually account for my work at all turns. Adrian Herman and Matthias Koenig were supremely kind and helpful to me during my time in Göttingen. Patrice Ladwig has been a true friend and an exceptional colleague. I am grateful to Tim Rosenkrantz and Leilah Vevaina, who provided not only friendship, but in many ways a home and family in Göttingen. My thanks also to Patrick Desplat, Nicole Itturiaga, Jane Kierst, and Gülay Türkmen for their friendship.

I can't really ever repay the kindness of those people in the Philippines I have worked with. I try, and will continue to try, but the balance sheet is off, my debt outstanding. I have benefited from untold friendship and care during my fieldwork in the Philippines. My debt to those people in Mindoro and Manila who welcomed me into their lives is immense. To name only some does a disservice to those unnamed. But first and foremost, the kindness and generosity of Eunice Novio Cordova and her family, Joma, Kitty, Karl, Kairos, and Ninang, for well over a decade now, continues to amaze me. I met Eunice in 2009, in Manila, and the very next day, we flew to Occidental Mindoro, where she brought me to her family home, which, a decade later, remains the center point of the circle, a space of calm, resolve, and support. Miguel Elausa tutored me in Tagalog, before becoming my closest friend and ally in Mindoro. This research would not have been possible without him. I am also grateful to the pastors and priests, the lay leaders, court clerks, and church administrators who helped me in my research.

In Mindoro, my thanks go to Kermit and Raquel Titrud, Keith and Grace McCune, Derek Daniels, John and Paula Richards, Mary Jane, Mary Grace, and Ninang Gumaod, Maan Villahermosa Reyes and her family, Shai Anne Tamares and her mother, Ric Festin, Marl Ramirez, Norman Novio, the late Rodolfo Acebes, Zenaido Solano Augustino and Pastor Augustino, and everyone at the CORD Foundation. In Manila, Raul Pertierra has always been a wonderful friend. My thanks also to Lisandro Claudio and Jayeel Cornelio.

The Flores family at the Bethany Evangelical Missionary Church, Labangan, in Occidental Mindoro, have been true friends, as have Teresita Benoza, Evedel Calay, Marlon de los Reyes, Melvin Domingo, Gloria, Kenneth, and Bel Pangilinan, Victorino Ruedes, Jonathan Velasco, and everyone at the United Methodist Church in Occidental Mindoro. To people at the United Methodist Church headquarters, and the Philippine Bible Society in Manila, I am thankful for their support. I am likewise grateful to Ofelia Estoya Aguilar, Angelito and Bobby Quinones, Mikaela Venturina, and everyone who allowed me to work closely with them. The late Silverio Importante could not have been more caring or generous.

All mistakes are my own.

My thanks and appreciation also to the Bentley Historical Library and the William L. Clements Library at the University of Michigan, the National Library of the Philippines, the National Archive of the Philippines, the United States Library of Congress, the United States National Archives, the Irish National Library, and the Rizal Library at the Ateneo de Manila University.

Parts of chapter 2 appeared in a different form in MacLochlainn (2019) ("Brand Displaced: Trademarking, Unmarking, and Making the Generic," *HAU: Journal of Ethnographic Theory* 9 [3]: 498–513); and chapter 6 in a different form in MacLochlainn (2015) ("Divinely Generic: Bible Translation and the Semiotics of Circulation," *Signs and Society* 3 [2]: 234–60); and chapter 4, which emerged in part from graduate studies at Maynooth University.

In a gesture to the backgrounds inherent in the generic, I want to thank those sonic backdrops to writing that often go unremarked upon but are, in the end, essential to many of us when we write, and which for me informed much of the spirit here: Alice Coltrane, Kelan Phil Cohran, Joe Henderson, Pharoah Sanders, Thundercat, Philip Glass, Tomasz

Stanko, Calvin Keys, Dirty Three, Future Islands, and Sons of Kemet. Miles Davis's *In a Silent Way* was a constant companion, as was Lloyd McNeil, and funnily enough, Bruce Springsteen. These were the sounds in my head, the ambient forms that I argue are so important in the world.

I cannot begin to adequately thank my family, Tristan, Dolores, and John, for their support throughout my life. And to Sabine Mohamed, who has been by my side, in my heart and in my head, and often in the next chair or room, while I wrote this book. And finally, as I write these words, to Sesuna as yet unborn, I can't wait to meet you.

Notes

Part I Introduction

1. Interestingly, Pierre Bourdieu, in his book *Distinction*, viewed the generic as a synonym for "common" (1984 [1979], 32).

2. The "ordinary" is, of course, an essential conceptual component within any ethnographic engagement, and has been foregrounded as such (Das 2020, 2007), often within spaces that see the ordinary ruptured, for example, those characterized by violence and trauma.

3. This is not necessarily true. Not only could East Timor be classified as Christian, but to label the Philippines "Christian" elides the substantial populations who identify as other faiths. It is a Christian majority—but with a famous Muslim minority, as well as a multitude of indigenous religious forms.

4. See also Paul Kockelman's (2013) discussion of the concept of the "sieve" as a means, not only of category making, but also of sorting, and its ontological consequences.

5. "Whassup" is a term that Michael Warner discussed in his "Publics and Counterpublics" (2002), noting how it highlights certain types of circulation, in this case its affective "talk value." As he notes, "you don't just mechanically repeat signature catchphrases. You perform through them your social placement. Different social styles can be created through different levels of reflexivity in this performance" (Warner 2002: 73).

6. Although there are examples when such technology is thought about in explicit ways. For example, the artist Lucie Davis created fake fingernails that have the RFID chips of the London Oyster metro cards in them, allowing people to simply wave their hand across the scanners as payment.

7. The bands are loose amalgamations of Hillsong musicians, with names such as Hillsong Worship, Hillsong Live, Hillsong United, and so on. The system of shared writers and musicians echoes the production systems of Motown and Tin Pan Alley.

8. The difference in usage between Kroeber and Sapir appeared to have little to do with their different theoretical views on locating the individual within a cultural model (as in their well-known exchange on the concept of the "superorganic" [Kroeber 1917; Sapir 1917]).

9. Such scholarship underlines the different traditions that enable one to engage the nature of cultural replication. For example, think of the semiotics of Charles

Peirce; Mikhail Bakhtin's work on genre, multiple voicing, and heteroglossia; Erving Goffman's work on framing; as well as Jürgen Habermas's famous work on the public sphere, and Walter Benjamin's writing on reproduction.

10. See Sadre-Orafai (2020) for an overview of how "type" has been taken up in anthropology.

11. See Francis Cody's examination of print capitalism in India for a discussion of how publics and their self-abstractions interact (Cody 2015).

Chapter 1

1. A literature that continues to expand, although not within the general remit of sociocultural anthropology.

2. Genus and genera have a somewhat similar issue regarding definition, perhaps highlighted best in 1978, when Colin Booth, a mycologist (fungi specialist), asked in an academic president address, "do you believe in genera?" The history of the classificatory slippage in biological taxonomies is described by Tod Stuessy (2009).

3. The history of twentieth-century anthropological research in the Philippines is unsurprisingly shot through with a contemporary history of American colonialism, as well as its Spanish antecedents. For an overview of the colonial entanglements of the American colonial project and twentieth-century anthropology in the Philippines, see Hutterer (1978). As I describe in chapter 4, the US colonial gaze and treatment of Indigenous Mangyan groups manifested through a particular ideology of cultural evolution. However, as Vicente Rafael has described, the inheritances and perdurances of such colonialism continue in basic if nuanced ways, for example, in the category and object of "Southeast Asia" itself (Rafael 1994a). For a discussion of the colonial ideologies that have suffused discourses on knowledge, education, and pedagogy in the Philippines, see Constantino (1970) and later discussions by Kramer (2006) and Claudio (2015). See also the recent work of Kathleen Cruz Gutierrez, examining the colonial histories of botany in the Philippines (2018a, 2018b).

4. And risked repeating classic forms of subjugation of large-scale colonial projects that celebrated classificatory forms. In the Philippine context, see Vicente Rafael's discussion of a US colonial census in the Philippines and how they began to epistemologically order Filipinos (1994). As Rafael describes, it was not so much a debate over race that played out in the census, but of the very nature of category.

5. For some, "color" itself among Hanunoo communities would be a covert category. See also Charles O. Frake's work on cognitive systems in the Philippines for an important parallel to Conklin's work.

6. For a detailed discussion of Whorf and his understanding of "covert categories" and crypto types, see Penny Lee's *The Whorf Theory Complex* (1996: chap. 4, 160–92).

7. Interestingly, within linguistics there is the concept of "generic is specific," which raises the question as to what extent metaphors are actually metaphorical, if that metaphor has become, for example, proverbial. Similarly, as described in more detail in chapter 2, is asking for a Kleenex, really all that metaphorical—given that the term Kleenex has been famously genericized? (See Lakoff 1994; Sullivan and Sweetser 2009.)

8. See Achille Mbembe, for example, for a discussion of race and naming (2017). See also John Jackson (2008), Anna Bax (2018), and Krystal A. Smalls (2018) for explorations of euphemism, indirectness, and the refusal to name.

9. Benjamin Lee Whorf's own use of "Standard Average European" gestures to

such ideologies of unmarked norms, and famous "voice from nowhere" or "news anchor" accents, and the broader, often more formal practices of standardizing languages, for example, in language textbooks.

10. For example, see Barrett, Hanna, and Palomar's recent article, "In Defense of the X"(2021), on some of the political contestations around the use of "Filipinx."

11. The generic is not fully tethered to the unmarked, however. Even in relation to "whiteness," the marked is also, and famously, circulated in generic ways. For example, if whiteness is the unmarked category in most European spaces, the marked, the nonwhite, is equally subjected to generic representations. Thus, whether it is South Asian immigration to the United Kingdom in the 1960s, or Turkish immigration to Germany in the 1970s, or Syrian refugees in the 2010s, they are often socially and politically constituted in generic ways.

Chapter 2

1. I would argue that even if this is true, it concerns not just ideologies of brand consumption and advertising, but also particular types of linguistic play that are common in the Philippines.

2. "Generic drugs" can actually be one of two things. The first is related to the actual active ingredient in the drug, and whether that is patented or not (generic). The second relates to the brand name of the drug, or whether a nonproprietary name is used.

3. One might use "fake brands," but I think "nonbrands" and "prop-brands" avoid the reification of a real/unreal, fake/authentic opposition, something I am trying to push back against here.

4. The "fake" itself has garnered increasing anthropological attention; see, for example, Crăciun (2008) and Copeman and da Col (2017), in which the fake itself exists as a proxy for a constellation of concerns regarding sincerity, falsity, self-deception, and ultimately how acts of recognition are tethered to assertions and negations of authenticity.

5. Anthropology's engagement with branding came surprisingly late—for example, in the hugely influential edited collection *The Social Life of Things* (Appadurai 1988)—and only now has the previous absence of the topic become notable.

6. For example, the Ikea brand and the Ikea wooden chair are generally much more closely aligned in their meaning than the unbranded chair and its carpenter. For critics of branding, this is of course much more than a semiotic coalescing, and instead constitutes erasure of the labor involved in production. Where the unbranded chair might index and exist as an icon of the labor and the carpenter involved in its production (one could imagine its production), the branded aspect of an Ikea chair conceals its production to the extent that it suggests it had no history before its presence in a store. Added to this is the nature of Ikea branding, which has pushed past the necessity of an insignia, and instead is formed through its design aesthetic.

7. Although, as I discuss later in terms of materiality and its replication in generic products, such expertise is deemed by the prop makers to be limited.

8. Interestingly, as I describe in chapter 3, "milk" as generic category is itself increasingly contested, with multiple legal cases in the United States and the European Union seeking to limit use of "milk" to identify only dairy milk, and not alternative milks, such as soy, almond, oat, and so on.

9. I say "ostensibly" here because alcohol brands are heavily and knowingly dependent on these generic representations of alcoholic consumption to bolster, if not their brand, then the consumption of alcohol in general, and, moreover, to frame the contexts in which one drinks. Consider, for example, the television show *Cheers* (1982–93). While undoubtedly influential in how Americans perceive the sociality of alcohol consumption, the show relied wholly on generic forms and nonbranded alcohol.

10. However, it appears that ISS has no interest in protecting its trademarks, and the company has, as far as I know, never attempted to prohibit anyone from using its brands. Although ISS has a legal department, no copyright or trademark lawyers are employed by the company.

11. Daniel Miller has also, with Sophie Woodward, deftly explored the ideologies and practices of a close cousin of the generic—the "ordinary" (2012).

12. Although see such cases as Shepard Fairey's Obama "Hope" poster, discussed in chapter 3, for a contrary position regarding the instability of the icon.

Chapter 3

1. See Whitaker (2019) for an overview of the legal aspects of the case and of "fair use." See Holland (2011) for an interesting legal semiotics of the case.

2. The literature on authorship is vast, but for the intersection of authorship and the legalities of copyright and open source, see Christopher Kelty (2008, 2004), Rosemary Coombe (1998), Gabriella Coleman (2009), Coleman and Golub (2008); and for a thoroughly ethnographic engagement, see Boateng (2011).

3. For an engagement with replication in a Filipino Christian context, see also de la Cruz (2009) and Cannell (1995).

4. In the literature on world's fairs, Stocking (1987), Benedict (1983), Rydell (1984), and Greenhalgh (1998) were foundational and overarching texts. See also Timothy Mitchell (1992) and Raymond Fogelson (1991) as important early interventions.

5. For a literature on Irish exhibitions and displays at world's fairs, see Crooke (2000), Hutchinson (2001), Meloy (2018), Mulligan (2014), O'Connor (2014), Saris (2000), Turpin (1981).

6. In describing these world's fairs, and exploring how a type of identity emerged from replication and mimesis—how, within the play between form and content, token and type, a new kind of quasi-authored, quasi-owned kind of self circulated—it is worth noting the connection to literature on how communities (and the forms of heritage, authenticity, inalienability, and value aligned with them) circulate like other types of things. Notable here, for example, is Jessica Cattelino's work on the fungibility of sovereignty and money among Seminole communities in the United States (2008), Comaroff and Comaroff's description of how authenticity and heritage become commodified (2009), and my own work on how Christian communities in the Philippines circulate as corporations (2019).

7. See Povinelli (2002) for how forms of social commensurability and alterity are inevitably ideologically loaded, embedded in state projects, and how commensurability is often a violent flattening of difference. Povinelli's work on incommensurability opens up a space in which to think about boundedness and limitations of the generic.

8. The name Ballymaclinton was named after the soap company, McClinton Soap Company. Interestingly, some authors, such as Phillip O'Connor (2014) have argued that the concoction of Ballymaclinton was an anti-nationalist move, sanitizing Irish heritage for an English market. But again, this only highlights the space between intentionality and the multivalent nature of signs.

Part II Introduction

1. See Hanegraaff 2018 [1998] for a discussion of how "new age" religious esoteric forms emerged in just such generic ways, through a process of amalgamation, mirroring, and formatting.

2. Mindoro, which was allotted to the Jesuits under Spanish rule, was in the early years of the twentieth century allotted anew to a collection of Baptist groups. The Baptists, however, finding Mindoro inhospitable, never really tried to establish much of a presence on the island.

3. Santa Teresita is where I conducted most of my research over the years and where I lived. I anonymize the town here, and aside from public figures, the names of people as well. I do so not because of any sensitivity or promise of confidentiality (nobody I have ever talked to asked me to protect their identity), but simply as a means of affording some privacy to those who opened their lives to me.

Chapter 4

1. Also referred to as "Araw ng mga Katutubo," and "Araw na Katutubo."

2. "Mangyan" is the appellation for seven or eight distinct ethnolinguistic Indigenous communities that traditionally live in the upland regions of Mindoro. "Mangyan," often preceded by the definite article ("the Mangyan"), is ubiquitous in Mindoro, and used by Mangyan people themselves, although more often when self-consciously aligning with and against lowland Filipinos. That is, "Mangyan" is the accepted and unproblematic term for the collective of the individual ethnolinguistic groups. However, Mangyan people are identified collectively by others far more often than by themselves, and thus the problematic edge to the term. Mangyan "communities" or "groups" are generally preferable to "the Mangyan." I move between both here, highlighting actual groups of people and the circulating idea and category of "Mangyan." The politics are to some extent similar to the case of "Native American," with all the complexities of that term. However, Indigeneity in the Philippines, and especially among Mangyan groups, mostly stands outside of a more intense politics of identity found elsewhere, at least so far.

3. Although Bennett Bean would push for the role of racialization in science and anthropology longer than most (Bean 1932). See Stocking (1968) for a detailed and nuanced discussion of racial approaches to ethnology early in the discipline; and recently King (2019).

4. See Michel Trouillot's (2003) noted discussion of the "savage slot" for how such ideological categories and compartments are created for the "other" and can remain static while appellations and descriptors can change.

5. It is worth noting that in the United States, the term "religion" itself has a long history of marking and unmarking certain groups, often as a generic (Protestant) Christianity (Asad 1993).

6. Interestingly, Rosaldo views the bureau, and Dean Worcester, its chief architect, as laying the groundwork for a later fetish of primitive and untouched Indigenous groups, which resulted in the famous Tasaday controversy in the 1970s that revolved around the discovery of a "new Stone Age" tribe, subsequently found to be fraudulent (Hemley 2006).

7. See Tomoko Masuzawa (2005) for a description of how generic religious rubrics and types emerged within a history of ordering the religious, and for a critical discussion of how projects of classifying and ordering people according to "religious beliefs" emerged in the first place.

8. See Deirdre de la Cruz (2015) for how Catholics engage with and mediate contemporary ideologies of universalism in Christianity; see Janet McIntosh (2009) for similar plays between universalized and differentiated Islamic forms and religious identities. See Saba Mahmood (2015) for a broader reading of how religious difference and pluralism has been encapsulated by secularist backdrops, and Niloofar Haeri (2021) for an important engagement in how Islam is debated and explicitly constituted as a circulating religious form.

9. Again, recalling a deep history of how religious selves have been commonly constituted through the religious other.

10. In Santa Teresita, the Witnesses members learned ASL, but by the end of my fieldwork, the Witnesses had actually translated their teachings into Filipino Sign Language (FSL), a burgeoning variant that language advocates in Manila are attempting to use to replace ASL and SEE throughout the country. However, FSL, in 2019, was yet to reach Occidental Mindoro through any pedagogical means.

11. The Jehovah's Witnesses Bible, the *New World Translation* (NWT) is perhaps most famous for its translation of John 1:1, which reads: "In the beginning was the Word, and the Word was with God and the Word was a god." The difference between this translation and most others is the use of the phrase "the word was a god," rather than "the word was God." This insertion of the indefinite article is taken to be a dividing theological line. Without it, Jesus is one and the same as God; with it, he is separate. The verse relating to the Tower of Babel in the NWT reads: "Then Jehovah went down to see the city and the tower that the sons of men had built. Jehovah then said: 'Look! They are one people with one language, and this is what they have started to do. Now there is nothing that they may have in mind to do that will be impossible for them. Come! Let us go down there and confuse their language in order that they may not understand one another's language.' So Jehovah scattered them from there over the entire face of the earth, and they gradually left off building the city. That is why it was named Babel, because there Jehovah confused the language of all the earth, and Jehovah scattered them from there over the entire face of the earth."

12. For a literature on the emergence of particular language ideologies and perceived boundaries between speakers and nonspeakers of sign language, see Hoffman-Dilloway (2011), Reno (2012), and Friedner (2015). For iconicity in language, see Mannheim and Newfield (1982), Nuckolls (1996), and Perniss et al. (2010).

13. Of course, while the generic in this case is viewed as unmediated, as we have seen in other chapters, and indeed in the work of a range of scholars from Jürgen Habermas to Michael Warner and William Mazzarella, the ease of intelligibility of social forms across contexts is at the core of mass-mediated publics. See Eisenlohr (2009) for an important discussion of media (and immediacy) in the manifestations of religious publics.

Chapter 5

1. See Eric Auerbach's famous genealogy and conceptualization of figura (1984). His work highlights the structural forms of replication in Christianity, from templates and models inherent in Christian texts, to how people stand in for biblical persons, for example, the long history of kings enacted as David figures. More broadly, figura allows us to think through the nature of substitutability, tropes, and analogy in Christianity. See also Bedos-Rezak (2010) and Leone and Parmentier (2014) on the semiotics of substitution in Christian history. In a Philippine context, Deirdre de la Cruz describes the emergence and circulation of the figure and of Mary, replicated through apparitions (de la Cruz 2015). Fenella Cannell (1995) and Julius Bautista (2010) have described how acts of bodily devotion are often explicitly imitational of Jesus. Thus, the forms of replication and figures in "standing for" and "standing in for" are critical to constituting a religious self.

2. Of course, most modern Christians do not live within the geographical confines of so-called biblical societies. However, while the olive might similarly exist outside of, for example, a Scandinavian milieu of connotational value, the historical relationship Scandinavians have with multiple translations of the Bible has undoubtedly given the term (and object) a locatable symbolic value.

3. As Carson (2009: 69) notes, while translation theories in English have diverged in the last two decades from dynamic or functional equivalence toward, for example, an incorporation of "relevance theory" and cognitive linguistics (e.g., the work of Dan Sperber and Deirdre Wilson [Sperber and Wilson1997; Wilson and Sperber 2004]), as well as Skopos theory (Cheung 2013; Reiss and Vermeer 2014), for Bible translators working among language groups that have no history of Bible translation, this theory of dynamic equivalence has remained the guiding and foundational approach to translation.

4. There has never previously existed a full Bible in any of these languages, although by 2009 the New Testament in each language had been completed. In 2022, the Bible in Occidental Tawbuid had been completed and was in press. These translators are also working on a new Tagalog translation of the Bible. In addition to the various Bible translation drafts discussed in the text, I cite from the following editions: New English Translation (NET), Contemporary English Version (CEV), King James Bible (KJV), Today's English Version (TEV), Ang Magandang Balita (AMB), and Ang Salita ng Dios (ASND).

5. While this separation of the American (and European) translators and the Mangyan native speakers in living arrangements suggests a spatial assertion of common missionary/native tropes of preferentiality and disparity of treatment, I am wary of making such a claim in this setting. There are numerous and varying reasons why the Mangyan remain separate from the translators throughout the workshop, including the desire to cook their own food, as well as privacy. Nevertheless, the separation is notable.

6. Compare a formal/literal version, the New English Translation (NET), what Annie called "extreme form based, and clunky though reliable." While I also include the NET translation in the text, I list here the other Bible translations that the translators were using:

> NET: "The king's heart is in the hand of the Lord like channels of water; he turns it wherever he wants."

CEV: "The Lord controls rulers, just as he determines the course of rivers."

TEV: "The Lord controls the mind of a king as easily as he directs the course of a stream."

KJV: "The king's heart is in the hand of the Lord, as the rivers of water: he turneth it whithersoever he will."

ASND: "Kayang hawakan ng panginoon ang isipan ng hari na gaya ng isang ilog pinaaagos niya ito saan man niya naisin" (It is in the hand of the lord that the king's thoughts lay, like how he directs the river to his wishes [Note the similarity, even on a lexico-semantic level, between Tagalog and Hanunoo.]).

AMB: "Hawak ni Yahweh ang isip ng isang hari at naibabaling niya ito kung saan igawi" (Yahweh holds a king's thoughts and can turn him as he directs).

7. I appreciate the difficulty and indeed irony here in providing an English gloss for the Hanunoo in a discussion of the problems in the semiotic mediation of language through translation.

8. NET: "All of a person's ways seem right in his own opinion, but the Lord evaluates the motives."

CEV: "We may think we are doing the right thing, but the Lord always knows what is in our hearts."

TEV: "You may think that everything you do is right, but remember that the Lord judges your motives."

CET: "We may think we are doing the right thing, but the Lord always knows what is in our hearts."

KJV: "Every way of a man is right in his own eyes: but the Lord pondereth the hearts."

ASND: "Inaakala ng tao na tama ang lahat ng kanyang ginagawa ngunit puso nila'y sinasaliksik ng panginoon" (A person can imagine that all they do is right but their hearts are searched/seen by the lord).

AMB: "Ang akala ng tao lahat ng kilos niya'y wasto, ngunit si Yahweh lang ang nakakasaliksik ng puso" (A person might think all of their actions are correct, but only Yahweh can search/see the heart).

9. NET: "The appetite of the wicked desires evil; his neighbor is shown no favor in his eyes."

CEV: "Evil people want to do wrong, even to their friends."

KJV: "The soul of the wicked desireth evil: his neighbour findeth no favour in his eyes."

ASND: "Gawain ng taong masama ay lagging masama at sa kanyang kapwa'y wala siyang awa" (The acts of the wicked will always be wicked and they have no mercy for their neighbors).

AMB: "Ang isip ng masama'y lagi sa kalikuan, kahit na kanino'y walang pakundangan" (The thoughts of the wicked are always unrighteous, they have no reverence for others).

10. NET: "The one who wanders from the way of wisdom will end up in the company of the departed."

CEV: "If you stop using good sense, you will find yourself in the grave."

TEV: "Death is waiting for anyone who wanders away from good sense."

KJV: "The man that wandereth out of the way of understanding shall remain in the congregation of the dead."

ASND: "Ang taong lumilihis sa daan ng katarungan ay hahantong sa kamatayan" (The person who leaves the path of justice will be led to death). AMB: "Nawawala't nalalagas, kapag ito'y nahanginan, nawawala na nga ito at hindi na mamamasdan" (The one who strays will be exposed, and now lost and not saved).

11. I use the term "transduction" here to emphasize the expansive semiotic modalities in which translation practices occur outside of strict denotational correspondence between languages. Silverstein takes "transduction" to be a "process of reorganizing the source semiotic organization (here . . . denotationally meaningful words and expressions of a source language occurring in co(n)text by target expressions-in-co(n)text) of another language presented through perhaps semiotically diverse modalities differently organized" (2003b, 83).

12. For example, see Nicholas Harkness's exploration of a Billy Graham speech in South Korea in the 1970s, for just how expansive such "transduction" in Christian speech and text can be, pulling together a massive swath of linguistic, religious, and political imaginaries (Harkness 2017b). In a similar vein but different context, Graham Jones has described an expansiveness in how very different, even contrary, spaces (in his case, magic and Christianity) are invoked and brought into interrelatedness (or "bundled" as per Keane 2003) to productive ends (Jones 2012).

Chapter 6

1. As with Santa Teresita, I am anonymizing the situ, or neighborhood, that I call Kulaman, not for any particular sensitivity of information or because anyone I have known has ever asked me to, but simply for a general affordance of privacy.

2. The literature on Christianity and social rupture in the Philippines has mostly focused, unsurprisingly, on Catholicism, and has tended to emphasize underlying practices of continuity outside of religion. Often nationalist in sentiment, this literature not only points to syncretic aspects of religious and social change, but has often presented Filipino Catholicism as a rupturing entity in sociopolitical terms, and as syncretic "folk Catholicism" in religious terms (the work of Landa Jocano stands out here as having been particularly influential; see Jocano 1981). For an important text on the transnational circulations of Catholicism, see Napolitano (2015).

3. Although as some have argued, in cases of conversionary rupture, the relationship between Christianity and culture is often seen to be severed, with the former assuming a universality and thus at once fundamentally causal of sociality, while at the same time once removed from it. For example see Webb Keane's discussion of E. B. Tylor (2007), and Robbins (2004), and Bialecki (2017).

4. In many respects, discursive omission may be aligned with the concept of erasure (Irvine and Gal 2000) and intertextual gaps (Briggs and Bauman 1992). Indeed, discursive omission can be seen to be a type of erasure, with the focus of the erasure on the object and concern that is being erased. Of course, as I hope to show here, the omission is never permanent, and not truly erased, as all parties are often consciously aware of what is being omitted. See also Judith Irvine's discussion of the "unmentionable" and topic avoidance (Irvine 2011). For an ethnographic engagement with silence within a Christian setting, Richard Bauman's *Let Your Words Be Few* (1983) continues to be unrivaled.

5. See Naveeda Khan (2012) for a critical comparison to Christian spaces of reli-

gious contestation and universalizing, in her description of how skepticism and aspiration in Islam in Pakistan contribute to conceptualizing future oriented religious spaces as "open."

6. While Sazon was at this time affiliated with JIL, he had been a pastor in numerous other born-again churches, and never appeared to be deeply involved in the JIL organization. He received no money from the church, and while JIL is known in the Philippines for having charismatic leanings, Sazon's JIL did not. In many ways, his church was generically born-again Evangelical.

7. It is the most uncommon of occurrences to find a Filipino outside of the main cities who would claim any form of atheism or agnosticism. In my two years of fieldwork, I came across only one person who said they did not believe in God, and even then they attended church regularly out of obligation to their family. However, amid generally educated circles in Manila, for example, one is likely to find a spectrum of religious beliefs that would mirror their Euro-American counterparts.

8. Criticisms of born-again churches most often emanate from a pro-Catholic stance, but not always. In general, for those with anti–born again sentiments, criticisms mostly concerned the self-interest of the pastors—that theirs was a money-making endeavor, taking advantage of the needy and poor. Of course, most people were quite willing to lay the same accusations, if not at the Catholic Church, then at least at many of its clergy.

9. The first two chapters of Daniel are concerned with how the three Jews mentioned here, along with Daniel himself, were taken to the court of Nebuchadnezzar, trained in the ways of the court, and taught to read and write the Babylonian language. The names of the three Jews were changed on arrival to the court from Hananiah, Mishael, and Azariah, to Shadrach, Meschach, and Abednego. Daniel's name was changed to Belteshazzar, although he does not figure as a character in the third chapter.

10. Sazon's services were conducted in Tagalog. Miguel Elausa was immensely helpful with translation and transcription, but the author is responsible for any errors.

11. As Judith Irvine notes in terms of "leakage": "Bear in mind, however, that although registers leak, not all leakage is necessarily undesirable. The speaker who quotes the Bible may, in some circles, be socially elevated by the use of sacred words, even though it is clear to all that he or she is not their author" (Irvine 2011: 26).

12. In early 2012, Santa Teresita was flooded with free Bibles, collectively provided by the born-again churches in Santa Teresita and the Philippine Bible Society in Manila.

13. Also, see Goffman (1983) for an early exposition on the problems of indirectness, and Ochs (Keenan) (1977) for a discussion of conversational implicatures.

14. Like "indirectness," "politeness" is a problematic term, encompassing all manner of social interactions, discursive and otherwise, and risks a cross-context mismatch of intentionality.

Bibliography

Agha, Asif. 2005. "Voice, Footing, Enregisterment." *Journal of Linguistic Anthropology* 15 (1): 38–59.

Al-Kadi, T. 2013. "Product Placement: A Booming Industry in Search of Appropriate Regulation," *Journal of Marketing Research and Case Studies*, 1–13.

Allert, Craig. 1999. "Is a Translation Inspired? The Problems of Verbal Inspiration for Translation and a Proposed Solution." In *Translating the Bible: Problems and Prospects*, ed. Stanley Porter and Richard Hess, 85–113. Sheffield, UK: Sheffield University Press.

Allison, Anne. 2004. "Cuteness as Japan's Millennial Product." In *Pikachu's Global Adventure: The Rise and Fall of Pokémon*, ed. Joseph Tobin, 35–49. Durham, NC: Duke University Press.

Anderson, Warwick. 2006. *Colonial Pathologies: American Tropical Medicine, Race, and Hygiene in the Philippines*. Durham, NC: Duke University Press.

Anderson, Warwick, and Hans Pols. 2012. "Scientific Patriotism: Medical Science and National Self-Fashioning in Southeast Asia." *Comparative Studies in Society and History* 54 (01): 93–113.

Appadurai, Arjun, ed. 1988. *The Social Life of Things: Commodities in Cultural Perspective*. Cambridge: Cambridge University Press.

Asad, Talal. 1986. "The Concept of Cultural Translation in British Social Anthropology." In *Writing Culture: The Poetics and Politics of Ethnography*, ed. J. Clifford and G. E. Marcus, 141–64. Berkeley: University of California Press.

———. 1993. *Genealogies of Religion: Discipline and Reasons of Power in Christianity and Islam*. Baltimore: Johns Hopkins University Press.

———. 2003. *Formations of the Secular: Christianity, Islam, Modernity*. Stanford: Stanford University Press.

Atran, Scott. 1998. "Folk Biology and the Anthropology of Science: Cognitive Universals and Cultural Particulars." *Behavioral and Brain Sciences* 21 (4): 547–69.

———. 2010. *Talking to the Enemy: Violent Extremism, Sacred Values, and What It Means to Be Human*. London: Penguin UK.

Auerbach, Erich. 1984. "Figura." In *Scenes from the Drama of European Literature*, 11–78. Minneapolis: University of Minnesota Press.

———. 2003 [1953]. *Mimesis: The Representation of Reality in Western Literature: New and Expanded Edition*. Princeton: Princeton University Press.

Augé, Marc. 1995. *Non-Places: Introduction to an Anthropology of Supermodernity*. London: Verso.

Baguio Midland Courier. 1959. "Baguio Golden Anniversary Supplement."

Bakhtin, Mikhail Mikhailovich. 1981. *The Dialogic Imagination: Four Essays*. Ed. and trans. Michael Holquist. Austin: University of Texas Press.

———. 1986. *Speech Genres and Other Late Essays*. Trans. Vern W. McGee. Austin: University of Texas Press.

Baldwin, James Mark. 1902. *Dictionary of Philosophy and Psychology, Vol. 2*. London: Macmillan.

Banfield, Ann. 1973. "Narrative Style and the Grammar of Direct and Indirect Speech." *Foundations of Language* 10 (1): 1–39.

Barnes, Stephen H. 1988. *Muzak, the Hidden Messages in Music: A Social Psychology of Culture*. Lewiston, NY: Edwin Mellen Press.

Barney, Darin David, Jonathan Sterne, E. Gabriella Coleman, Christine Ross, and Tamar Tembeck. 2016. *The Participatory Condition in the Digital Age*. Minneapolis: University of Minnesota Press.

Barrett, Kay Ulanday, Karen Buenavista Hanna, and Anang Palomar. 2021. "In Defense of the X: Centering Queer, Trans, and Non-Binary Pilipina/x/Os, Queer Vernacular, and the Politics of Naming." *Alon: Journal for Filipinx American and Diasporic Studies* 1 (2).

Barrows, David Prescott. 1901. *The Bureau of Non-Christian Tribes for the Philippine Islands: Circular of Information, Instructions for Volunteer Field Workers, the Museum of Ethnology, Natural History and Commerce*. Published by the Bureau of Non-Christian Tribes for the Philippine Islands.

Bartlett, Harley Harris. 1940. "The Concept of the Genus: I. History of the Generic Concept in Botany." *Bulletin of the Torrey Botanical Club* 67 (5): 349–62.

Bateson, Gregory. 1958 [1936]. *Naven: A Survey of the Problems Suggested by a Composite Picture of the Culture of a New Guinea Tribe Drawn from Three Points of View*. Stanford: Stanford University Press.

Baudrillard, Jean. 1994 [1981]. *Simulacra and Simulation*. Ann Arbor: University of Michigan Press.

———. 2016 [1976]. *Symbolic Exchange and Death*. London: Sage.

Bauman, Richard. 1983. *Let Your Words Be Few: Symbolism of Speaking and Silence among Seventeenth-Century Quakers*. Cambridge: Cambridge University Press.

Bautista, Julius. 2010. *Figuring Catholicism: An Ethnohistory of the Santo Niño de Cebu*. Manila: Ateneo de Manila University Press.

Bax, Anna. 2018. "'The C-Word' Meets 'the N-Word': The Slur-Once-Removed and the Discursive Construction of 'Reverse Racism.'" *Journal of Linguistic Anthropology* 28 (2): 114–36.

Baynton, Douglas C. 1996. *Forbidden Signs: American Culture and the Campaign against Sign Language*. Chicago: University of Chicago Press.

Bean, Robert Bennett. 1932. *The Races of Man: Differentiation and Dispersal of Man*. New York: University Society, Inc.

Bedos-Rezak, Brigitte. 2010. *When Ego Was Imago: Signs of Identity in the Middle Ages*. Leiden: Brill.

Benedict, Burton. 1983. *The Anthropology of World's Fairs: San Francisco's Panama Pacific International Exposition of 1915*. Berkeley, CA: Lowie Museum of Anthropology.

Benedict, Ruth. 2005 [1934]. *Patterns of Culture*. Boston: Houghton Mifflin Harcourt.

———. 2006 [1942]. *The Chrysanthemum and the Sword*. Boston: Houghton Mifflin Harcourt.

Benjamin, Walter. 1968. *Illuminations: Essays and Reflections*. Boston: Houghton Mifflin Harcourt.

———. 1999. *The Arcades Project*. Cambridge, MA: Harvard University Press.

Berlant, Lauren. 1993. "National brands/national body: Imitation of life." In *The Phantom Public Sphere*, ed. Bruce Robbins, 173–208. Minneapolis: University of Minnesota Press.

Berlin, Brent. 1976. "The Concept of Rank in Ethnobiological Classification: Some Evidence from Aguaruna Folk Botany." *American Ethnologist* 3 (3): 381–99.

———. 1992. *Ethnobiological Classification: Principles of Categorization of Plants and Animals in Traditional Societies*. Princeton: Princeton University Press.

Berlin, Brent, Dennis E. Breedlove, and Peter H. Raven. 1973. "General Principles of Classification and Nomenclature in Folk Biology." *American Anthropologist* 75 (1): 214–42.

Berlin, Brent, and Paul Kay. 1969. *Basic Color Terms: Their Universality and Evolution*. Berkeley: University of California Press.

Beyer, Otley. 1918. *Ethnography of the Mindoro-Palawan Peoples: A Collection of Original Sources 1* (Parts 1 and 2). Manila.

Bialecki, Jon. 2017. *A Diagram for Fire: Miracles and Variation in an American Charismatic Movement*. Berkeley: University of California Press.

Bialecki, Jon, and Eric Hoenes del Pinal. 2011. "Introduction: Beyond Logos: Extensions of the Language Ideology Paradigm in the Study of Global Christianity." *Anthropological Quarterly* 84, no. 3: 575–93.

Bloch, Stefano. 2005. "Properties and Prop-House Geography: One Aspect of the Film Industrial Complex in Los Angeles." MA thesis, UCLA.

Boateng, Boatema. 2011. *The Copyright Thing Doesn't Work Here: Adinkra and Kente Cloth and Intellectual Property in Ghana*. Minneapolis: University of Minnesota Press.

Bourdieu, Pierre. 1984 [1979]. *Distinction: A Social Critique of the Judgment of Taste*. Cambridge, MA: Harvard University Press.

Bowker, Geoffrey C., and Susan Leigh Star. 2000. *Sorting Things Out: Classification and Its Consequences*. Cambridge, MA: MIT Press.

Boyer, Dominic C. 2000. "On the Sedimentation and Accreditation of Social Knowledges of Difference: Mass Media, Journalism, and the Reproduction of East/West Alterities in Unified Germany." *Cultural Anthropology* 15 (4): 459–91.

———. 2013. *The Life Informatic: Newsmaking in the Digital Era*. Ithaca, NY: Cornell University Press.

Briggs, Charles L., and Richard Bauman. 1992. "Genre, Intertextuality, and Social Power." *Journal of Linguistic Anthropology* 2 (2): 131–72.

Brodwin, Paul. 2003. "Pentecostalism in Translation: Religion and the Production of Community in the Haitian Diaspora." *American Ethnologist* 30 (1): 85–101.

Brody, David. 2010. *Visualizing American Empire: Orientalism and Imperialism in the Philippines*. Chicago: University of Chicago Press.

Bucholtz, Mary. 2019. "The Public Life of White Affects." *Journal of Sociolinguistics* 23 (5): 485–504.

Burnham, Daniel H., and Pierce Anderson. 1905. "Improvement of Manila," Department, United States War. *Annual Reports of the Secretary of War*, vol. 10, exhibit B.

Burrow-Giles Lithographic Co. v. Sarony. 1884. 111 US 53. Supreme Court.

Callon, Michel. 1986. "Some Elements of a Sociology of Translation: Domestication of the Scallops and the Fishermen of St. Brieuc Bay." In *Power, Action and Belief: A New Sociology of Knowledge?* ed. J. Law, 196–223. London: Routledge.

Cannell, Fenella. 1995. "The Imitation of Christ in Bicol, Philippines." *Journal of the Royal Anthropological Institute* 1 (2): 377.

———. 2005. "The Christianity of Anthropology." *Journal of the Royal Anthropological Institute* 11, no. 2: 335–56.

Carlson, Gregor, and Francis Jeffry Pelletier. 1995. *The Generic Book*. Chicago: University of Chicago Press.

Carr, E. Summerson, and Michael Lempert. 2016. *Scale: Discourse and Dimensions of Social Life*. Berkeley: University of California Press.

Carson, D. A. 2009. "The Limits of Functional Equivalence in Bible Translation—and Other Limits Too." In *The Challenge of Bible Translation: Communicating God's Word to the World*, ed. Glen G. Scorgie, Mark L. Strauss, and Steven M. Voth Zondervan, 65–114. Grand Rapids, MI: Zondervan.

Cartwright, Lisa, and Stephen Mandiberg. 2009. "Obama and Shepard Fairey: The Copy and Political Iconography in the Age of the Demake." *Journal of Visual Culture* 8 (2): 172–76.

Case & Co. 1964. *Effects of Muzak on Industrial Efficiency*. Muzak.

Cattelino, Jessica. 2008. *High Stakes: Florida Seminole Gaming and Sovereignty*. Durham, NC: Duke University Press.

Cheung, Andy. 2013. "A History of Twentieth Century Translation Theory and Its Application to Bible Translation." *Journal of Translation* 9 (1): 1.

Clarke, Kamari. 2010. "Rethinking Africa through Its Exclusions: The Politics of Naming Criminal Responsibility." *Anthropological Quarterly* 83 (3): 625–51.

Claudio, Lisandro E. 2015. "Beyond Colonial Miseducation Internationalism and Deweyan Pedagogy in the American-Era Philippines." *Philippine Studies: Historical and Ethnographic Viewpoints* 63 (2): 193–221.

Clifford, James. 1982. *Person and Myth: Maurice Leenhardt in the Melanesian World*. Berkeley: University of California Press.

Clymer, Kenton J. 1986. *Protestant Missionaries in the Philippines, 1898–1916: An Inquiry into the American Colonial Mentality*. Urbana: University of Illinois Press.

Cody, Francis. 2013. *The Light of Knowledge: Literacy Activism and the Politics of Writing in South India*. Ithaca, NY: Cornell University Press.

———. 2015. "Populist Publics: Print Capitalism and Crowd Violence beyond Liberal Frameworks." *Comparative Studies of South Asia, Africa and the Middle East* 35 (1): 50–65.

Coleman, Gabriella. 2009. "CODE IS SPEECH: Legal Tinkering, Expertise, and Protest among Free and Open Source Software Developers." *Cultural Anthropology* 24 (3): 420–54.

———. 2013. *Coding Freedom: The Ethics and Aesthetics of Hacking*. Princeton: Princeton University Press.

Coleman, Gabriella, and Alex Golub. 2008. "Hacker Practice: Moral Genres and the Cultural Articulation of Liberalism." *Anthropological Theory* 8 (3): 255–77.

Coleman, Simon. 2000. *The Globalization of Charismatic Christianity*. Cambridge: Cambridge University Press.

———. 2003. "Continuous Conversion: The Rhetoric, Practice, and Rhetorical Practice of Charismatic Protestant Conversion." In *The Anthropology of Religious Conversion*, ed. Andrew Buckser and Stephen D. Glazier, 15–28. Lanham, MD: Rowman & Littlefield.

Coleman, Simon, and Peter Jeffrey Collins, eds. 2004. *Religion, Identity and Change: Perspectives on Global Transformations*. Farnham, Surrey, UK: Ashgate Publishing.

Collins, John J. 1984. *Daniel, with an introduction to Apocalyptic Literature*. Grand Rapids, MI: Wm. B. Eerdmans Publishing.

Comaroff, Jean, and John Comaroff. 1991a. *Of Revelation and Revolution, Vol. 1: Christianity, Colonialism, and Consciousness in South Africa*. Chicago: University of Chicago Press.

———. 1991b. *Of Revelation and Revolution, Vol. 2: The Dialectics of Modernity on a South African Frontier*. Chicago: University of Chicago Press.

———. 2009. *Ethnicity, Inc.* Chicago: University of Chicago Press.

Conklin, Harold C. 1949. "Preliminary Report on Field Work on the Islands of Mindoro and Palawan, Philippines." *American Anthropologist* 51 (2): 268–73.

———. 1955a. "The Relation of Hanunóo Culture to the Plant World." PhD diss., Yale University.

———. 1955b. "Hanunoo Color Categories." *Southwestern Journal of Anthropology* 11 (4): 339–44.

———. 1957. *Hanunoo Agriculture. A Report on an Integral System of Shifting Cultivation in the Philippines. Vol. 2.*

———. 1959. "Linguistic Play in Its Cultural Context." *Language* 35 (4): 631–36.

———. 1969. "An Ethnoecological Approach to Shifting Agriculture." In *Environment and Cultural Behavior: Ecological Studies in Cultural Anthropology*, ed. A. P. Vayda, 221–33. Garden City, NY: Natural History Press.

Constantino, Renato. 1970. "The Mis-Education of the Filipino." *Journal of Contemporary Asia* 1 (1): 20–36.

Conti, Rena M., and Ernst R. Berndt. 2020. "Four Facts concerning Competition in US Generic Prescription Drug Markets." *International Journal of the Economics of Business* 27 (1): 27–48.

Coombe, Rosemary J. 1996. "Embodied Trademarks: Mimesis and Alterity on American Commercial Frontiers." *Cultural Anthropology* 11 (2): 202–24.

———. 1998. *The Cultural Life of Intellectual Properties: Authorship, Appropriation, and the Law*. Durham, NC: Duke University Press.

Copeman, Jacob, and Giovanni da Col, eds. 2017. *Fake: Anthropological Keywords*. Chicago: Hau Books/University of Chicago Press.

Crăciun, Magdalena. 2008. "Researching Fakes: Practising Anthropology Out of the Corner of One's Eye." *Anthropology Matters* 10 (2).

———. 2012. "Rethinking Fakes, Authenticating Selves." *Journal of the Royal Anthropological Institute* 18 (4): 846–63.

Croft, William, and D. Alan Cruse. 2004. *Cognitive Linguistics*. Cambridge: Cambridge University Press.

Crooke, Elizabeth M. 2000. *Politics, Archaeology, and the Creation of a National Museum in Ireland: An Expression of National Life*. Newbridge, Co. Kildare, Ireland: Irish Academic Press.

Csordas, Thomas J. 1997. *Language, Charisma, and Creativity: Ritual Life in the Catholic Charismatic Renewal*. New York: Palgrave.

Cullen, Fintan. 2017. *Ireland on Show: Art, Union, and Nationhood*. London: Routledge.

Darnell, Regna. 1998. *And Along Came Boas: Continuity and Revolution in Americanist Anthropology*. Amsterdam: John Benjamins Publishing.

Darwin, Charles. 2009 [1859]. *The Origin of Species; And, the Descent of Man*. Cambridge: Cambridge University Press.

Das, Veena. 2007. *Life and Words: Violence and the Descent into the Ordinary*. Berkeley: University of California Press.

———. 2020. *Textures of the Ordinary: Doing Anthropology after Wittgenstein*. New York: Fordham University Press.

Daswani, Girish. 2013. "On Christianity and Ethics: Rupture as Ethical Practice in Ghanaian Pentecostalism." *American Ethnologist* 40 (3): 467–79.

Dávila, Arlene M. 2008. *Latino Spin: Public Image and the Whitewashing of Race*. New York: NYU Press.

Davis, Catherine. 1998. *The Spirits of Mindoro: The True Story of How the Gospel Came to a Strangely Prepared Demon-Fearing People*. Oxford: Monarch Books.

de la Cruz, Deirdre. 2009. "Coincidence and Consequence: Marianism and the Mass Media in the Global Philippines." *Cultural Anthropology* 24 (3): 455–88.

———. 2015. *Mother Figured: Marian Apparitions and the Making of a Filipino Universal*. Chicago: University of Chicago Press.

Deleuze, Gilles. 1988 [1966]. *Bergsonism*. New York: Zone Books.

———. 2004 [1968]. *Difference and Repetition*. London: A&C Black.

Derrida, Jacques. 1976 [1967]. *Of Grammatology*. Trans. Gayatri Chakravorty Spivak. Baltimore: Johns Hopkins University Press.

———. 1977 [1972]. "Signature Event Context." *Glyph* 1: 172–97.

Doeppers, Daniel F. 1976. "The Philippine Revolution and the Geography of Schism." *Geographical Review* 66 (2): 158–77.

Dumont, Louis. 1980. *Homo Hierarchicus: The Caste System and Its Implications*. Chicago: University of Chicago Press.

Durkheim, Émile. 2012 [1915]. *The Elementary Forms of the Religious Life*. London: Courier Corp.

Durkheim, Émile, and Marcel Mauss. 1963 [1903]. *Primitive Classification*. London: Cohn & West.

Eisenlohr, Patrick. 2009. "Technologies of the Spirit: Devotional Islam, Sound Reproduction and the Dialectics of Mediation and Immediacy in Mauritius." *Anthropological Theory* 9 (3): 273–96.

———. 2018. *Sounding Islam: Voice, Media, and Sonic Atmospheres in an Indian Ocean World*. Berkeley: University of California Press.

Engelke, Matthew. 2004. "Text and Performance in an African Church: The Book, 'Live and Direct.'" *American Ethnologist* 31 (1): 76–91.

———. 2007. *A Problem of Presence: Beyond Scripture in an African Church*. Berkeley: University of California Press.

———. 2013. *God's Agents: Biblical Publicity in Contemporary England*. Berkeley: University of California Press.

Eriksson, Maria, Rasmus Fleischer, Anna Johansson, Pelle Snickars, and Patrick

Vonderau. 2019. *Spotify Teardown: Inside the Black Box of Streaming Music*. Cambridge, MA: MIT Press.

European Court of Justice, Case C-422/16, *Verband Sozialer Wettbewerb ev v TofuTown GmbH* ECLI:EU:C:2017:458.

Evans-Pritchard, Edward. 1965. *Theories of Primitive Religion*. Oxford: Clarendon Press.

The Exhibition Expositor and Advertiser, nos. 1–25. 1853. Dublin.

Fehérváry, Krisztina. 2009. "Goods and States: The Political Logic of State-Socialist Material Culture." *Comparative Studies in Society and History* 51 (2): 426–59.

———. 2012. "From Socialist Modern to Super-Natural Organicism: Cosmological Transformations through Home Décor." *Cultural Anthropology* 27 (4): 615–40.

———. 2013. *Politics in Color and Concrete: Socialist Materialities and the Middle Class in Hungary*. Bloomington: Indiana University Press.

Fernandez, James. 1974. "The Mission of Metaphor in Expressive Culture [and Comments and Reply]." *Current Anthropology* 15 (2): 119–45.

———. 1991. *Beyond Metaphor: The Theory of Tropes in Anthropology*. Stanford: Stanford University Press.

Fernando, Mayanthi L. 2014. *The Republic Unsettled: Muslim French and the Contradictions of Secularism*. Durham, NC: Duke University Press.

Fisher, William W., III, Frank Cost, and Meir Feder. 2012. "Reflections on the Hope Poster Case." *Harvard Journal of Law and Technology* 25: 243.

Fixico, Donald Lee. 2012. *Bureau of Indian Affairs*. Santa Barbara, CA: ABC-CLIO.

Fogelson, Raymond. 1991. "The Red Man in the White City." In *Columbian Consequences, Vol. 3*, ed. D. H. Thomas, 73–90. Washington, DC: Smithsonian Institution.

Forth, Gregory. 2010. "Symbolic Classification: Retrospective Remarks on an Unrecognized Invention." *Journal of the Royal Anthropological Institute* 16 (4): 707–25.

———. 2016. *Why the Porcupine Is Not a Bird: Explorations in the Folk Zoology of an Eastern Indonesian People*. Toronto: University of Toronto Press.

Foucault, Michel. 1979. "Authorship: What Is an Author?" *Screen* 20 (1): 13–34.

Frake, Charles O. 1961. "The Diagnosis of Disease among the Subanun of Mindanao." *American Anthropologist* 63 (1): 113–32.

———. 1995 [1962]. "The Ethnographic Study of Cognitive Systems." In *Language, Culture, and Society: A Book of Readings*, 2nd ed., ed. Ben Blount, 125–42. Long Grove, IL: Waveland Press.

Friedner, Michele Ilana. 2015. *Valuing Deaf Worlds in Urban India*. New Brunswick, NJ: Rutgers University Press.

Gal, Susan. 2019. "Making Registers in Politics: Circulation and Ideologies of Linguistic Authority." *Journal of Sociolinguistics* 23 (5): 450–66.

Gal, Susan, and Judith T. Irvine. 2019. *Signs of Difference: Language and Ideology in Social Life*. Cambridge: Cambridge University Press.

Gal, Susan, and Kathryn Woolard. 2001. *Languages and Publics: The Making of Authority*. London: Routledge.

Geertz, Clifford. 1973. *The Interpretation of Cultures: Selected Essays*. New York: Basic Books.

Gelman, Susan A. 2009. "Learning from Others: Children's Construction of Concepts." *Annual Review of Psychology* 60 (1): 115–40.

Gershon, Ilana. 2017. *Down and Out in the New Economy: How People Find (or Don't Find) Work Today.* Chicago: University of Chicago Press.

Gershon, Ilana, and Michael M. Prentice. 2021. "Genres in New Economies of Language." *International Journal of the Sociology of Language* 267–68: 117–24.

Gibson, Thomas Paul. 1983. *Religion, Kinship and Society among the Buid of Mindoro, Philippines.* London: London School of Economics.

Goffman, Erving. 1974. *Frame Analysis: An Essay on the Organization of Experience.* New York: Harper & Row.

———. 1983. "Felicity's Condition." *American Journal of Sociology* 89 (1): 1–53.

Greene, Jeremy A. 2014. *Generic: The Unbranding of Modern Medicine.* Baltimore: Johns Hopkins University Press.

Greenhalgh, Paul. 1998. *Fair World: A History of World's Fairs and Expositions, from London to Shanghai, 1851–2010.* Winterbourne, UK: Papadakis.

Guide to the Irish Industrial Village and Blarney Castle, the Exhibit of the Irish Industries Association at the World's Columbian Exposition. 1893. Chicago: n.p.

Gumperz, John Joseph. 1971. *Language in Social Groups.* Vol. 3. Stanford: Stanford University Press.

Gursel, Zeynep Devrim. 2016. *Image Brokers: Visualizing World News in the Age of Digital Circulation.* Berkeley: University of California Press.

Gutierrez, Kathleen Cruz. 2018a. "Rehabilitating Botany in the Postwar Moment: National Promise and the Encyclopedism of Eduardo Quisumbing's Medicinal Plants of the Philippines (1951)." *Asian Review of World Histories* 6 (1): 33–67.

———. 2018b. "What's in a Latin Name?: Cycas Wadei & the Politics of Nomenclature." *Philippine Journal of Systematic Biology* 12 (2): 24–35.

Haeri, Niloofar. 2021. *Say What Your Longing Heart Desires: Women, Prayer, and Poetry in Iran.* Stanford: Stanford University Press.

Handman, Courtney. 2007. "Access to the Soul: Native Language and Authenticity in Papua New Guinea Bible Translation." In *Consequences of Contact: Language Ideologies and Sociocultural Transformations in Pacific Societies,* ed. Miki Makihara and Bambi B. Schieffelin, 166–88. Oxford: Oxford University Press.

———. 2010. "Events of Translation: Intertextuality and Christian Ethno-Theologies of Change among Guhu-Samane, Papua New Guinea." *American Anthropologist* 112 (4): 576–88.

———. 2014. *Critical Christianity: Translation and Denominational Conflict in Papua New Guinea.* Berkeley: University of California Press.

Hanegraaff, Wouter J. 2018 [1998]. *New Age Religion and Western Culture: Esotericism in the Mirror of Secular Thought.* Leiden: Brill.

Hanks, William F. 2010. *Converting Words: Maya in the Age of the Cross.* Berkeley: University of California Press.

Hansen, Thomas Blom. 2018. *Wages of Violence: Naming and Identity in Postcolonial Bombay.* Princeton: Princeton University Press.

Hardin, C. L., and Luisa Maffi. 1997. *Color Categories in Thought and Language.* Cambridge: Cambridge University Press.

Harding, Susan. 2000. *The Book of Jerry Falwell: Fundamentalist Language and Politics.* Princeton: Princeton University Press.

Harkness, Nicholas. 2010. "Words in Motion and the Semiotics of the Unseen in Two Korean Churches." *Language and Communication* 30 (2): 139–58.

———. 2014. *Songs of Seoul: An Ethnography of Voice and Voicing in Christian South Korea*. Berkeley: University of California Press.

———. 2017a. "Glossolalia and Cacophony in South Korea: Cultural Semiosis at the Limits of Language." *American Ethnologist* 44 (3): 476–89.

———. 2017b. "Transducing a Sermon, Inducing Conversion: Billy Graham, Billy Kim, and the 1973 Crusade in Seoul." *Representations* 137 (1): 112–42.

Haspelmath, Martin. 2006. "Against Markedness (and What to Replace It With)." *Journal of Linguistics* 42 (1): 25–70.

Hau, Caroline S., and Victoria L. Tinio. 2003. "Language Policy and Ethnic Relations in the Philippines." In *Fighting Words: Language Policy and Ethnic Relations in Asia*, ed. Michael Edward Brown and Sumit Ganguly. Cambridge, MA: MIT Press.

Haviland, John B. 1996. "Texts from Talk in Tzotzil." In *Natural Histories of Discourse*, ed. Michael Silverstein and Greg Urban, 45–79. Chicago: University of Chicago Press.

———. 1999. "Gesture." *Journal of Linguistic Anthropology* 9 (1–2): 88–91.

———. 2003. "Ideologies of Language: Some Reflections on Language and U.S. Law." *American Anthropologist* 105 (4): 764–74.

Hayden, Cori. 2007. "A Generic Solution?" *Current Anthropology* 48 (4): 475–95.

———. 2013. "Distinctively Similar: A Generic Problem." *University of California, Davis, Law Review* 47: 601.

Hefner, Robert, ed. 1993. *Conversion to Christianity: Historical and Anthropological Perspectives on a Great Transformation*. Berkeley: University of California Press.

Hemley, Robin. 2006. *Invented Eden: The Elusive, Disputed History of the Tasaday*. Lincoln: University of Nebraska Press.

Henare, Amiria, Martin Holbraad, and Sari Wastell. 2007. *Thinking through Things: Theorising Artefacts Ethnographically*. London: Routledge.

Hill, Jane H. 1998. "Language, Race, and White Public Space." *American Anthropologist* 100 (3): 680–89.

Hilliard, David C., Joseph Nye Welch II, and Uli Widmaier. 2012. *Trademarks and Unfair Competition*. New York: LexisNexis.

Hines, Thomas S. 1972. "The Imperial Façade: Daniel H. Burnham and American Architectural Planning in the Philippines." *Pacific Historical Review* 41 (1): 33–53.

Hoffmann-Dilloway, Erika. 2011. "Ordering Burgers, Reordering Relations: Gestural Interactions between Hearing and d/Deaf Nepalis." *Pragmatics* 21 (3): 373–91.

Holbraad, Martin. 2012. *Truth in Motion: The Recursive Anthropology of Cuban Divination*. Chicago: University of Chicago Press.

Holland, H. Brian. 2011. "Social Semiotics in the Fair Use Analysis." *Harvard Journal of Law and Technology* 24: 335.

Hunn, Eugene. 1976. "Toward a Perceptual Model of Folk Biological Classification." *American Ethnologist* 3 (3): 508–24.

Hutchinson, John. 2001. "Archaeology and the Irish Rediscovery of the Celtic Past." *Nations and Nationalism* 7 (4): 507–21.

Hutterer, Karl L. 1978. "Dean C. Worcester and Philippine Anthropology." *Philippine Quarterly of Culture and Society* 6 (3): 125–56.

Hymes, Dell. 1964. "Introduction: Toward Ethnographies of Communication." *American Anthropologist* 66 (6): 1–34.

———. 1974. *Foundations in Sociolinguistics: An Ethnographic Approach*. Philadelphia: University of Pennsylvania Press.

———. 1983. *Essays in the History of Linguistic Anthropology*. Amsterdam: John Benjamins Publishing.

The Illustrative and Descriptive Catalogue of the Dublin International Exhibition of 1865. 1865. London: n.p.

Inoue, Miyako. 2004. "What Does Language Remember? Indexical Inversion and the Naturalized History of Japanese Women." *Journal of Linguistic Anthropology* 14 (1): 39–56.

International Council on Biblical Inerrancy. 1978. "The Chicago Statement on Bible Inerrancy." *Journal of the Evangelical Theological Society* 21 (4): 289–96.

Ireland at the World's Fair. 1894. Pamphlet. N.p.

Ireland Department of Agriculture and Technical Instruction. 1904. *Irish Industrial Exhibition, World's Fair, St Louis 1904: Handbook and Catalogue of Exhibits*. N.p.

Irvine, Judith T. 1993. "Insult and Responsibility: Verbal Abuse in a Wolof Village." In *Responsibility and Evidence in Oral Discourse*, 105–34. Cambridge: Cambridge University Press.

———. 2011. "Leaky Registers and Eight-Hundred-Pound Gorillas." *Anthropological Quarterly* 84 (1): 15–39.

Irvine, Judith T., and Susan Gal. 2000. "Language Ideology and Linguistic Differentiation." In *Regimes of Language*, ed. Paul V. Kroskrity, 35–83. Santa Fe, NM: School of American Research.

Itten, Johannes. 1921. "Color Star in Seven Light Levels and Twelve Tones." Supplement to *Utopia: Documents of Reality*. Weimar: Utopia.

Jackson, John L., Jr. 2005. *Real Black: Adventures in Racial Sincerity*. Chicago: University of Chicago Press.

———. 2008. *Racial Paranoia: The Unintended Consequences of Political Correctness*. New York: Basic Books.

Jakobson, Roman. 1984 [1939]. *Russian and Slavic Grammar: Studies 1931–1981*. Berlin: Walter de Gruyter.

Jocano, F. Landa. 1981. *Folk Christianity*. Dublin: Trinity Research Institute.

Jolly, Margaret. 1996. "Devils, Holy Spirits, and the Swollen God: Translation, Conversion and Colonial Power in the Marist Mission, Vanuatu, 1887–1934." In *Conversion to Modernities: The Globalization of Christianity*, ed. Peter van der Veer, 231–62. London: Routledge.

Jones, Graham. 2011. *Trade of the Tricks: Inside the Magician's Craft*. Berkeley: University of California Press.

———. 2012. "Magic with a Message: The Poetics of Christian Conjuring." *Cultural Anthropology* 27 (2): 193–214.

———. 2017. *Magic's Reason: An Anthropology of Analogy*. Chicago: University of Chicago Press.

Kant, Immanuel. 2008 [1781]. *Critique of Pure Reason*. New York: Penguin.

Kardes, Frank, Maria Cronley, and Thomas Cline. 2014. *Consumer Behavior*. Mason, OH: Cengage Learning.

Keane, Webb. 1997. "Religious Language." *Annual Review of Anthropology* 26: 47–71.

———. 2002. "Sincerity, 'Modernity,' and the Protestants." *Cultural Anthropology* 17 (1): 65–92.

———. 2003. "Semiotics and the Social Analysis of Material Things." In *Words and Beyond: Linguistic and Semiotic Studies of Sociocultural Order*, 409–25. Special issue. *Language and Communication* 23 (3).

———. 2007. *Christian Moderns: Freedom and Fetish in the Mission Encounter*. Berkeley: University of California Press.

———. 2009. "On Multiple Ontologies and the Temporality of Things." *Material World Blog* 7.

———. 2013. "On Spirit Writing: Materialities of Language and the Religious Work of Transduction." *Journal of the Royal Anthropological Institute* 19 (1): 1–17.

———. 2018. "On Semiotic Ideology." *Signs and Society* 6 (1): 64–87.

Kelty, Christopher M. 2004. "Culture's Open Sources: Software, Copyright, and Cultural Critique." *Anthropological Quarterly* 77 (3): 499–506.

———. 2008. *Two Bits: The Cultural Significance of Free Software*. Durham, NC: Duke University Press.

———. 2019. *The Participant*. Chicago: University of Chicago Press.

Khan, Naveeda. 2012. *Muslim Becoming: Aspiration and Skepticism in Pakistan*. Durham, NC: Duke University Press.

King, Charles. 2019. *Gods of the Upper Air: How a Circle of Renegade Anthropologists Reinvented Race, Sex, and Gender in the Twentieth Century*. New York: Knopf Doubleday Publishing Group.

Kirsch, Thomas G. 2004. "Restaging the Will to Believe: Religious Pluralism, Anti-Syncretism, and the Problem of Belief." *American Anthropologist* n.s. 106 (4): 699–709.

Klein, Naomi. 2000. *No Logo: Taking Aim at the Brand Bullies*. Toronto: Knopf Canada.

Kockelman, Paul. 2013. "The Anthropology of an Equation: Sieves, Spam Filters, Agentive Algorithms, and Ontologies of Transformation." *HAU: Journal of Ethnographic Theory* 3 (3): 33–61.

Kohn, Eduardo. 2013. *How Forests Think: Toward an Anthropology beyond the Human*. Berkeley: University of California Press.

Koolhaas, Rem. 1998. "The Generic City." In Rem Koolhaas, Bruce Mau, and Office for Metropolitan Architecture, *S, M, L, XL*. New York: Monacelli Press.

Kramer, Paul Alexander. 2006. *The Blood of Government: Race, Empire, the United States, and the Philippines*. Chapel Hill: University of North Carolina Press.

Kroeber, Alfred Louis. 1917. "The Superorganic." *American Anthropologist* 19 (2): 163–213.

———. 1948. *Anthropology: Race, Language, Culture, Psychology, Prehistory*. New York: Harcourt, Brace & World, Inc.

Kroeber, Alfred Louis, and Clyde Kluckhohn. 1952. *Culture: A Critical Review of Concepts and Definitions*. New York: Vintage Books.

Kroskrity, Paul V. 2000. *Regimes of Language: Ideologies, Polities, and Identities*. Santa Fe, NM: School of American Research.

Lachica, Eddie. 1968. "'Burnham's Plan for Manila.'" *Philippine Herald*, July.

La Ferle, Carrie, and Steven M. Edwards. 2006. "Product Placement: How Brands Appear on Television." *Journal of Advertising* 35 (4): 65–86.

Lakoff, George. 1994. "What Is Metaphor?" In *Analogy, Metaphor, and Reminding*, ed. John A. Barnden and Keith James Holyoak. Bristol, UK: Intellect Books.

Lanza, Joseph. 2004. *Elevator Music: A Surreal History of Muzak, Easy-Listening, and*

Other Moodsong; Revised and expanded ed. Ann Arbor: University of Michigan Press.

Larkin, Brian. 2008. *Signal and Noise: Media, Infrastructure, and Urban Culture in Nigeria*. Durham, NC: Duke University Press.

Latour, Bruno. 1987. *Science in Action: How to Follow Scientists and Engineers through Society*. Cambridge, MA: Harvard University Press.

———. 1993. *We Have Never Been Modern*. Cambridge, MA: Harvard University Press.

Lee, Benjamin. 1997. *Talking Heads: Language, Metalanguage, and the Semiotics of Subjectivity*. Durham, NC: Duke University Press.

Lee, Benjamin, and Edward LiPuma. 2002. "Cultures of Circulation: The Imaginations of Modernity." *Public Culture* 14 (1): 191–213.

Lee, D. Demetracopoulou. 1944. "Categories of the Generic and the Particular in Wintŭ." *American Anthropologist* 46 (3): 362–69.

Lee, Penny. 1996. *The Whorf Theory Complex: A Critical Reconstruction*. Amsterdam: John Benjamins Publishing.

Lempert, Michael. 2012. "Indirectness." In *The Handbook of Intercultural Discourse and Communication*, ed. Christina B. Paulston, Scott Kiesling, and Elizabeth Rangel. Hoboken, NJ: Wiley Blackwell.

Leone, Massimo, and Richard J. Parmentier. 2014. "Representing Transcendence: The Semiosis of Real Presence." *Signs and Society* 2 (S1): S1–23.

Leslie, Sarah-Jane. 2007. "Generics and the Structure of the Mind." *Philosophical Perspectives* 21 (1): 375–403.

Lessig, Lawrence. 2008. *Remix: Making Art and Commerce Thrive in the Hybrid Economy*. New York: Penguin.

Lévi-Strauss, Claude. 1963a. *Structural Anthropology*. London: Hachette UK.

———. 1963b. *Totemism*. Boston: Beacon Press.

———. 1966. *The Savage Mind*. Chicago: University of Chicago Press.

Li, Darryl. 2019. *The Universal Enemy: Jihad, Empire, and the Challenge of Solidarity*. Stanford: Stanford University Press.

Linnaeus, Carolus. 2003 [1735]. *Systema Naturae 1735: Facsimile of the First Edition With an Introduction And a English Translation of the "Observationes."* Leiden: Brill.

López, Violeta B. 1976. *The Mangyans of Mindoro: An Ethnohistory*. Manila: University of the Philippines Press.

Louwrens, L. J. 2004. "On the Generic Nature of Common Northern Sotho Bird Names: A Probe into the Cognitive Systematization of Indigenous Knowledge." *South African Journal of African Languages* 24 (2): 95–117.

Lucy, John A. 1992. *Language Diversity and Thought: A Reformulation of the Linguistic Relativity Hypothesis*. Cambridge: Cambridge University Press.

Lury, Celia. 2004. *Brands: The Logos of the Global Economy*. New York: Routledge.

Luvaas, Brent. 2013. "Material Interventions: Indonesian DIY Fashion and the Regime of the Global Brand." *Cultural Anthropology* 28 (1): 127–43.

MacLaury, Robert E. 1997. *Color and Cognition in Mesoamerica: Constructing Categories as Vantages*. Austin: University of Texas Press.

MacLochlainn, Scott. 2019. "Of Congregations and Corporations: Schism, Transcendence, and the Religious Incorporate in the Philippines." *Anthropological Quarterly* 92 (4): 1039–68.

Mahmood, Saba. 2015. *Religious Difference in a Secular Age: A Minority Report*. Princeton: Princeton University Press.

Mannheim, Bruce, and Susan A. Gelman. 2013. "El aprendizaje de los conceptos genéricos entre niños quechuahablantes monolingües." *Bulletin de l'Institut Français d'Études Andines* 42 (3): 353–68.

Mannheim, Bruce, and Madeleine Newfield. 1982. "Iconicity in Phonological Change." In *Papers from the Fifth International Conference on Historical Linguistics, Galway, April 6–10 1981*, ed. Anders Ahlquist, 211. Amsterdam: John Benjamins Publishing.

Manning, Paul. 2007. Rose-Colored Glasses? Color Revolutions and Cartoon Chaos in Postsocialist Georgia. *Cultural Anthropology* 22 (2): 171–213.

———. 2010. "The Semiotics of Brand." *Annual Review of Anthropology* 39: 33–49.

———. 2012. *Semiotics of Drink and Drinking*. Edinburgh: A&C Black.

Manning, Paul, and Ann Uplisashvili. 2007. "'Our Beer': Ethnographic Brands in Postsocialist Georgia." *American Anthropologist* 109 (4): 626–41.

Mari, Alda, Claire Beyssade, and Fabio Del Prete. 2013. *Genericity*. Oxford: Oxford University Press.

Masuzawa, Tomoko. 2005. *The Invention of World Religions: Or, How European Universalism Was Preserved in the Language of Pluralism*. Chicago: University of Chicago Press.

Mattingly, Cheryl. 2008. "Pocahontas Goes to the Clinic: Popular Culture as Lingua Franca in a Cultural Borderland." *American Anthropologist* 108 (3): 494–501.

Mazzarella, William. 2003. *Shoveling Smoke: Advertising and Globalization in Contemporary India*. Durham, NC: Duke University Press.

———. 2013. *Censorium: Cinema and the Open Edge of Mass Publicity*. Durham, NC: Duke University Press.

———. 2017. *The Mana of Mass Society*. Chicago: University of Chicago Press.

———. 2019. "Brand(ish)ing the Name, or, Why is Trump So Enjoyable?" In *Sovereignty, Inc.: Three Inquiries in Politics and Enjoyment*, ed. William Mazzarella, Eric Santner, and Aaron Schuster, 113–60. Chicago: University of Chicago Press.

Mbembe, Achille. 2017. *Critique of Black Reason*. Durham, NC: Duke University Press.

McElhinny, Bonnie. 2001. "See No Evil, Speak No Evil: White Police Officers' Talk about Race and Affirmative Action." *Journal of Linguistic Anthropology* 11 (1): 65–78.

McIntosh, Janet. 2009. *The Edge of Islam: Power, Personhood, and Ethnoreligious Boundaries on the Kenya Coast*. Durham, NC: Duke University Press.

———. 2014. "Linguistic Atonement: Penitence and Privilege in White Kenyan Language Ideologies." *Anthropological Quarterly* 87 (4): 1165–99.

McLean, B. H. 2012. *Biblical Interpretation and Philosophical Hermeneutics*. Cambridge: Cambridge University Press.

McLean, Stuart J. 2017. *Fictionalizing Anthropology: Encounters and Fabulations at the Edges of the Human*. Minneapolis: University of Minnesota Press.

Meloy, Elizabeth. 2018. "'In the Dawn of a Brighter Day': Re-Presenting the Famine at the Irish International Exhibition of 1853." *New Hibernia Review* 22 (1): 19–44.

Meyer, Birgit. 1999. *Translating the Devil: Religion and Modernity among the Ewe in Ghana*. Edinburgh: Edinburgh University Press.

———. 2004. "Christianity in Africa: From African Independent to Pentecostal-Charismatic Churches." *Annual Review of Anthropology* 33: 447–74.

———. 2015. *Sensational Movies: Video, Vision, and Christianity in Ghana*. Berkeley: University of California Press.

Meyer, Jeffrey, Reo Song, and Kyoungnam Ha. 2016. "The Effect of Product Placement on the Evaluation of Movies." *European Journal of Marketing* 50 (3–4): 530–49.

Miller, Daniel, ed. 1998. *Material Cultures: Why Some Things Matter*. New York: Routledge.

Miller, Daniel, and Sophie Woodward. 2012. *Blue Jeans: The Art of the Ordinary*. Berkeley: University of California Press.

Mitchell, Timothy. 1989. "The World as Exhibition." *Comparative Studies in Society and History* 31 (2): 217–36.

———. 1991. *Colonising Egypt: With a New Preface*. Berkeley: University of California Press.

———. 1992. "Orientalism and the Exhibitionary Order." In *Colonialism and Culture*, ed. Nicholas Dirks, 289–316. Ann Arbor: University of Michigan Press.

Moore, Charles. 1921. *Daniel H. Burnham, Vol. 2*. New York: Houghton Mifflin.

Moore, Robert E. 2003. "From Genericide to Viral Marketing: On 'Brand.'" *Language and Communication* 23 (3–4): 331–57.

Mulligan, Fergus. 2014. "William Dargan, the 1853 Dublin Exhibition and the National Gallery of Ireland." *Dublin Historical Record* 67 (2): 54–70.

Murphy, Keith M. 2005. "Collaborative Imagining: The Interactive Use of Gestures, Talk, and Graphic Representation in Architectural Practice." *Semiotica* 2005 (156): 113–45.

———. 2015. *Swedish Design: An Ethnography*. Ithaca. NY: Cornell University Press.

Nakassis, Constantine V. 2012. "Counterfeiting What? Aesthetics of Brandedness and BRAND in Tamil Nadu, India." *Anthropological Quarterly* 85 (3): 701–21.

———. 2013. "Citation and Citationality." *Signs and Society* 1 (1): 51–77.

Napolitano, Valentina. 2015. *Migrant Hearts and the Atlantic Return: Transnationalism and the Roman Catholic Church*. New York: Fordham University Press.

Nida, Eugene. 1964. *Toward a Science of Translating: With Special Reference to Principles and Procedures Involved in Bible Translating*. Leiden: Brill.

———. 1966 [1959]. "Principles of Translation as Exemplified by Bible Translating." In *On Translation*, ed. Reuben A. Brower, 11–31. Cambridge, MA: Harvard University Press.

———. 1975. *Language Structure and Translation*. Stanford: Stanford University Press.

———. 2002. *Contexts in Translation*. Philadelphia: Benjamins.

Nida, Eugene, and Charles Russell Taber. 1982. *The Theory and Practice of Translation*. Leiden: Brill.

Nuckolls, Janis B. 1996. *Sounds Like Life: Sound-Symbolic Grammar, Performance, and Cognition in Pastaza Quechua*. Oxford: Oxford University Press.

Ochs (Keenan), Elinor. 1976. "The Universality of Conversational Postulates." *Language in Society* 5 (1): 67–80.

———. 1977. "On the Universality of Conversational Implicatures." In *Studies in Language Variation*, ed. R. W. Fasold and R. Shuy, 255–69. Washington, DC: Georgetown University Press.

——. 1979. "Transcription as Theory." *Developmental Pragmatics* 10 (1): 43–72.

O'Connor, John Philip. 2014. "'For a Colleen's Complexion': Soap and the Politicization of a Brand Personality, 1888–1916." *Journal of Historical Research in Marketing* 6 (1): 29–55.

Orlikowski, Wanda J., and JoAnne Yates. 1994. "Genre Repertoire: The Structuring of Communicative Practices in Organizations." *Administrative Science Quarterly* 39 (4): 541–74.

Ortner, Sherry B. 2016. "Dark Anthropology and Its Others: Theory since the Eighties." *HAU: Journal of Ethnographic Theory* 6 (1): 47–73.

Pakia, Mohamed. 2006. *African Traditional Plant Knowledge Today: An Ethnobotanical Study of the Digo at the Kenya Coast.* Münster: LIT Verlag.

Pandian, Anand. 2019. *A Possible Anthropology: Methods for Uneasy Times.* Durham, NC: Duke University Press.

Pang, L. 2008. "China Who Makes and Fakes: A Semiotics of the Counterfeit." *Theory, Culture and Society* 25 (6): 117–40.

Peirce, C. S. S. 2009 [1906]. *Prolegomena to An Apology for Pragmaticism; The Logic of Interdisciplinarity; "The Monist" Series.* Berlin: Akademie Verlag.

Pelletier, Francis Jeffry. 2010. *Kinds, Things, and Stuff: Mass Terms and Generics.* New York: Oxford University Press.

Perchonock, Norma, and Oswald Werner. 1969. "Navaho Systems of Classification: Some Implications for Ethnoscience." *Ethnology* 8 (3): 229–42.

Perniss, Pamela, Robin L. Thompson, and Gabriella Vigliocco. 2010. "Iconicity as a General Property of Language: Evidence from Spoken and Signed Languages." *Frontiers in Psychology* 1: 227.

Philips, Susan. 2010. "Semantic and Interactional Indirectness in Tongan Lexical Honorification." *Journal of Pragmatics* 42 (2): 317–36.

Povinelli, Elizabeth A. 2002. *The Cunning of Recognition: Indigenous Alterities and the Making of Australian Multiculturalism.* Durham, NC: Duke University Press.

Price, Robert M. 2009. *Inerrant the Wind: The Evangelical Crisis in Biblical Authority.* Amherst, NY: Prometheus Books.

Radin, Paul. 1972 [1956]. *The Trickster: A Study in American Indian Mythology.* New York: Schocken Books.

Radmacher, Earl D., and Robert D. Preus. 1984. *Hermeneutics, Inerrancy and the Bible.* Grand Rapids, MI: Academie Books.

Rafael, Vicente L. 1988. *Contracting Colonialism: Translation and Christian Conversion in Tagalog Society under Early Spanish Rule.* Ithaca, NY: Cornell University Press.

——. 1994a. "The Cultures of Area Studies in the United States." *Social Text* 41: 91–111.

——. 1994b. "White Love: Census and Melodrama in the United States Colonization of the Philippines." *History and Anthropology* 8 (1–4): 265–97.

——. 2000. *White Love and Other Events in Filipino History.* Durham, NC: Duke University Press.

Rains, Stephanie. 2008. "Here Be Monsters: The Irish Industrial Exhibition of 1853 and the Growth of Dublin Department Stores." *Irish Studies Review* 16 (4): 487–506.

Randall, Robert A. 1987. "The Nature of Highly Inclusive Folk-Botanical Categories." *American Anthropologist* 89 (1): 143–46.

Reiss, Katharina, and Hans J. Vermeer. 2014. *Towards a General Theory of Translational Action: Skopos Theory Explained.* London: Routledge.

Reno, Joshua. 2012. "Technically Speaking: On Equipping and Evaluating 'Unnatural' Language Learners." *American Anthropologist* 114 (3): 406–19.

Robbins, Joel. 2001. "God Is Nothing but Talk: Modernity, Language, and Prayer in a Papua New Guinea Society." *American Anthropologist* 104 (4): 901–12.

———. 2004. *Becoming Sinners: Christianity and Moral Torment in a Papua New Guinea Society.* Berkeley: University of California Press.

Rosa, Jonathan. 2019. *Looking Like a Language, Sounding Like a Race.* New York: Oxford University Press.

Rosaldo, Michelle Z. 1972. "Metaphors and Folk Classification." *Southwestern Journal of Anthropology* 28 (1): 83–99.

———. 1980a. *Knowledge and Passion.* Cambridge: Cambridge University Press.

———. 1980b. "The Use and Abuse of Anthropology: Reflections on Feminism and Cross-Cultural Understanding." *Signs: Journal of Women in Culture and Society* 5 (3): 389–417.

———. 1982. "The Things We Do with Words: Ilongot Speech Acts and Speech Act Theory in Philosophy." *Language in Society* 11 (2): 203–37.

———. 1984. "Words That Are Moving: The Social Meanings of Ilongot Verbal Art." In *Dangerous Words: Language and Politics in the Pacific,* ed. Donald Lawrence Brenneis and Fred R. Myers, 131–60. New York: New York University Press.

Rosaldo, Renato. 1982. "Utter Savages of Scientific Value." In *Politics and History in Band Societies,* ed. Eleanor Leacock and Richard Lee, 309–25. Cambridge: Cambridge University Press.

———. 1993. *Culture and Truth: The Remaking of Social Analysis: With a New Introduction.* Boston: Beacon Press.

Rubi v. Provincial Board. 1919. Supreme Court of the Philippines. G.R. No. L-14078.

Rutherford, Danilyn. 2006. "The Bible Meets the Idol: Writing and Conversion in Biak, Irian Jaya, Indonesia." In *The Anthropology of Christianity,* ed. Fenella Cannell, 240–72. Durham, NC: Duke University Press.

Rydell, Robert W. 1984. *All the World's a Fair: Visions of Empire at American International Expositions, 1876–1916.* Chicago: University of Chicago Press.

Sadre-Orafai, Stephanie. 2020. "Typologies, Typifications, and Types." *Annual Review of Anthropology* 49: 193–208.

Sanneh, Lamin. 1989. *Translating the Message: The Missionary Impact on Culture.* Ossining, NY: Orbis Books.

Sapir, Edward. 1917. "Do We Need a 'Superorganic'?" *American Anthropologist* 19 (3): 441–47.

Saris, A. Jamie. 2000. "Imagining Ireland in the Great Exhibition of 1853." In *Ireland in the Nineteenth Century: Regional Identity,* ed. Leon Litvack and Glenn Hooper. Dublin: Four Courts Press.

Saunders, Barbara A. C., and Jaap van Brakel. 1988. "Re-evaluating Basic Color Terms." *Cultural Dynamics* 1: 359–78.

Saunders, George R., ed. 1988. *Culture and Christianity: The Dialectics of Transformation.* Westport, CT: Greenwood Press.

Schieffelin, Bambi. 2007. "Found in Translating: Reflexive Language across Time and Texts." In *Consequences of Contact: Language Ideologies and Sociocultural Trans-*

formations in Pacific Societies, ed. M. Makihara and Bambi B. Schieffelin, 140–65. Oxford: Oxford University Press.

Schult, Volker. 1997. "Mindoro and North Luzon under American Colonial Rule." *Philippine Studies* 45 (4): 477–99.

Scott, Geoffrey R., and Karen E. Maull. 2012. "Kryptonite, Duff Beer and the Protection of Fictional Characters and Products in the Global Community." *Monash University Law Review* 38 (1): 228–82.

Scott, Susie. 2017. "A Sociology of Nothing: Understanding the Unmarked." *Sociology* 52 (February).

Searle, John R. 2002. *Consciousness and Language.* Cambridge: Cambridge University Press.

Seaver, Nick. 2022. *Computing Taste: Algorithms and the Makers of Music Recommendation.* Chicago: University of Chicago Press.

Seiter, Bill, and Ellen Seiter. 2012. *The Creative Artist's Legal Guide: Copyright, Trademark and Contracts in Film and Digital Media Production.* New Haven: Yale University Press.

Shankar, Shalini. 2019. "Nothing Sells Like Whiteness: Race, Ontology, and American Advertising." *American Anthropologist* 122.

Shryock, Andrew. 2004. "Other Conscious/Self Aware: First Thoughts on Cultural Intimacy and Mass Mediation." In *Off Stage/On Display: Intimacy and Ethnography in the Age of Public Culture,* ed. Andrew Shryock. Stanford: Stanford University Press.

Silverstein, Michael. 2003a. "Indexical Order and the Dialectics of Sociolinguistic Life." In *Words and Beyond: Linguistic and Semiotic Studies of Sociocultural Order.* Special issue. *Language and Communication* 23 (3): 193–229.

———. 2003b. "Translation, Transduction, Transformation: Skating 'Glossando' on Thin Semiotic Ice." In *Translating Cultures: Perspectives on Translation and Anthropology,* ed. Paula G. Rubel and Abraham Rosman, 75–105. New York: Berg.

———. 2005. "Axes of Evals." *Journal of Linguistic Anthropology* 15 (1): 6–22.

———. 2010. "'Direct' and 'Indirect' Communicative Acts in Semiotic Perspective." *Journal of Pragmatics* 42 (2): 337–53.

Silverstein, Michael, and Greg Urban, eds. 1996. *Natural Histories of Discourse.* Chicago: University of Chicago Press.

Simone, AbdouMaliq. 2016. "Urbanity and Generic Blackness." *Theory, Culture and Society* 33 (7–8): 183–203.

Sinaltrainal v. Coca-Cola Co. 578 F3d 1252 (11th Cir. 2009).

Smalls, Krystal A. 2018. "Fighting Words: Antiblackness and Discursive Violence in an American High School." *Journal of Linguistic Anthropology* 28 (3): 356–83.

Sperber, D., and D. Wilson. 1997. "Remarks on Relevance Theory and the Social Sciences." *Multilingua* 16:145–52.

Spivak, Gayatri Chakravorty. 1988. "Can the Subaltern Speak?" In *Marxism and the Interpretation of Culture,* ed. Cary Nelson and Lawrence Grossberg, 271–313. Basingstoke, UK: Macmillan.

Sproule, John. 1854. *The Irish Industrial Exhibition of 1853: a detailed catalogue of its contents, with critical dissertations, statistical information, and accounts of manufacturing processes in the different departments.* Dublin: James McGlashan.

Stocking, George. 1968. *Race, Culture, and Evolution: Essays in the History of Anthropology.* Chicago: University of Chicago Press.

——. 1987. *Victorian Anthropology*. New York: Free Press.

——. 1991. *Victorian Anthropology*. New York: Simon & Schuster.

Strassler, Karen. 2020. *Demanding Images: Democracy, Mediation, and the Image-Event in Indonesia*. Durham, NC: Duke University Press.

Strathern, Marilyn. 2014. "Reading Relations Backwards." *Journal of the Royal Anthropological Institute* 20: 3–19.

Stuessy, Tod F. 2009. *Plant Taxonomy: The Systematic Evaluation of Comparative Data*. New York: Columbia University Press.

Sullivan, Karen, and Eve Sweetser. 2009. "Is 'Generic Is Specific' a Metaphor?" Rochester, NY: Social Science Research Network (SSRN).

Tadiar, Neferti XM. 2016. "City Everywhere." *Theory, Culture & Society* 33 (7–8): 57–83.

Taussig, Michael T. 1993. *Mimesis and Alterity: A Particular History of the Senses*. Hove, East Sussex, UK: Psychology Press.

——. 2010. *What Color Is the Sacred?* Chicago: University of Chicago Press.

Tomlinson, Matt. 2006. "Retheorizing Mana: Bible Translation and Discourse of Loss in Fiji." *Oceania* 76 (2): 173–85.

Trawick, Margaret. 1988. "Ambiguity in the Oral Exegesis of a Sacred Text: Tirukkovaiyar (or, the Guru in the Garden, Being an Account of a Tamil Informant's Responses to Homesteading in Central New York State)." *Cultural Anthropology* 3 (3): 316–51.

Trouillot, Michel-Rolph. 2003. "Anthropology and the Savage Slot: The Poetics and Politics of Otherness." In *Global Transformations: Anthropology and the Modern World*, ed. Michel-Rolph Trouillot, 7–28. New York: Palgrave Macmillan.

Tsing, Anna Lowenhaupt. 2005. *Friction: An Ethnography of Global Connection*. Princeton: Princeton University Press.

Tupas, Ruanni. 2015. "The Politics of 'p' and 'f': A Linguistic History of Nation-Building in the Philippines." *Journal of Multilingual and Multicultural Development* 36 (6): 587–97.

Turpin, John. 1981. "Exhibitions of Art and Industries in Victorian Ireland: Part I: The Irish Arts and Industries Exhibition Movement 1834–1864." *Dublin Historical Record* 35 (1): 2–13.

20th Century Fox Film Corporation and Matt Groening Productions Inc. v. The South Australian Brewing Company Ltd. and Lion Nathan Australia Pty Ltd. No. NG 155 of 1996 FED No. 365/96 Australia.

Tylor, Edward Burnett. 1871. *Primitive Culture: Researches into the Development of Mythology, Philosophy, Religion, Art, and Custom*. London: J. Murray.

United States v. Paramount Pictures, Inc. 1948. 334 U.S 131.

Untitled pamphlet on Irish Village at World's Columbian Exposition. 1893. Held at National Library of Ireland.

Urban, Greg. 2001. *Metaculture: How Culture Moves through the World*. Minneapolis: University of Minnesota Press.

Urciuoli, Bonnie. 2009. "Talking/Not Talking about Race: The Enregisterments of Culture in Higher Education Discourses." *Journal of Linguistic Anthropology* 19 (1): 21–39.

VanPool, Christine S., and Todd L. VanPool. 2009. "The Semantics of Local Knowledge: Using Ethnosemantics to Study Folk Taxonomies Represented in the Archaeological Record." *Journal of Anthropological Research* 65 (4): 529–54.

Villanueva, Elaine Loreen C., and Inocencio E. Buot Jr. 2020. "Useful Plants of the Alangan Mangyan of Halcon Range, Mindoro Island, Philippines." *Journal of Marine and Island Cultures.*

Viveiros de Castro, Eduardo. 1998. "Cosmological Deixis and Amerindian Perspectivism." *Journal of the Royal Anthropological Institute* 4 (3): 469–88.

———. 2004. "Exchanging Perspectives: The Transformation of Objects into Subjects in Amerindian Ontologies." *Common Knowledge* 10 (October): 463–84.

Warner, Michael. 2002. "Publics and Counterpublics." *Public Culture* 14 (1): 49–90.

———. 2005. *Publics and Counterpublics.* New York: Zone Books.

Waugh, Linda R. 1980. "The Poetic Function in the Theory of Roman Jakobson." *Poetics Today*: 57–82.

———. 1982. "Marked and Unmarked: A Choice between Unequals in Semiotic Structure." *Semiotica* 38 (3–4): 299–318.

Weber, Max. 1978 [1921]. *Economy and Society: An Outline of Interpretive Sociology.* Berkeley: University of California Press.

Wengrow, David. 2008. "Prehistories of Commodity Branding." *Current Anthropology* 49 (1): 7–34.

Werner, Abraham Gottlob. 1805. *A Treatise on the External Characters of Fossils.* Dublin: M. N. Mahon.

Whitaker, Amy. 2019. "Shared Value over Fair Use: Technology, Added Value, and the Reinvention of Copyright." *Cardozo Arts & Entertainment Law Journal* 37: 635.

Whorf, Benjamin Lee. 1945. "Grammatical Categories." *Language* 21 (1): 1–11.

Wilf, Eitan Y. 2014. *School for Cool: The Academic Jazz Program and the Paradox of Institutionalized Creativity.* Chicago: University of Chicago Press.

———. 2016. "The Post-It Note Economy: Understanding Post-Fordist Business Innovation through One of Its Key Semiotic Technologies." *Current Anthropology* 57 (6): 732–60.

Wilson, Deirdre, and Dan Sperber. 2004. "Relevance Theory." In *Handbook of Pragmatics*, ed. Laurence R. Horn and Gregory Ward, 607–32. Malden, MA: Blackwell.

Witkowski, Stanley R., and Cecil H. Brown. 1977. "An Explanation of Color Nomenclature Universale." *American Anthropologist* 79 (1): 50–57.

Wittgenstein, Ludwig. 2010 [1953]. *Philosophical Investigations.* New York: John Wiley & Sons.

Zerubavel, Eviatar. 2018. *Taken for Granted: The Remarkable Power of the Unremarkable.* Princeton: Princeton University Press.

Zuckerman, Charles. 2020. "'Don't Gamble for Money with Friends': Moral-Economic Types and Their Uses." *American Ethnologist* 47, no. 4: 432–46.

———. 2021. "On the Unity of Types: Lao Gambling, Ethno-Metapragmatics, and Generic and Specific Modes of Typification." *Language in Society* 50 (4): 557–82.

Index

Page numbers in italics refer to figures.

cognition and, 4, 7, 12, 23, 33, 35, 38–41, 44, 48, 55; color, 28, 31, 33, 38–41, 42, 46, 48, 53; Conklin and, 39–41, 48; covert, 12, 27, 31–34, 45, 48, 53, 165, 192nn5–6; general, 33, 48, 195n2; genre, 14–15, 18, 25, 29, 79, 185; highland Filipinos, 120; ideological, 7, 26, 40, 52, 192n3, 195n4; Kockelman on, 191n4; legal issues and, 30, 82, 193n8; lowland Filipinos, 113–17, 120–24, 128, 142, 146, 195n2; marked, 28, 34, 50–58, 72, 74, 78, 119, 122, 128–29, 162, 184, 193n11; milk, 62, 67–68, 81–82, 193n8; mimesis and, 81–82, 84, 87–88; naming and, 31, 33–34, 52, 88; order and, 4, 7, 9–12, 20–27, 30–55; race and, 192n4; religion and, 181; Rosaldo on, 45–49; sieve for, 191n4

Catholicism: ambience of, 31, 163–82, 199n2; Bible studies and, 137; big faith and, 168, 172–78; born-again Evangelicals and, 31, 200n8; catechism and, 118–19, 181; charismatic, 112, 200n6; CHESC and, 131; colonialism and, 126; converts to, 114, 166–67, 172; Deuterocanonical, 155; dominance of, 8, 112–13, 121, 128–29; exclusion of God's name and, 155; failures of, 179; folk, 199n2; Franciscan Missionaries of Mary (FMM) and, 117–19; Hail Mary, 181; idolatry and, 130, 176–78; Irish, 100; Jesuit, 121, 195; Kulaman and, 163–82; lowland Filipinos and, 114, 117; Mangyan people and, 30, 114–21; mass and, 163, 171; Mindoro and, 30–31, 115, 118, 164, 167, 173–74, 180–81; missionaries and, 30, 117–18, 128; as monopoly, 129; Orthodox, 112; pharmacies and, 183; pluralism and, 8, 112, 118, 128–29; Protestants and, 112–13, 118, 128, 130, 144, 152, 166, 174, 195n5; Roman, 112, 165; Rosary, 181; Sazon and, 162–82; self-interest of pastors and, 200n8; social rupture and, 199n2; Spain and, 112, 126, 128, 182; state support of, 112–13, 128–29; universalism and, 5, 128, 166, 196n8

Cattelino, Jessica, 194n6
charismatics, 112, 200n6
Charles I, 98
CHESC: Arnels and, 131–33, 138; Bible and,

131–32, 138; born-again Evangelicals and, 131, 138; deaf people and, 138; Jesus and, 138; Signed Exact English (SEE) and, 133

Chicago Statement on Biblical Inerrancy, 152–53

Chicago World's Fair, 91, 95, 100

Christians: anthropology and, 112, 114, 124, 140, 143, 165–67; big faith and, 168, 172–78; brands and, 121, 128, 141, 160, 169; categories and, 119–21, 127, 129, 165, 167, 174, 178–81; classification and, 30–31, 107, 112, 122, 126–29, 185, 191n3, 196n7; codification of, 120–21; colonialism and, 8, 111–12, 120, 124, 145, 183; commensurability and, 112, 138, 142, 150, 153, 156–62, 166, 172, 174; Durkheim on, 21; equivalency and, 171; ethnography and, 8, 17, 29–30, 111–16; Hanunoo people and, 114, 117–18, 142, 145–50, 155, 159, 197n6, 198n7; Holy Spirit and, 30, 142–43, 146, 153–54, 161; ideologies and, 8, 121–22, 133, 137, 140–45, 150, 160–62, 167, 177, 179–80, 195n4, 196n8, 196n12; idolatry and, 130, 176–78; Irish, 95; language and, 140–62; lowland Filipinos and, 113–17, 120–24, 128, 142, 146, 195n2; Mangyan people and, 113–29, 140–46, 153–56, 160–62, 195n2, 197n5; marked and, 119, 122, 128–29, 162, 184; media and, 8; mimesis and, 30, 113, 118–19; Mindoro and, 17, 29–31, 111–46, 152–54, 159–61, 164, 167, 173–74, 180–84, 195n2, 196n10; music and, 14–19, 132, 175; order and, 192nn3–6, 193n11; ownership and, 16–17, 19, 119; Protestant, 112–13, 118, 128, 130, 144, 152, 166, 174, 195n5; social rupture and, 199n2; Tagalog and, 113, 116–21, 124, 133, 146–50, 155, 157–60, 188, 197n4, 197n6, 200n10; templates and, 197n1; tokens and, 172, 181; translation and, 16, 30, 129, 134, 136, 140–62, 196nn10–11, 197nn2–6, 198n7, 199n11, 200n10; types and, 114, 119, 121, 123, 128–31, 150, 159, 163, 167, 176, 178–81; universalism and, 8, 128, 139, 166, 196n8; unmarked and, 30, 119–22, 129, 162, 167–68, 176–77, 195n5. *See also specific religions*